Lecture Notes in Computer Science 1797

Edited by G. Goos, J. Hartmanis and J. van Leeuwen

W0042392

Springer
Berlin
Heidelberg
New York
Barcelona
Hong Kong
London
Milan
Paris
Singapore
Tokyo

Babak Falsafi   Mario Lauria (Eds.)

Network-Based Parallel Computing

Communication, Architecture and Applications

4th International Workshop, CANPC 2000
Toulouse, France, January 8, 2000
Proceedings

 Springer

Series Editors

Gerhard Goos, Karlsruhe University, Germany
Juris Hartmanis, Cornell University, NY, USA
Jan van Leeuwen, Utrecht University, The Netherlands

Volume Editors

Babak Falsafi
Purdue University, School of Electrical & Computer Engineering
1258 Electrical Engineering Building, West Lafayette, Indiana 47907-1285, USA
E-mail: babak@ecn.purdue.edu

Mario Lauria
Ohio State University, Department of Computer and Information Science
Dreese Lab 395, 2015 Neil Avenue, Columbus, OH 43210-1277, USA
E-mail: lauria@cis.ohio-state.edu

Cataloging-in-Publication Data applied for

Die Deutsche Bibliothek - CIP-Einheitsaufnahme

Network based parallel computing : communication, architecture, and
applications ; 4th international workshop ; proceedings / CANPC 2000,
Toulouse, France, January 8, 2000. Babak Falsafi ; Mario Lauria (ed.).
- Berlin ; Heidelberg ; New York ; Barcelona ; Hong Kong ; London ;
Milan ; Paris ; Singapore ; Tokyo : Springer, 2000
  (Lecture notes in computer science ; Vol. 1797)
  ISBN 3-540-67879-4

CR Subject Classification (1998): C.2, D.1.3, F.1.2, D.4.4

ISSN 0302-9743
ISBN 3-540-67879-4 Springer-Verlag Berlin Heidelberg New York

Springer-Verlag is a company in the BertelsmannSpringer publishing group.
© Springer-Verlag Berlin Heidelberg 2000
Printed in Germany

Typesetting: Camera-ready by author, data conversion by Christian Grosche, Hamburg
Printed on acid-free paper   SPIN: 10720115   06/3142   5 4 3 2 1 0

Preface

Clusters of workstations/PCs connected by off-the-shelf networks have become popular as platforms for cost-effective parallel computing. Technological advances in both hardware and software have made such a network-based parallel computing platform an affordable alternative to commercial supercomputers for an increasing number of scientific applications.

Continuing in the tradition of the three previously successful workshops, this fourth Workshop on Communication, Architecture and Applications for Network-based Parallel Computing (CANPC 2000) brought together researchers and practitioners working in architecture, system software, applications, and performance evaluation to discuss state-of-the-art solutions for network-based parallel computing. This year, the workshop was held in conjunction with the sixth International Symposium on High-Performance Computer Architecture (HPCA-6).

As in prior editions, the papers presented here are representative of a spectrum of research efforts from groups in academia and industry to further improve cluster computing's viability, performance, cost-effectiveness, and usability. Specifically, we have arranged the contributions in this edition into four groups: (1) program development and execution support, (2) network router architecture, (3) system support for communication abstractions, and (4) network software and interface architecture.

The first group contains three papers that focus on programming and usability of clusters. Unlike tightly-coupled parallel supercomputers, clusters are built with commodity networking technology and operating systems. As such, clusters require additional support in the areas of program deployment and transparent and robust network connectivity. The specific contributions include a remote execution facility to deploy programs in a cluster in a transparent, secured, and decentralized manner; and a transparent mechanism to virtualize network connectivity in dynamic cluster environments. This group also includes a paper on a visual parallel programming tool for the BSP distributed programming model.

The second and third groups of papers improve on crucial aspects of the cluster technology such as routing (papers on Up*/Down* routing, dynamic routing reconfiguration, deadlock-free routing), and system support for derived data types and collective communication. These efforts show how the cluster concept is influencing research on topics that for years have been associated with traditional large-scale supercomputers, like interconnect topologies, routing schemes, parallel libraries.

The fourth group addresses the high software and network interface communication overheads characteristic of clusters. One paper goes back to the root of the network computing approach, and performs an in-depth analysis of existing gigabit architectures (VIA, Gigabit Ethernet). Another evaluates various design

points for the emerging industry standard for interface architectures, VIA. The
third paper in this section proposes a novel messaging implementation in which
the system learns and predicts patterns of message sequences to reduce the processing overhead.

Our excellent program this year was only made possible with the help and
great efforts of many people. First, we would like to thank all of the authors
for submitting papers, the program committee for their timely and meticulous
reviewing and selection of the papers, and the HPCA-6 organizing committee
for their support of this workshop. Special thanks to Henri Bal for giving an
excellent keynote address. Finally, we would like to thank the editorial staff of
Springer-Verlag for agreeing to publish the final version of these proceedings.

April 2000   Babak Falsafi and Mario Lauria
                                                     Program Co-chairs

CANPC 2000 Program Committee

Babak Falsafi, *Purdue University (co-chair)*
Mario Lauria, *The Ohio State Univeristy (co-chair)*

Henri Bal, *Vrije University*
Angelos Bilas, *University of Toronto*
Alok Choudhary, *Northwestern University*
Robert Clay, *Sandia National Labratories*
Jose Duato, *Universidad Politécnica de Valencia*
Rudolf Eigenmann, *Purdue University*
Bob Horst, *3Ware Inc.*
Giulio Iannello, *Università di Napoli*
Liviu Iftode, *Rutgers University*
Alain Kägi, *Intel MRL*
Vijay Karamcheti, *New York University*
Steve Lumetta, *University of Illinois*
Dhabaleswar Panda, *The Ohio State University*
Phil Papadopoulos, *University of California*
Ioannis Schoinas, *Intel SAL*
Anand Sivasubramaniam, *The Penn State University*
Peter Steenkiste, *Carnegie Mellon University*
Robert Stets, *Compaq WRL*
Craig Stunkel, *IBM T.J. Watson*
Jaspal Subhlok, *University of Houston*
Rich Wolski, *University of Tennessee*

Table of Contents

Program Development and Execution Support

Network Router Architecture

System Support for Communication Abstractions

Network Software and Interface Architecture

REXEC: A Decentralized, Secure Remote Execution Environment for Clusters

Brent N. Chun and David E. Culler

University of California at Berkeley
Computer Science Division, Berkeley, CA 94720
Tel: +1 510 642 8299, Fax: +1 510 642 5775
{bnc,culler}@cs.berkeley.edu
http://www.cs.berkeley.edu/~{bnc,culler}

Abstract. Bringing clusters of computers into the mainstream as general-purpose computing systems requires that better facilities for transparent remote execution of parallel and sequential applications be developed. While much research has been done in this area, most of this work remains inaccessible for clusters built using contemporary hardware and operating systems. Implementations are either too old and/or not publicly available, require use of operating systems which are not supported by modern hardware, or simply do not meet the functional requirements demanded by practical use in real world settings. To address these issues, we designed REXEC, a decentralized, secure remote execution facility. It provides high availability, scalability, transparent remote execution, dynamic cluster configuration, decoupled node discovery and selection, a well-defined failure and cleanup model, parallel and distributed program support, and strong authentication and encryption. The system is implemented and is currently installed and in use on a 32-node cluster of 2-way SMPs running the Linux 2.2.5 operating system.

Keywords: Clusters, Remote execution, Distributed systems, Decentralized control

1   Introduction

We have designed and implemented a new remote execution environment called REXEC [1] to address the lack of a sufficient remote execution facility for parallel and sequential jobs on clusters of computers. Building on previous work in remote execution and practical experience with the Berkeley NOW and Millennium clusters, the system provides decentralized control, transparent remote execution, dynamic cluster membership, decoupled node discovery and selection, a well-defined error and cleanup model, support for sequential programs as well as parallel and distributed programs, and user authentication and encryption. It takes advantage of modern systems technologies such as IP multicast and mature OS support for threads to simplify its design and implementation. It is implemented almost entirely at user-level with small modifications to the

---

[1] Our REXEC system has no relation to the 4.2 BSD rexec function, nor does it have any relation to the rexec command used in the Butler [13] system or the rexec function in NEST [1].

B. Falsafi and M. Lauria (Eds.): CANPC 2000, LNCS 1797, pp. 1–14, 2000.

Linux 2.2.5 kernel. The system is currently installed and in use on a 32-node cluster of 2-way SMPs as part of the UC Berkeley Millennium Project.

The rest of this paper is organized as follows. In Section 2, we state our design goals and assumptions for the REXEC system. In Section 3, we describe the REXEC system architecture and our implementation on a 32-node cluster of 2-way SMPs running the Linux operating system. In Section 4, we discuss three examples of how REXEC has been applied to provide remote execution facilities to applications. In Section 5, we discuss related work. Section 6 describes future work and in Section 7 we conclude the paper.

2   Design Goals and Assumptions

In this section, we describe our design goals and the assumptions made in designing REXEC. Our design goals are based on several years of practical experience as users of the Berkeley NOW cluster, a thorough examination of previous systems work in remote execution, and a desire to combine and extend key features in each of the systems into a single remote execution environment. Our goals are as follows:

- *High availability.* The system should be highly available and provide graceful degradation of service in the presence of failures.
- *Scalability.* As more nodes are added and more applications are run, remote execution overhead should scale gracefully.
- *Transparent remote execution.* Execution on remote nodes should be as transparent as possible.
- *Minimal use of static configuration files.* The remote execution system should rely on as few static configuration files as possible.
- *Decoupled discovery and selection.* The process of discovering which nodes are in the cluster and what their state is should be separated from the selection of which nodes to run an application on.
- *Well-defined failure and cleanup models.* The system should provide well-defined models for failure and cleanup.
- *Parallel and distributed program support.* The remote execution environment should provide a minimal set of hooks that allow parallel and distributed runtime environments to be built.
- *Security.* The system should provide user authentication and encryption of all communication.

Our assumptions are typical of remote execution systems and not overly restricting or extensive. Modern clusters built using off-the-shelf hardware and contemporary operating systems are easily configured to satisfy these assumptions. Our assumptions are as follows:

- *Uniform file pathnames.* We assume that all shared files are accessible on all nodes using the same pathnames and that most local files on each node are also accessible under the same pathnames (e.g., /bin/ls).

- *Compatible OS and software configurations.* We assume all nodes in the cluster run compatible versions of the operating system and have compatible software configurations.
- *Common user ID/account database.* We assume each user has a unique user ID and an account which is the same on all the nodes in the cluster.

3   System Architecture

The REXEC system architecture is organized around three types of entities: *rexecd*, a daemon which runs on each cluster node; *rexec*, a client program that users run to execute jobs using REXEC; and *vexecd*, a replicated daemon which provides node discovery and selection services (Fig. 1). Users run jobs on the system using the rexec client. The rexec client performs two functions: (i) selection of nodes based on user preferences (e.g., lowest CPU load) and (ii) remote execution of the user's application on those nodes through direct SSL-encrypted TCP connections to node rexecd daemons. REXEC is implemented and currently installed and running on a 32-node cluster of 2-way Dell Poweredge 2300 SMPs running a modified version of the Linux 2.2.5 operating system. In this section, we provide details on the key features of REXEC and show how these features address our design goals.

3.1   Decentralized Control

REXEC uses decentralized control for graceful scaling of system overhead as more cluster nodes are added and more applications are being run. Upon selecting a set of remote nodes to run on, the rexec client opens TCP connections to each of the nodes and executes the remote execution protocol with the rexecd daemons directly. These direct client to daemon connections allow the work (e.g., forwarding to stdin, stdout, and stderr, networking and process resources, etc.) of managing the remote execution to be distributed between the rexec client and the rexecd daemons. With a large number of nodes, having a centralized entity act as an intermediary between users and cluster nodes can easily become a bottleneck as single node resources become an issue. Our scheme avoids this problem by distributing this work.

In addition to scalability, a decentralized design by definition avoids single points of failure. By freeing users from depending on intermediate entities to access the nodes they need to run their programs, we ensure that any functional node in the system which is reachable over the network and running an rexecd daemon can always be used to run user applications. REXEC can have any number of "front end" machines. This is in contrast to previous systems such as GLUnix [7] and SCore-D [8], which use a centralized entity as the intermediary between clients and the cluster. In GLUnix, for example, when the master crashes, all 115 nodes of the Berkeley NOW cluster become unavailable for running programs through the GLUnix system. In practice, centralized entities with no backup or failover capabilities can decrease system availability significantly.

3.2   Transparent Remote Execution

REXEC provides transparent remote execution which allows processes running on remote nodes to execute and be controlled as if they were running locally. It uses four

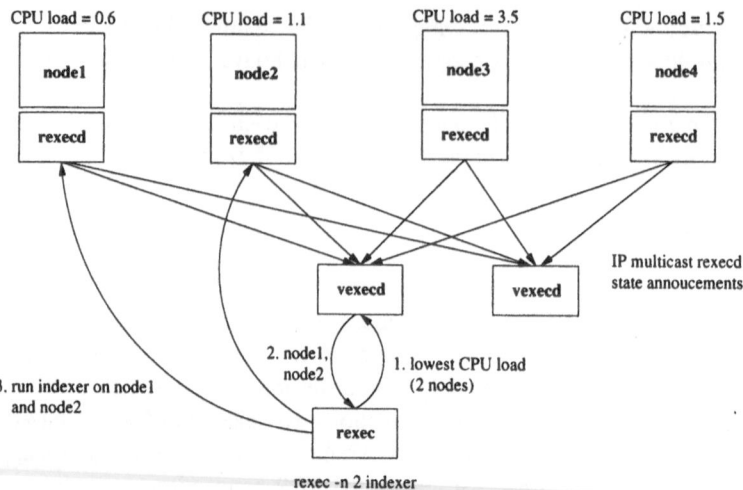

Fig. 1. Overall organization of the REXEC remote execution environment. The system is organized around three types of entities: *rexecd*, a daemon which runs on each cluster node; *rexec*, a client program that users run to execute jobs using REXEC; and *vexecd*, a replicated daemon which provides node discovery and selection services. Users run jobs in REXEC using the rexec client which performs two functions: (i) selection of which nodes to run on based on user preferences and (ii) remote execution of the user's application on those nodes through direct SSL-encrypted TCP connections to the node rexecd daemons. In this example, there are four nodes in the system: node1, node2, node3, and node4 and two instances of vexecd, each of which implements a lowest CPU load policy. A user wishes to run a program called indexer on the two nodes with the lowest CPU load. Contacting a vexecd daemon, rexec obtains the names of the two machines with the lowest CPU load, node1 and node2. rexec then establishes SSL-encrypted TCP connections directly to those nodes to run indexer on them.

mechanisms to accomplish this: (i) propagation and recreation of the user's local environment on remote nodes, (ii) forwarding of local signals to remote processes, (iii) forwarding of stdin, stdout, and stderr between the rexec client and remote processes and (iv) local job control to control remote processes.

The implementation of these mechanisms is centered around a collection of rexec client and per-rexec-client rexecd threads. Referring to Fig. 2, propagation and recreation of the user's local environment is done by having the node thread in rexec package up the user's local environment and having the rexec thread in rexecd recreate it after forking and before execing the user's job. Forwarding of local signals and stdin is done by having the signals thread and stdin thread in rexec forward signals and stdin to each of the remote stdin/sig threads in the rexecds, which then deliver them to the user's application using signals and Unix pipes. Forwarding of remote stdout and stderr is done by having stdout and stderr threads in rexecd read from stdout and stderr Unix pipes connected to the user's process and forward that data back to node threads in the rexec client. Local job control is done by forwarding signals as usual but also by translating certain signals to ones which have meaning for remote processes not attached to a terminal. (For example, SIGTSTP (C-z) is translated to SIGSTOP.)

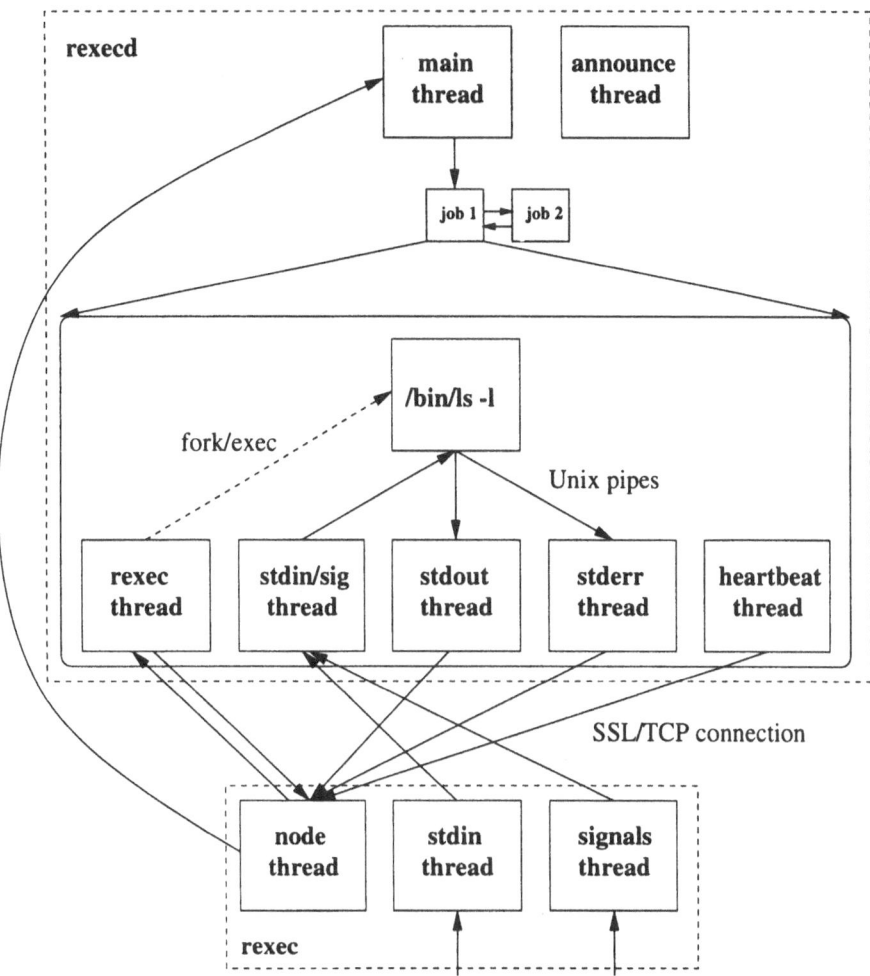

Fig. 2. Internal thread structure and data flows for rexec and rexecd. rexec consists of a stdin thread for forwarding of stdin, a signals thread for forwarding of signals, and one node thread per node for managing remote process execution including propagation of the user's environment, the request to start the user's application, printing remotely forwarded stdout and stderr to the user's local terminal, receiving heartbeat packets (and rexec client monitoring of the TCP connection), and receiving the exit status of the remote process. (In this example, rexec is running '/bin/ls -l' on a single node so there is only one node thread.) rexecd consists of a main thread which creates new threads for new rexec clients and maintains a list of running jobs, an announce thread for sending multicast state announcements, and a collection of per-rexec-client threads. These per-rexec-client threads include an rexec thread for the client, the user process forked and execed by the rexec thread, a stdin/signals thread for forwarding stdin/signals from rexec to the user process, stdout and stderr threads for forwarding stdout and stderr from the user process to rexec, and a heartbeat thread for sending of periodic heartbeat packets to detect failures in the SSL-encrypted TCP connection between rexec and rexecd.

3.3 Dynamic Cluster Membership

REXEC uses a dynamic cluster membership service to discover nodes as they join and leave the cluster using a well-known cluster multicast address. In our experience with large clusters of computers, we have found that over time the set of available nodes tends to vary as nodes are added, removed, rebooted, and so forth. Using static configuration files or manual intervention to track cluster membership is error-prone and inefficient. A dynamic membership service based on multicast avoids this and also has the desirable property that processes can communicate with interested receivers without explicitly naming them. Senders who wish to communicate information simply send it on the multicast address with a unique message type. Interested parties can elect to receive and interpret information of interest by examining incoming message types. If necessary, processes can even use the multicast channel to bootstrap point-to-point connections.

Approximate membership of the cluster is maintained by replicated vexecd daemons by using the reception of a multicast rexecd announcement packet as a sign that a node is available and the non-reception of an announcement over a small multiple of a periodic announcement interval as a sign that a node is unavailable. Each rexecd sends announcement packets periodically (once every minute) and also whenever a significant change in state is observed. Currently, announcements based on state changes are sent for job arrivals and job departures. vexecd daemons discover and maintain the node membership in the cluster by caching and timing out node announcement information.

3.4 Decoupled Discovery and Selection

REXEC decouples node discovery from the selection of which nodes an application should run on. Replicated vexecd daemons are responsible for discovering and maintaining the node membership of the cluster. Within one state announcement period, a new vexecd discovers the entire instantaneous membership of the cluster. With multiple vexecd daemons keeping track of all the nodes, their configuration, and state, a selection policy is simply a mapping that applies some criteria to that list of available hosts and returns a set of hosts.

Because users may have different criteria in how they want nodes to be selected for their applications, discovery and selection are decoupled. The vexecd daemons which do discovery can implement any number of selection policies. The idea with vexecds implementing selection services as well is that we envision that most users will probably choose from a small set of policies in deciding where to run their applications. In a community composed largely of scientific computing users, for example, lowest CPU load may be the most common criteria.

vexecds precompute and cache orderings on the list of available nodes so clients can quickly obtain the results of common selection policies. Under most circumstances, users will contact prewritten vexecd daemons asking for the n "best" nodes, where best is defined according to some selection criteria. The vexecds simply return the top n nodes on their ordered list, which is recomputed each time a state change occurs with adjustments. vexecds (and end users) are free to implement arbitrarily complex selection policies.

Since users will want to use vexecds based on the selection policies the vexecds implement, the discovery of vexecd daemons and use of their services cannot be completely transparent. More information is needed from the user either in the form of a list of suitable vexecd servers or a criteria which is expressed in a way that the system can automatically discover which vexecd daemons implement that criteria. Currently, we take the former approach. Users specify a list of suitable vexecd daemons using an environment variable, VEXEC_SVRS.

Discovery of vexecd hosts that implement suitable selection policies can be done through out-of-band means (e.g., posting on a web page) or it can be done semi-automatically. We offer both approaches. The former is self-explanatory. The latter involves using the cluster IP multicast channel to multicast to all vexecd daemons in the system asking them what selection policy they implement. Each vexecd, upon receiving a such a request, returns a string that provides a textual description of its policy which the user can then use to construct a suitable list for setting the VEXEC_SVRS environment variable.

3.5   Error and Cleanup Model

REXEC provides a well-defined error handling and cleanup model for applications. If an error occurs on the rexec client, in any of the remote processes, or on any of the TCP connections between the rexec client and any of the remote rexecd daemons, the entire application exits, all resources are reclaimed, and a textual error message is printed to the user. A common shortcoming in many previous remote execution systems, especially those that support parallel execution, is lack of a precise error and cleanup model and insufficient implementations of remote cleanup. REXEC addresses this by defining a model, addressing the new failure modes associated with remote execution and parallel and distributed programs, and providing a robust implementation.

Transparent remote execution of parallel and sequential applications introduces new two classes of failures. First, failures can occur in the rexec client (the local point of control) and between the rexec client and the daemons. Since the rexec client logically represents an applications' remote process(es), failure of the rexec client is interpreted as failure of the application and the application is aborted. Second, failures can occur in individual processes of a parallel or distributed program. Since for all but the most trivially parallelizable and distributed programs there will be communication between processes and failure of one process usually means failure of the entire application, we interpret failure of an individual process in the program as a failure of the entire application. While these interpretations may not be true for all applications, we feel they are reasonable assumptions for a large class of programs.

In general, there are many potential error and cleanup models the system could support. However, only a handful of them make practical sense to real applications. For example, another useful failure model which we are considering supporting but currently do not implement is the model where all processes are completely decoupled and we leave it up to the application to deal with failures. Such a model might be appropriate, for example, for a parallel application with its own error detection and the ability to grow and shrink based on resource availability and faults.

The implementation of the error and cleanup model is done mainly at user-level but also involves some small kernel modifications. At user-level, the rexec client and rexecd daemons monitor each other through their TCP connections. Upon detecting an error, the rexec client exits. Upon detecting an error with some rexec client, rexecd frees all resources associated with that client and kills all its threads.

To ensure that proper process cleanup is performed on remote nodes, REXEC uses small modifications to the Linux kernel to track and control a logical set of processes whose first member is a user process forked by rexecd and other members are descendents of that process. To do this, we added a new system call to specify the first member of a logical set of processes (all descendents of that process inherit the fact that they are part of the same set) and a system call to deliver signals to all members of that set, regardless of changes in Unix process group, intermediate parents exiting causing their children to be inherited by init, and so forth. When performing cleanup in response to an error, REXEC simply sends SIGKILL to all processes in the logical set of processes, which results in all resources for all processes in the set being freed. We also modified the wait system call to deal with logical sets of processes so a process p_x blocked on a wait call waiting for another process p_y to exit does not return until all processes in p_y's logical process set have exited. This feature is used by the per-rexec-client thread (Fig. 3.2) so it returns only when all processes forked by the user's original process (i.e., the process which the per-rexec-client thread did a fork/exec on), including itself, have exited.

An alternative approach to cleanup, one which would have resulted in better portability of the system, would have been to send SIGKILL to the process group for the user's process that was forked by rexecd. An implementation of this approach uses standard POSIX interfaces. However, there are limitations and consequences. The biggest limitation is the inability to keep track of process relationships when process groups change. An example of this is a user process forked by rexecd which then forks a child and exits. rexecd would keep track of the parent's process group but since the parent has exited, the child now becomes inherited by init and becomes a member of an orphaned process group. Consequently, it becomes impossible to send a signal to the original process group. The orphaned child will not receive it and thus rexecd has lost track of a process. User processes could also call setpgrp themselves and a similar problem results. By keeping tracking process relationships in the kernel using our new system calls, we ensure that we always are able to kill all processes associated with a user process forked by rexecd.

3.6 Parallel and Distributed Applications

REXEC supports parallel and distributed applications by allowing users to launch and control multiple instances of the same program on multiple nodes and by providing a set of hooks that allow parallel runtime environments to be built. Starting #nodes instances of the same program is accomplished by adding a -n #nodes switch to the rexec client program which allows the user to specify a program should be run on #nodes nodes of the cluster.

The hooks we provide for runtime environments are a fairly minimal set. Each remote process has four environment variables set by REXEC: REXEC_GPID,

REXEC_PAR_DEGREE, REXEC_MY_VNN, and REXEC_SVRS. REXEC_GPID is a globally unique identifier for a particular execution of a user's application. It is implemented as a 64-bit concatenation of the 32-bit IP address of the interface the rexec client uses to communicate with rexecds and the local 32-bit process ID of the rexec client. REXEC_PAR_DEGREE is a 32-bit integer which specifies the number of nodes the application is running on. Within an n node program, REXEC assigns an ordering on the nodes from 0 to REXEC_PAR_DEGREE - 1. On each node, REXEC_MY_VNN specifies the position of that node in that ordering. Finally, REXEC_SVRS contains a list of REXEC_PAR_DEGREE hostnames (or IP addresses) for each of the nodes the user's application is running on.

3.7 Authentication and Encryption

REXEC provides user authentication and encryption of all communication between rexec clients and rexecd daemons. More specifically, REXEC uses the SSLeay version 0.9.0b implementation of the Secure Socket Layer (SSL) protocol [6] for authentication and encryption of all TCP connections between these entities. Each user has a private key, encrypted with 3DES, and a certificate containing the user's identity and a public key that is signed by a well-known certificate authority who verifies user identities. In our system, we use a single trusted certificate authority for certificate signing and use user names as identifies in certificates.

Each time a user wants to run an application using REXEC, the user invokes the rexec client on the command line and types in a passphrase which decrypts the user's private key. The system then performs a handshake between the rexec client and rexecd, negotiates a cipher, uses a Diffie-Hellman key exchange to establish a session key, uses RSA to verify that the user's certificate was signed by the trusted certificate authority, and checks that the username in the certificate exists and that it matches that of corresponding local user ID that was propagated from the rexec client. Once the user's identity has been established, all communication over the corresponding TCP connection is encrypted with 3DES using the shared session key.

4 REXEC Applications

In this section, we present three examples of how REXEC has been applied to provide remote execution facilities to applications. In the first example, we describe how the REXEC system is used in its basic form to provide remote execution for parallel and sequential jobs. In the second example, we describe an MPI implementation using a fast communication layer on Myrinet that uses REXEC as its underlying remote execution facility. Finally, in the third example, we provide an example of how REXEC has been extended to provide remote execution on Berkeley's Millennium cluster which uses market-based resource management techniques [4].

4.1 Parallel and Sequential Jobs

The rexec client provides the minimal amount of support needed to transparently run and control parallel and sequential programs on a cluster. Users run the rexec client as follows: rexec -n #nodes progname arg1 arg2 .. argn, where #nodes is the number of nodes the program should be executed on and progname arg1 arg2 .. argn is the command line the user would type to run program progname with arguments arg1, arg2, .., argn on a single node. Node selection is done through use of vexecd daemons by specifying a list of suitable vexecd daemons through the VEXEC_SVRS environment variable. Alternatively, if the user wants to run an application on a specific set of nodes, the user can set the REXEC_SVRS environment variable. A non-null REXEC_SVRS always takes precedence over VEXEC_SVRS. Parallel and distributed programs can be launched using the basic rexec client. It is responsibility of runtime layers or the application to make use of REXEC's environment variable support for parallel and distributed programs to decide how data and computation should be partitioned and how communication between processes is established.

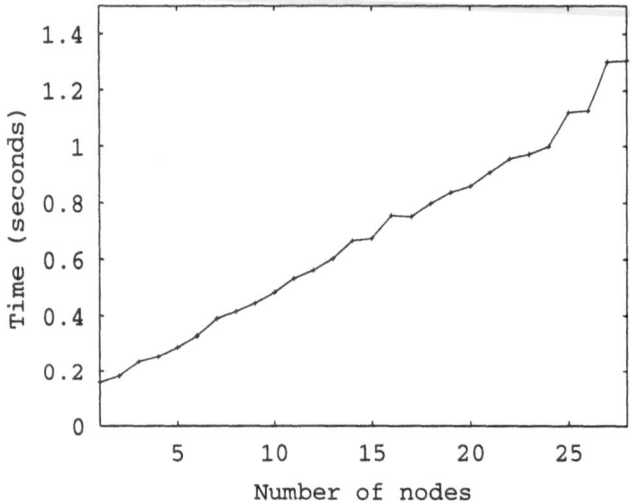

Fig. 3. Measured execution time to run a null parallel program with REXEC as a function of number of nodes. This graph shows the measured execution time of a parallel program that starts and immediately exits on multiple nodes of the cluster. The measurements illustrate the basic costs associated with running jobs through the REXEC system. The start-up and cleanup cost for a running a single node program with REXEC is 158 ms. As the number of nodes increases, total execution time scales linearly with an average per-node cost of 42.8 ms.

Figure 3 illustrates the basic performance and scalability characteristics of REXEC. It shows the measured execution time of running a null parallel program that starts and immediately exits versus the number nodes the program was run on. The measurements illustrate the basic costs associated with running jobs through the REXEC system. The start-up and cleanup cost for a running a single node program with REXEC is 158 ms. As the number of nodes increases, total execution time scales linearly with an average per-node cost of 42.8 ms. Note that, to date, we have mainly focused on other aspects of

REXEC's design as stated in Section 2. We have not aggressively pursued performance optimizations on the system. Thus, absolute performance numbers as shown still have considerable room for improvement. The key point here is that the costs are scaling linearly with the number of nodes. Per-node costs will be optimized in a future version of REXEC.

4.2 MPI/GM on Myrinet

Using REXEC's basic hooks for parallel and distributed programs, we modified Myricom's MPI implementation over the GM (MPI/GM) fast communication layer [12] to use REXEC as its underlying remote execution mechanism. MPI rank and size are set using the REXEC_PAR_DEGREE and REXEC_MY_VNN environment variables. Communication is set up using REXEC_GPID and REXEC_SVRS to do an all-to-all exchange of GM port names using a centralized nameserver. Upon creating a GM port, each process binds a (key,value) = (REXEC_GPID:REXEC_MY_VNN, GM port number) pair in the nameserver then does REXEC_PAR_DEGREE lookups on keys REXEC_GPID:vnn (vnn = 0,1,..,REXEC_PAR_DEGREE-1). Since each GM network address is an IP address and a GM port number and each process knows the hostname (IP address) to VNN mapping from REXEC_SVRS, each process thus knows the GM network address of each process in the program and can then communicate. Using MPI/GM over REXEC, MPI programs can be started and controlled just like any other application run through REXEC.

4.3 Computational Economy

As part of the Berkeley Millennium Project, we extended the REXEC remote execution environment to operate in the context of a market-based resource management system. In this system, users compete for shared cluster resources in a *computational economy* where nodes are sellers of computational resources, user applications are buyers, and each user sets a willingness to pay for each application based on the personal utility of running it. By managing resources according to personal value, we hypothesize that market-based sharing can deliver significantly more value to users than traditional approaches to resource management. To support a computational economy, we extended the REXEC system in three ways. First, a new command line switch (-r maxrate) was added to the rexec client to specify the maximum rate, expressed in credits per minute, the application is willing to pay for CPU time. Second, rexecd was modified to use an economic front end (a collection of functions that implement the CPU market) which performs proportional-share CPU allocation using a stride scheduler [20] and charging of user accounts for CPU usage. Third, we modified rexecd to include in its announcement packets the current aggregate willingness to pay of all REXEC applications competing for its resources for building selection policies based on the economy.

5   Related Work

Research efforts in remote execution environments for clusters have been going on for over a decade. Each has succeeded in addressing and to various extents solving different subsets of the key problems in remote execution systems. None of these systems, however, has addressed the range of problems that REXEC does. Built on previous work and practical experience with a large-scale research cluster, REXEC addresses a wide range of practical needs while providing useful features which address important issues such as error handling and cleanup, high availability, and dynamic cluster configuration. To accomplish its goals, REXEC is implemented at user-level on a commodity operating system with small modifications to the OS kernel. Such an approach is an example of one of three distinct implementation strategies: (i) user-level approaches (ii) modification of existing operating systems, and (iii) completely new distributed operating systems.

GLUnix [7], SCore-D [8], Sidle [9], Butler [13], HetNOS [3], and Load Sharing Facility (LSF) [22] are examples of user-level implementations. Compared to REXEC, each of these systems implements a subset of REXEC's features. GLUnix and Score-D, for example, are the only two systems in the list that support parallel programs. However, both of them also rely on centralized control and manually updated cluster configuration. Butler and LSF support different forms of replicated discovery and selection. However, neither supports an error and cleanup model as extensive as REXEC or strong authentication and encryption. One notable feature that has been implemented in some of these systems which REXEC currently does not support is a programmatic interface to the system. GLUnix, Butler, HetNOS, and LSF, for example, allow users to write applications which link with a C library of remote execution related functions. Using this model, applications such as a shell which automatically decides whether to execute a job locally or remotely have been developed.

MOSIX [2], NEST [1], COCANET Unix [16], and Solaris MC [10, 17] are examples of modifying and extending an existing operating system. Again, each of the systems supports only a subset of REXEC's features. NEST, for example, supports transparent remote execution but does not support features such as dynamic cluster membership or parallel and distributed application support. MOSIX, for example, provides transparent remote execution but does so in a fairly limited context which is mainly targeted for load balancing amongst a set of desktop machines to exploit idle time. One notable feature supported by MOSIX which REXEC currently does not support is process migration. Mechanisms to implement it, however, are well-known [5, 11, 15, 19] in both user-level and kernel-level implementations and under various constraints. Another notable difference between REXEC and these kernel-level implementations is the degree of transparency in the remote execution system. Kernel-level implementations can achieve greater levels of transparency than user-level approaches. Solaris MC, for example, implements a true single system image with real global PIDs, a global /proc filesystem, and a global cluster-wide filesystem.

Sprite [14], V [18, 19], and LOCUS [21] are examples of completely new distributed operating systems which support transparent remote execution. Like the other systems described, these distributed operating systems also support only a subset of REXEC's features. V, for example, supports a publish-based, decentralized state announcement scheme very much like REXEC. On the hand, V does not support parallel applications, does not support flexible selection policies, nor does it implement strong authentication and encryption. Like MOSIX, all three of these systems support process migration which REXEC currently does not implement. In addition, like the kernel-level implementations previously described, these new operating systems also achieve greater levels of transparency due to implementations at the operating system level and, in the case of Sprite and LOCUS, cluster-wide global filesystems.

6 Future Work

Future work on the REXEC system comes in four areas. First, we intend to add a programmatic interface to REXEC that exposes REXEC's functionality to user applications though a user library. Using this interface, one of the applications we are planning to build is a shell that understands remote execution through REXEC and, in particular, makes it easier and more natural for users to use the computational economy. Second, we intend to add support for transparent remote execution of X applications and secure tunneling of X traffic over SSL. Techniques for implementing such support are well-known and already exist in programs such as the secure shell client (ssh). Third, we plan to pursue performance optimizations of the system to bring per-node costs down. As the Millennium system scales to hundreds of nodes as planned, optimization of such costs will become increasingly important for highly parallel applications. Finally, we intend to work on making REXEC portable across multiple operating systems and eventually plan on making a public release of the source code so others can use it and improve on it.

7 Conclusion

To bring clusters of computers into the mainstream as general-purpose computing systems, better facilities are needed for transparent remote execution of parallel and sequential applications. While much research has been done in the area of remote execution, much of this work remains inaccessible for clusters built using contemporary hardware and operating systems. To address this, we designed and implemented a new remote execution environment called REXEC. Building on previous work in remote execution and practical experience with the Berkeley NOW and Millennium clusters, it provides decentralized control, transparent remote execution, dynamic cluster configuration, decoupled node discovery and selection, a well-defined failure and cleanup model, parallel and distributed program support, and strong authentication and encryption. The system is implemented and is currently installed on a 32-node cluster of 2-way SMPs running the Linux 2.2.5 operating system. It currently serves as the remote execution facility for market-based resource management studies as part of the UC Berkeley Millennium Project.

References

1. AGRAWAL, R., AND EZZAT, A. K. Location independent remote execution in nest. *IEEE Transactions on Software Engineering 13*, 8 (August 1987), 905–912.
2. BARAK, A., LA'ADAN, O., AND SMITH, A. Scalable cluster computing with mosix for linux. In *Proceedings of Linux Expo '99* (May 1999), pp. 95–100.

3. BARCELLOS, A. M. P., SCHRAMM, J. F. L., FILHO, V. R. B., AND GEYER, C. F. R. The hetnos network operating system: a tool for writing distributed applications. *Operating Systems Review* (October 1994).

4. CHUN, B. N., AND CULLER, D. E. Market-based proportional resource sharing for clusters. Submitted for publication, September 1999.

5. DOUGLIS, F., AND OUSTERHOUT, J. Transparent process migration: Design alternatives and the sprite implementation. *Software—Practice and Experience 21*, 8 (August 1991).

6. FREIER, A. O., KARLTON, P., AND KOCHER, P. C. The ssl protocol version 3.0 (internet-draft). 1996.

7. GHORMLEY, D. P., PETROU, D., RODRIGUES, S. H., VAHDAT, A. M., AND ANDERSON, T. E. Glunix: a global layer unix for a network of workstations. *Software—Practice and Experience* (Apr. 1998).

8. HORI, A., TEZUKA, H., , AND ISHIKAWA, Y. An implementation of parallel operating system for clustered commodity computers. In *Proceedings of Cluster Computing Conference '97* (March 1997).

9. JU, J., XU, G., AND TAO, J. Parallel computing using idle workstations. *Operating Systems Review* (July 1993).

10. KHALIDI, Y. A., BERNABEU, J. M., MATENA, V., SHIRRIFF, K., AND THADANI, M. Solaris mc: A multi computer os. In *Proceedings of the 1996 USENIX Conference* (1996).

11. LITZKOW, M., TANNENBAUM, T., BASNEY, J., AND LIVNY, M. Checkpoint and migration of unix processes in the condor distributed processing system. Tech. Rep. 1346, University of Wisconsin-Madison, April 1997.

12. MYRICOM. The gm api. 1999.

13. NICHOLS, D. A. Using idle workstations in a shared computing environment. In *Proceedings of the 11th ACM Symposium on Operating Systems Principles* (1987).

14. OUSTERHOUT, J. K., CHERENSON, A. R., DOUGLIS, F., NELSON, M. N., AND WELCH, B. B. The sprite network operating system. *IEEE Computer 21*, 2 (February 1988).

15. PLANK, J. S., BECK, M., KINGSLEY, G., AND LI, K. Libckpt: Transparent checkpointing under unix. In *Proceedings of the 1995 USENIX Winter Conference* (1995).

16. ROWE, L. A., AND BIRMAN, K. P. A local network based on the unix operating system. *IEEE Transactions on Software Engineering 8*, 2 (March 1982).

17. SHIRRIFF, K. Building distributed process management on an object-oriented framework. In *Proceedings of the 1997 USENIX Conference* (1997).

18. STUMM, M. The design and implementation of a decentralized scheduling facility for a workstation cluster. In *Proceedings of the 2nd IEEE Conference on Computer Workstations* (March 1988), pp. 12–22.

19 THEIMER, M. M., LANTZ, K. A., , AND CHERITON, D. R. Preemptable remote execution facilities for the v-system. In *Proceedings of the 10th ACM Symposium on Operating Systems Principles* (1985).

20. WALDSPURGER, C. A., AND WEIHL, W. E. Stride scheduling: Deterministic proportional-share resource management. Tech. Rep. MIT/LCS/TM-528, Massachusetts Institute of Technology, 1995.

21. WALKER, B., POPEK, G., ENGLISH, R., KLINE, C., AND THIEL, G. The locus distributed operating system. In *Proceedings of the 9th ACM Symposium on Operating Systems Principles* (1983), pp. 49–70.

22. ZHOU, S., WANG, J., ZHENG, X., AND DELISLE, P. Utopia: A load sharing facility for large, heterogenous distributed computer systems. *Software—Practice and Experience* (1992).

A Visual BSP Programming Environment for Distributed Computing

Jeremy Martin[1] and Alex Wilson[2]

[1] Oxford Supercomputing Centre
Wolfson Building, Parks Road
Oxford, OX1 3QD, UK
jeremy.martin@computing-services.oxford.ac.uk
[2] Embedded Solutions Ltd, 7/8 Milton Park
Abingdon, Oxfordshire, OX14 4RT, UK
awilson@EMBEDDEDSOL.com

Abstract. The idea of network-based parallel computing, using commodity components, is not new. However, until recently, the communication performance of such systems was inadequate for the efficient parallelisation of most algorithms. With the advent of *fast ethernet* and affordable switching technology, this is no longer the case and there is much work in progress to exploit the potential for cut-price supercomputing.

Now that the hardware issues are being resolved there is still a clear requirement for suitable programming models and software development tools to make it easy to use this emerging generation of parallel computers effectively. We believe that the BSP programming paradigm is ideally suited for network parallel computing due its elegance, simplicity and performance prediction feature. We are developing a visual tool to facilitate the development of BSP programs in a distributed environment. In this paper we describe the operation of this tool in a tutorial style, and we discuss additional features that are planned for the future.

1 Introduction

The structure of this paper is as follows. First we shall review the Bulk Synchronous Parallel (BSP) model of computation and illustrate its cost-prediction model in the context of NOW ('network-of-workstations') parallel computers. Then we shall run through a tutorial of using the BSP visual development system. This is followed by a description of implementation issues. At the moment this tool consists primarily of a debugger, but we plan to add some extra features, which are discussed in the final section.

The BSP Computation Model

The BSP computer[7] consists of a number of processor/memory pairs connected by a communication network. Each processor has fast access to local memory and *uniformly slow* access to remote memory.

B. Falsafi and M. Lauria (Eds.): CANPC 2000, LNCS 1797, pp. 15–29, 2000.

The BSP programming model is a prominent example of the use of *remote memory transfer*. This is an alternative to message passing, in a distributed memory environment. Each process can directly write and read to the memory of a remote process. These actions are one-sided with no action by the remote process and hence there is no potential for deadlock.

Execution of a BSP program proceeds in *supersteps* separated by *global synchronisations*. A superstep consists of each process doing some calculation, using local data, *and/or* communicating some data by direct memory transfer. The global synchronisation event guarantees that all communication has completed before the commencement of the next superstep.

BSP programs are SPMD, which stands for *single program multiple data*. Each processor runs an identical program, but the programmer has access to the current process id (which is in the range 0 to *nprocs* − 1, where *nprocs* is the total number of processes) to allow different behaviour to be implemented at each node if required.

The main BSP commands are as follows:

bsp_begin, bsp_end define start and end of SPMD code
bsp_pid get local process id
bsp_nprocs get total number of threads
bsp_sync perform barrier synchronisation
bsp_push_reg make a data structure globally visible
bsp_pop_reg remove the global visibility of a data structure
bsp_put, bsp_get transfer data to/from other processes. If the *high-performance* option is selected this may take place at any time during superstep so one must not change/use the data until after the next global synchronisation.

Let us consider a C program for the numerical solution to Laplace's equation over a rectangular domain, with fixed values on the boundary, using the technique of Jacobi iteration[2]. The sequential code for a single iteration is as follows:

```
for (row = 1; row < HEIGHT - 1; row++) {
  for (col = 1; col < WIDTH - 1; col++) {
    unew[row][col] =
    0.25*(u[row - 1][col] + u[row + 1][col] +
        u[row][col - 1] + u[row][col + 1]);
  }
}
```

We could parallelise this using BSP by arranging the grid into overlapping strips, each to be worked on by a separate process.

Each iteration involves a computation phase, then a communication phase, and finally a global synchronisation. Each process updates its internal nodes and then transmits 'halo' data to its neighbours.

```
for (row = 1; row < STRIPS - 1; row++) {
  for (col = 1; col < WIDTH - 1; col++) {
    unew[row][col] =
    0.25*(u[row - 1][col] + u[row + 1][col] +
          u[row][col - 1] + u[row][col + 1]);
  }
}
pid = bsp_pid();
if (pid != NPROCS - 1) { /*update next strip*/
  bsp_put(pid + 1, unew[STRIPS-2],
  unew[0], 0, 4 * WIDTH);
}
if (pid != 0) { /*update previous strip*/
  bsp_put(pid - 1, unew[1],
  unew[STRIPS-1], 0, 4 * WIDTH);
}
bsp_sync();
```

BSP Cost Modelling

Perhaps the most important feature of BSP is its cost-prediction model, which makes it relatively easy to evaluate the potential efficiency of an algorithm prior to implementation. In this model the parallel computer is reduced to four constants (s, p, l, g) where

s = processor speed (Mflops)

p = number of processors

$l = \dfrac{\text{latency/synchronisation time}}{\text{time for 1 floating point op}}$

$$g = \frac{\text{time to get/send 1 fp. value}}{\text{time to do 1 floating point op.}}$$

The cost of a single superstep is then

$$n_o + n_c g + l$$

where
n_o = max number of f.p. operations performed by any process
n_c = max number of real values communicated by any process
and the predicted execution time is given by

$$s^{-1}(n_o + n_c g + l)$$

The BSP cost of the whole task is just the sum of the individual supersteps.

In the case of the above Jacobi iteration example we evaluate the BSP cost function as follows. Let us assume that the grid has dimension I in each direction. Then the amount of data points to be updated by each processor is $\frac{I^2}{p}$. Each update requires four arithmetic operations so we have:

$$n_o = \frac{4I^2}{p}$$

The most communication that any processor has to do is to output two complete rows of data to its neighbours (and simultaneously to input two new rows from the same parties). So we have:

$$n_c = 2I$$

This leads to an overall cost function, for a single iteration, of

$$\frac{4I^2}{p} + 2Ig + l$$

Note that we could reduce the cost by partitioning the data grid into squares rather than strips. In that case the cost would be

$$\frac{4I^2}{p} + \frac{4Ig}{\sqrt{p}} + l$$

Using the Oxford implementation of BSP[5], parameters (s, p, l, g) have been measured for a wide variety of architectures. These may be used to predict the likely performance of a BSP algorithm prior to execution (or even program construction). Certain algorithms can be immediately consigned to the waste-bin, perhaps avoiding months of futile effort.

Here are some examples of BSP parameters for some particular architectures, based on the Oxford BSPlib benchmarks[12].

Machine	s	p	l	g
Origin 2000	101	4	1789	10.24
		32	39057	66.7
Cray T3E	46.7	4	357	1.77
		16	751	1.66
Pentium NOW	61	4	139981	1128.5
10Mbit shared ether		8	539139	1994.1
Pentium II NOW	88	4	11757	31.5
100Mbit switched ether		8	18347	30.9

The latter two rows of this table show that the advent of fast-ethernet and switching technology has led to a huge reduction in the l and g communication parameters for a PC cluster. In particular, for an 8-processor system the g parameter, which represents the cost of entering data into the network, is improved by a factor of around 70. There are two reasons for this. Firstly fast ethernet has ten times the bandwidth of standard ethernet. Secondly using a switch allows each processor to have a dedicated cable, virtually eliminating collisions. There is further potential for reducing the g parameter by using multiple ethernet connections per processor node. The BSP parameters for such machines are now in the league of purpose-built supercomputers, but they cost far less to build. Network-based parallel computing has finally come of age!

To emphasise this point, let us now compare the likely performance of the Jacobi iteration program running on an 'old-style' NOW with its performance on a state-of-the art machine.

Consider running the program on a 1000×1000 data grid. On an 8-processor Pentium NOW, connected by a 10 Mbit shared ethernet, the predicted running time for a single iteration would be

$$\frac{1}{61} \left(\frac{4 \times 1000^2}{8} + 2000 \times 1994.1 + 539139 \right) \times 10^{-6}\text{s}$$
$$= 0.082\text{s}$$

which is longer than the predicted single processor execution time of

$$\frac{1}{61} \left(4 \times 1000^2 \right) \times 10^{-6}\text{s} = 0.066\text{s}$$

In fact the application under consideration is an example of a program that parallelises particularly well. For many algorithms the story would be even worse. So the BSP cost-prediction model gives us a clear indication as to why network-based parallel computing has been slow to take off.

Now consider running the same parallel code on an 8-processor Pentium-II NOW connected by 100 Mbit switched ethernet. The predicted running time is 0.0066s compared with the predicted single-processor time of 0.045s, giving a speedup factor of 6.8 and a parallel efficiency of 85%.

2 The BSP Development System

Parallel programming is a tricky business. Pathological problems such as deadlock, livelock, and race conditions are the bane of its practitioners[6]. The simplicity of the BSP model has been a major step towards making parallel programming more accessible. But in order for BSP to succeed in gaining worldwide prominence there is a requirement for a supporting suite of professional software development tools. We are in the process of developing such tools. The main component in place is a visual debugger. Further work is planned to incorporate facilities for parallel performance profiling[3, 4], visualisation, and computational steering.

Now let us illustrate the operation of the BSP debugger by considering its application to the parallel program described in section 2. When the program is executed in 'debug mode' a graphical console appears and the program halts at the call to **bsp_begin**, which marks the start of its parallel region. A process display window is created to depict the processes that have been spawned and their subsequent communication actions. A window onto the source code is also provided, showing the current point of execution that has been reached.

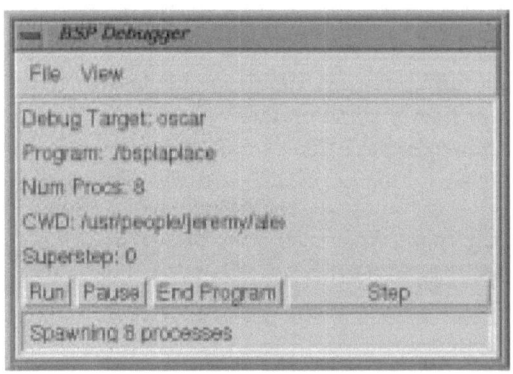
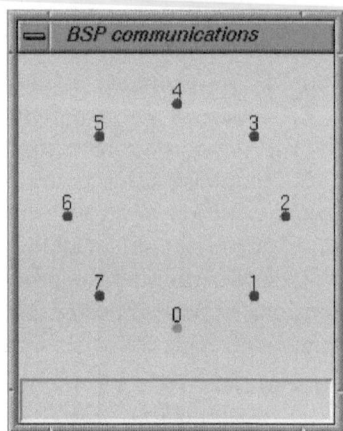

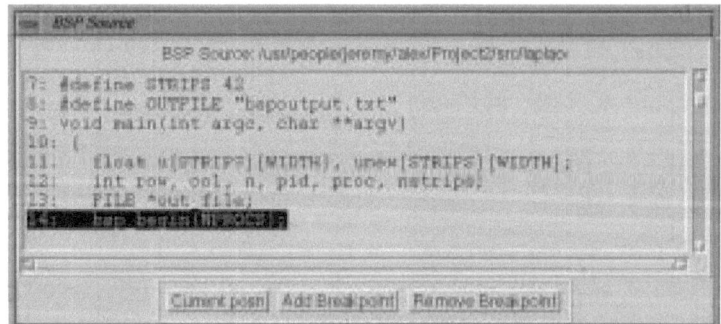

Henceforth the BSP superstep is taken as the quantum of computation and, using the console buttons, it is possible to advance the computation one step at a time, and to examine the source, destination and content of all communication events that take place.

After superstep one the program is yet to perform any communication; registration of data has just taken place (using calls to **bsp_push_reg**).

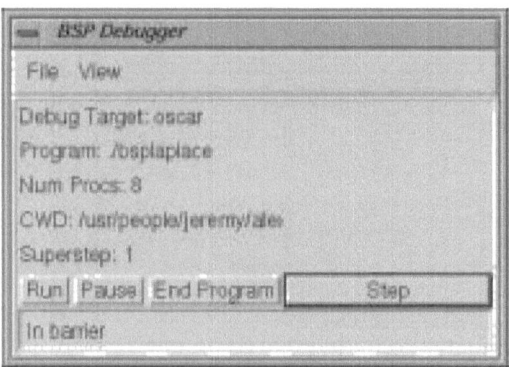

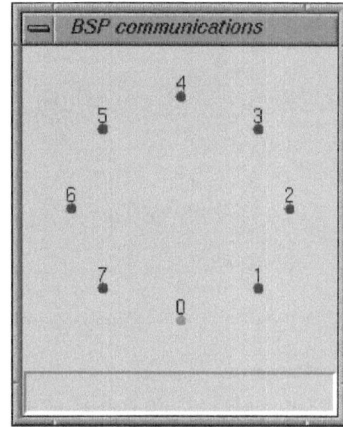

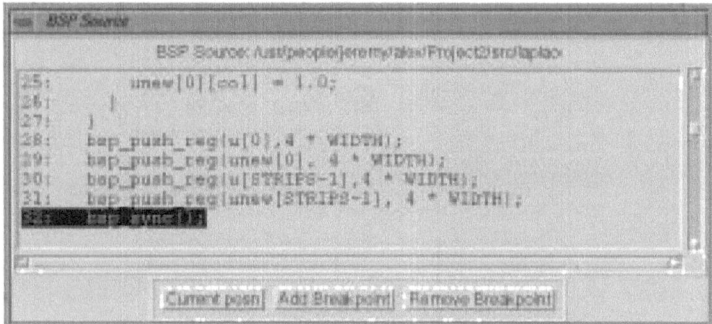

After superstep two we see, from the communication display, that data have been transmitted between adjacent processes in the manner that we would expect.

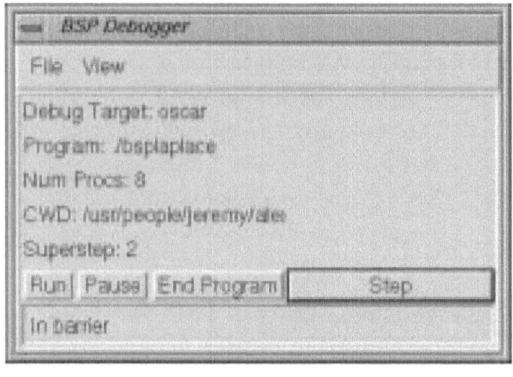

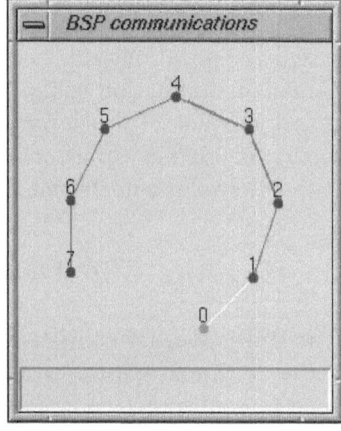

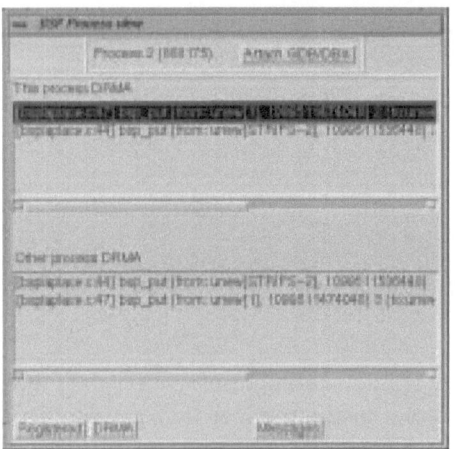

It is now possible to examine the content of individual communication events. At this early stage in the computation the actual data being transmitted are not particularly interesting, all being zero. It will require a number of iterations for non-zero values to propagate from the boundaries.

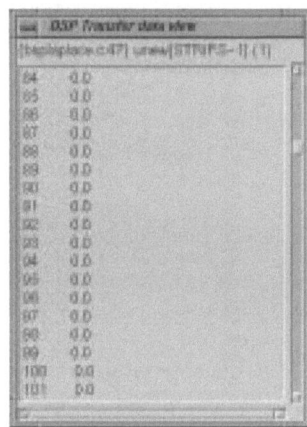

Satisfied that all is in order, we may click the console's 'run' button to allow the program to proceed without interruption. However we are free to intercept it at any later stage using the 'pause' button.

The development tool has been used to program a number of sophisticated parallel applications[10], such as parallel sorting using regular sampling[8] and Gaussian elimination using partial pivoting[9]. We believe it has saved an immense amount of development time. Note that, for fine-grained debugging, a facility is provided to attach a serial debugger to any thread, and interact with it remotely through the console.

3   How the BSP Debugger Works

The BSP debugger consists of a high-level debug library of BSP commands together with a graphical user interface programmed in java[1]. Around six thousand lines of source code have been written so far.

The Debug Library

The debug library was designed to be as easy to use as possible. Thus the user is only required to include the BSPlib debugging header **db_bsp.h** (see Figure 1) instead of the standard BSPlib header **bsp.h**, and to link with the library file **libdb_bsp.a**.

The debugger header file (see figure 1) redefines all the BSP functions (using C preprocessor macros) so that they are replaced with debugging functions instead (e.g. any instances of **bsp_sync** are redefined to **db_bsp_sync** etc.). Note that some of the debugging functions have additional arguments, for specifying the actual names of variables and the file and line number of source code from which the function is called. The values for these variables may be automatically generated using standard C macros (**#**, **_FILE_**, and **_LINE_**). This enables the BSP debugger to locate the source code from which all BSP calls are made and to display the names of variables that are registered and communicated.

In order to know the name of the running program (required for attaching **gdb** and other sequential debuggers to individual processes) the **main** function is redefined to **program_main**, and a new main function is defined in the debug library. The latter takes a copy of the program arguments (including the name of the executable) before passing them unchanged to the debugged program's main function.

```
/* db_bsp.h - Include this file instead of bsp.h to use the BSP debugger */

/* We have to redefine main so that we can use our own function and thus get */
/* the name of the running program */
  #define main(a, b)            program_main(a, b)
/* We use #a to pass the name of variable a */
  #define bsp_push_reg(a,b)     db_bsp_push_reg(a,b,#a)
  #define bsp_pop_reg(a)        db_bsp_pop_reg(a)
  #define bsp_put(a,b,c,d,e)    db_bsp_put(a,b,c,d,e, #b, #c, NORMAL, __FILE__, __LINE__ )
  #define bsp_get(a,b,c,d,e)    db_bsp_get(a,b,c,d,e, #b, #d, NORMAL, __FILE__, __LINE__ )
  #define bsp_bcast(a,b,c,d)    db_bsp_bcast(a,b,c,d, #b, #c, __FILE__, __LINE__ )
  #define bsp_hpput(a,b,c,d,e)  db_bsp_put(a,b,c,d,e, #b, #c, HIGH, __FILE__, __LINE__ )
  #define bsp_hpget(a,b,c,d,e)  db_bsp_get(a,b,c,d,e, #b, #d, HIGH, __FILE__, __LINE__ )
  #define bsp_sync()            db_bsp_sync( __FILE__, __LINE__ )
  #define bsp_begin(a)          db_bsp_begin(a, __FILE__, __LINE__ )
  #define bsp_end()             db_bsp_end( __FILE__, __LINE__ )
  #define bsp_pid()             db_bsp_pid()
  #define bsp_nprocs()          db_bsp_nprocs()
  #define bsp_init              db_bsp_init
  #define bsp_abort             db_bsp_abort
#endif
```

Fig. 1. The debug library header file

Providing a full picture of the communications taking place during the running of any BSP program requires that a considerable amount of information be obtained, updated, and sent to the graphical interface on demand. The constraints of a debugging library mean that this data can only be managed and exported upon calling the library functions. So each debug BSP function has to perform various additional tasks, as well as executing the corresponding BSP command. A hidden layer of communication has been added to allow each process in a program to be controlled and interrogated while retaining its original semantics. This is done using only the original BSP inter-process communication functions[10].

The BSP library guarantees only that process number zero has use of a machine's I/O capability. Thus it is that process only which is linked to the java graphical interface. This means that if data is required from the other processes then there must be some form of internal communication (using BSP) in order to pipe the data into process zero and then out to the graphical interface. This also works in reverse with queries and commands from the graphical interface arriving at process zero before being distributed to the other processes.

When a program compiled with the debugging library enters a barrier synchronisation, it is temporarily halted (unless the console's 'run' button has been pressed), and the user is able to send requests for further information about the program. This capability, and that of returning the requested information from all processes is achieved by implementing a 'false barrier' which allows information to pass from the graphical interface through process zero to the other processes. In order to do this, the debugging library registers a variable called **barrier_command** at the beginning of the program (in **db_bsp_begin**).

When **db_bsp_sync** is called, all the processes enter a loop in which process zero awaits commands from the graphical interface, before copying them into **barrier_command** on all the other processes. All processes then synchronise and carry out the appropriate command (for example '**QUERY_TRANSFERS**'), synchronise and then await the next command (e.g. '**SEND_SOURCE**'). On receipt of the command '**END_BSP_SYNC**' (the user having pressed the 'step' or 'run' button on the graphical interface) all processes exit their loop and the main BSP program continues to run.

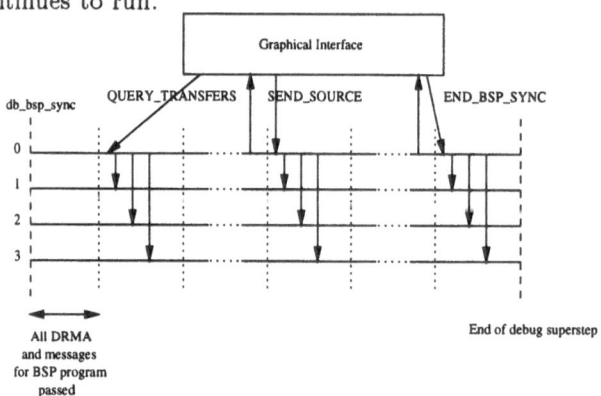

The Graphical Interface

The java GUI component interacts with BSP process number zero using TCP/IP sockets. At the outset of the project it was decided that the implementation provided should be as portable as possible and should run on every platform which is supported by the current version of BSPlib. However, graphical interfaces tend to be highly specific to particular platforms. The graphical part of the debugger was expected to be fairly complex visually but not to require a particularly large amount of processing power. Therefore it was decided that java would suit the requirements very well (being extensively portable, with built-in networking capabilities, easy to use to implement graphical interfaces, and sufficiently powerful for the task required[1]).

Several possible methods were considered before it was decided that the best way of communicating between the C library and the java graphical interface was through the use of TCP-IP data-stream sockets[1]. Socket communications are simple to implement in java, and there are a set of standard C socket libraries available across all major UNIX platforms. Moreover, employing sockets also allows the user to run the debugger on a machine separate from the BSP code if so desired (useful, as not all parallel machines come with a java virtual machine, and high-performance programs do not benefit from having the added overhead of a java virtual machine running on one of their processors).

Although the basic data-types in java are represented in the same way on every machine (one of the benefits of the language), the way that different machines (and compilers) store C data-types can vary substantially. So as to maintain the portability of the debug library, the code for communicating with the java interface has been kept separate. There are several functions defined to convert C types to a format which java can readily read. Messages passed consist of a 32 bit integer indicating the type of the message, followed by a variable length buffer containing the main body of the communication.

Displaying the Communication Topology. Providing a graphical representation of the communications between processes required us to implement an appropriate graph-drawing algorithm. The method chosen is a physical simulation of a number of balls (the processors) connected by springs (the communications links between processors). The balls are placed at an initial starting position and then the simulation allowed to run. Once the root mean square velocity of the balls has fallen below a certain threshold the simulation is stopped and the physical arrangement drawn to the screen. The algorithm is designed to use the positions of balls at the end of one superstep as the start position of the simulation for the next. This is so that processors change position as little as possible, making the evolution of communications over time easier to see.

Displaying Transfer Data. The approach taken for displaying transfer data is to extract it from the system only on demand. If, for example, the user of the debugger wishes to display the contents of a message that has been written to process five, then process zero is instructed, via the TCP-IP socket, to obtain that information. Process zero, in turn, issues a request to process five to supply the data. A global synchronisation is then applied. Next process five sends back the requested data and another synchronisation is applied. Finally process zero returns the data to the user interface along the socket. This internal protocol is enclosed within the **db_bsp_sync** command, as described above.

An alternative approach would be to attempt to buffer all data that are communicated during each superstep for perousal at the user interface. However this would not be at all scalable, easily leading to memory overflows.

Handling Type Information. Unlike most contemporary parallel programming libraries, the inter-process communication in the BSP library is untyped – communications are treated purely as transfers of sequences of bytes and the actual data type is unknown. However, for debugging purposes, it is useful to know the types of all variables that are communicated, so as to be able to inspect and display their values and also to check for type mismatches. Unfortunately there is no standard C macro available for this purpose so we have implemented a preprocessor which scans the source code of the BSP program and builds a database of the types of the variables used in each BSP function call. These are written out to a database which is subsequently used by the java graphical user interface component to display data correctly.

Automatic Error Checking

Debuggers tend to have facilities built-in for the automatic detection of common errors and potential errors. The BSP debugger is capable of detecting a number of commonly-occurring, pathological errors, principally:

- *Registration* errors, where not all processors register a particular variable. The debug version of **bsp_push_reg** is supplied with the actual name of the variable being registered as an argument (see figure 1). Hence it is simple to detect such errors at the point of cross-correlating addresses for use in data transfers.
- *Out of bounds communication* errors, where a communication operation attempts to write to an area of memory that has not been registered. This check is currently supported by the underlying BSP library[5] and so we have not implemented it as part of the debugger, although to do so would be straightforward.
- *Synchronisation* errors, where code is compiled with the assumption that processors will synchronise at the same place in the code, and yet they do not. The debug version of **bsp_sync** is supplied with the location in source code from which it is called as an argument. Hence the current source-code locations of all the processes may easily be cross-correlated between supersteps.
- *High performance transfer* errors, where an area of memory is changed after it has been given as the source to a high-performance **bsp_put** or **bsp_get** and before a **bsp_sync**. The debugger can be set to catch such errors by comparing the data stored at both the source and destination addresses of each high-performance transfer event after the processors have synchronised. If they are different then this is likely to indicate an error.

- *Type* errors, where the source and destination address of a communication operation do not hold the same type of data.
  When the user calls either the **bsp_put** or **bsp_get** function, it is almost certain that the source and destination variables should be of the same type as they are both used to contain the same information. Thus in most cases if data is transferred between two memory locations of different type it is because of an error in the program being executed. As the debugger has access to the type of each variable used for data transfer, it is able to detect type inconsistencies at the end of each superstep.
- *Overwrite* errors, where a location on a particular process is written by more than one process in a superstep.
  The debug versions of the communication routines keep track of the source, destination, and size of all data transfers during each superstep. Upon entering **db_bsp_sync**, all this information is communicated to process zero, where it may be correlated and overwrite errors be detected.

4   Conclusions and Areas for Future Development

Commodity supercomputing is now a reality. The promise of scalable price/performance ratios will surely be very appealing. However existing serial programs (or even shared-memory parallel programs) will have to be laboriously parallelised if they are to use NOWs effectively. We believe that the parallelisation effort will usually be simplified using BSP, rather than the industry standard MPI library[1][11]. BSP has no deadlocks to worry about. It has far fewer commands than MPI, and its cost/prediction model is a vital aid towards achieving good parallel speedup. We have developed a visual debugger to assist with conversion to BSP and have demonstrated its effectiveness in increasing productivity. Further facilities are planned as follows:

Profiling: The ability to analyse parallel efficiency and highlight troublesome areas of load imbalance at run-time,
   An excellent visual profiling tool for BSP programs is already in existence[3, 4]. It is used to analyse imbalance in either computation or communication in the execution of BSP programs, and specific problematic areas of code can be pinpointed. It can also derive a BSP cost expression for an existing BSP program, which may then be used to predict its likely performance on other systems.
   It is our intention to combine these features with the BSP debugger in due course. We envisage that an additional display window would be offered to show a histogram representing the costs of computation, communication and synchronisation in all supersteps to have occurred so far. An accumulated BSP cost function could also be displayed.

---

[1] But note that BSP functionality is included as a subset of MPI version 2.

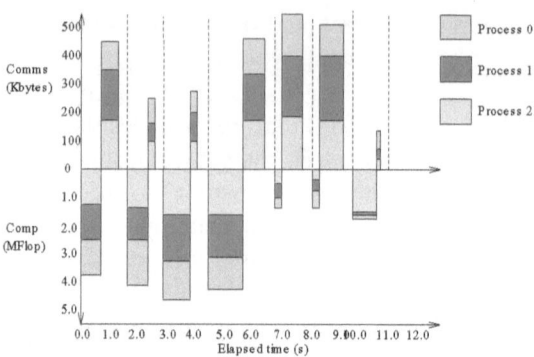

Visualisation: The ability to visualise data from a parallel computation in progress, and also to allow the programmer to create graphical user interfaces to the application,

The standard java libraries incorporate portable software for visualisation and manipulation of two and three dimensional geometric objects, and also for building graphical user interfaces. Hence an obvious extension to our BSP programming enviroment would be to provide direct and easy access to these facilities from within BSP parallel programs. This could then be used as the basis for developing parallel BSP graphical algorithms to perform tasks such as ray tracing or construction of iso-surfaces within data fields.

Computational Steering: The ability to modify future behaviour of a program in response to data visualisation.

There is much interest at present in constructing *virtual laboratories*, whereby complex mathematical simulations in progress are visualised and interacted with. It has been found that huge amounts of computer time and money may be saved using this simple technique. It would be straightforward to modify the BSP debugger to accept commands to change the values of parameters at superstep boundaries controlled by widgets from the user interface. We have two current projects in progress in the Oxford Supercomputing Centre of this nature. One is related to techniques for extracting oil from porous rocks, the other is concerned with molecular dynamics simulations.

At present our BSP development system works only with C programs. In due course we would like to provide support for other languages, such as FORTRAN.

References

1. David Flanagan: Java in a Nutshell. O'Reilly, Second edition (1997)
2. Gene Golub and James M. Ortega: Scientific Computing: An introduction with Parallel Computing. Academic Press, ISBN 0-1-289253-4 (1993)
3. Jonathan M. D. Hill, Paul I. Crumpton and David A. Burgess: The theory, practice and a tool for BSP performance prediction. EuroPar'96, LNCS Springer-Verlag, Volume 1124, pp697-705, (1996)

4. Jonathan M.D. Hill, Stephen Jarvis, Constantinos Siniolakis, and Vasil P. Vasilev: Portable and architecture independent parallel performance tuning using a call-graph profiling tool. 6th EuroMicro Workshop on Parallel and Distributed Processing (PDP'98) IEEE Computer Society (1998)
5. Jonathan M. D. Hill, Bill McColl, Dan C. Stefanescu, Mark W. Goudreau, Kevin Lang, Satish B. Rao, Torsten Suel, Thanasis Tsantilas, and Rob Bisseling: BSPLib: The BSP Programming Library. to appear in Parallel Computing.
6. J. M. R. Martin: The Design and Construction of Deadlock-Free Concurrent Systems. University of Buckingham D. Phil thesis (1996)
7. W.F. McColl: Scalable Computing. In: Computer Science Today: Recent Trends and Developments, ed: J. van Leeuwen. Springer-Verlag LNCS, Volume 1000, pp46-61. (1995)
8. H. Shi and J. Schaeffer: Parallel Sorting by Regular Sampling, Journal of Parallel and Distributed Computing. Volume 14(4), pp361-372 (1992)
9. A. Tiskin: Bulk-synchronous parallel Gaussian elimination. Proceedings of CASC (1998)
10. A. Wilson: A Visual Debugger for BSPlib. Oxford University MSc thesis, 1999.
11. MPI: A message passing interface in Proc. Supercomputing '93, IEEE Computer Society, Message Passing Interface Forum series, pp878-883, (1993)
12. BSP Machine Parameters, see URL
    http://www.BSP-Worldwide.org/implmnts/oxtool.htm

Transparent Network Connectivity in Dynamic Cluster Environments

Xiaodong Fu, Hua Wang, and Vijay Karamcheti

New York University, New York, NY 10012, USA
{xiaodong,wanghua,vijayk}@cs.nyu.edu
http://www.cs.nyu.edu/pdsg

Abstract. This paper presents the design, implementation, and performance of a transparent network connectivity layer for dynamic cluster environments. Our design uses the techniques of API interception and virtualization to construct a transparent layer in user space; use of the layer requires no modification either to the application or the underlying operating system and messaging layers. Our layer enables the migration of application components without breaking network connections, and additionally permits adaptation to the characteristics of the underlying networking substrate. Experiments with supporting a persistent socket interface in two environments—an Ethernet LAN on top of TCP/IP, and a Myrinet LAN on top of Fast Messages—show that our approach incurs minimal overheads and can effectively select the best substrate for implementing application communication requirements.

1 Introduction

With improvements in microprocessor and networking performance, cluster environments have become an increasingly cost-effective option for general parallel and distributed computing. Despite demonstrations of effectiveness in controlled situations (e.g., a dedicated cluster of workstations employed for scientific computations), wider-scale use of cluster environments for general applications has been hampered by the need to handle two characteristics of such environments: *heterogeneous resource capabilities* and *dynamic availability*. The former is a consequence of both the incremental construction of cluster installations over an extended time period and the emerging trend towards integrating mobile resource-constrained devices in such environments. The latter characteristic primarily arises due to the fact that cluster environments are not dedicated to a single application to permit optimal use of shared resources.

The traditional method of addressing these characteristics relies on being able to migrate application components among the cluster resources and efficiently adapting to the underlying resource capabilities. Such migration capability effectively supports the distribution of computational load among nodes in a cluster, the dynamic addition and removal of computing nodes to a running application, and the migratability of applications between fixed and mobile devices. However, to fully realize these benefits, the migration must be supported as transparent

B. Falsafi and M. Lauria (Eds.): CANPC 2000, LNCS 1797, pp. 30–44, 2000.
© Springer-Verlag Berlin Heidelberg 2000

to the application as possible. In particular, network connectivity must be maintained, both within application components and between the application and the outside world. Unfortunately, maintaining connectivity is complicated by the fact that (1) sending and receiving network messages changes the state of operating system (OS) buffers, and (2) an application typically internalizes several operating system handles (such as socket identifiers and IP addresses), which stop being relevant upon migration.

Existing approaches deal with the above problems either by relying on extensive modifications to OS structures to support migration [6,12,13,10], or by requiring the use of a new application programming interface (API) [2,4,3,7] whose implementation isolates the application from the consequences of migration. Neither of these choices is ideal because they cannot be applied to existing OSes and applications. Moreover, most such solutions do not address the issue of adapting to changes in resource characteristics (e.g., the availability of networking substrates with different capabilities).

In this paper we present the design, implementation, and performance of a network connectivity layer that addresses the above shortcomings. Our layer operates *transparently* between the application and the underlying communication layer or operating system (our specific context is Win32 applications running on top of Windows NT). This layer interfaces with the application and the operating system using API interception techniques [1,8], which permits calls made to system APIs to be diverted to a set of routines provided by our layer. This facility permits our layer to maintain network connectivity across application component migrations without requiring modification to either the applications that sit on top, or the communication layers and operating systems that sit below. In particular, this network connectivity layer manages the mapping between physical and virtual handles and the uninterrupted transfer of required state whenever a component is migrated.

Moreover, using the same techniques, this layer can also support the dynamic adaptation of the application to changing underlying resource characteristics. For instance, upon detecting that the network connection after migration is slow, the layer can transparently introduce compression and decompression steps at the two ends of the connection, thereby trading off additional processing for network bandwidth. Thus, this layer provides a natural place for incorporating several policies for customizing application use of underlying resources.

To assess the complexity and performance overheads of the network connectivity layer, we describe its implementation in the concrete context of two environments—an Ethernet LAN on top of TCP/IP, and a Myrinet LAN on top of Fast Messages [11,9]. Our results show that the layer incurs minimal overheads and can effectively select the best substrate for implementing application communication requirements.

The rest of this paper is organized as follows. Section 2 presents relevant background and related approaches for maintaining network connectivity. Section 3 presents the design and implementation details of our transparent communication layer. The performance overheads of the layer are analyzed in Section 4.

Section 5 briefly describes the packaging of the network connectivity functionality as a stand-alone software module. Section 6 discusses the applicability of our approach to other related problems and we conclude in Section 7.

2   Background

The context for this research is applications written to the Win32 and WinSock interfaces running on top of the Windows NT operating system. Our goal is to provide transparent network connectivity across migration of such applications, and constitutes one component of a larger research project called *Computing Communities (CC)* [5]. CC articulates a novel method of middleware development, which does not suffer from the excruciating problem of having to redesign, recode, or even recompile the applications. The binaries of all existing applications can run on a new, distributed platform without modification. This distributed platform realizes a "computing community", in which all of the physical resources such as CPU, display, file system, network are virtualized and provide the application with a view of running on a virtual multiprocessor system.

2.1   Related Work

Previous approaches for maintaining network connectivity fall into two broad categories: modifications to the OS network protocol stack, and introduction of a new API for accessing underlying resources.

Modifying the OS network layer. Several researchers [13,12,6] have successfully demonstrated transparent network connectivity by across process migrations by incorporating changes to kernel data structures and protocols. For instance [13,12], the implementation of network migration on top of the Chorus operating system modifies the network manager so that a migrating process' ports are marked as migrating. Messages sent to the port of a migrating process results in the requesting node being informed of the migration, causing the request to be reissued. While such solutions provide required functionality, their reliance on kernel modifications restricts their applicability in the case of commodity OSes.

Modifying the API interface. An alternative approach isolates the application from changes in its mapping to underlying resources. Typically, this requires modifying application abstractions using new APIs. For instance, the application can use only connectionless protocols (using global target identifiers that are guaranteed to remain unchanged across migrations) or fault-tolerant group communication primitives [3,7]. Some other systems rely on appropriate run-time support to construct a global name space for all structures [2,4] where the application remains unaware that its mapping to underlying physical resources has changed. The primary handicap of such approaches is their limited applicability to commodity applications that are written using standard APIs.

2.2 API Interception

Our approach addresses the above shortcomings by maintaining network connectivity using a user-level middleware layer that is *transparently* inserted between the application and the underlying OS; neither the application nor the OS needs to be modified. In fact, the application does not even need to be recompiled or relinked.

Our middleware layer is inserted using a recently developed technique [1,8] called API interception. This technique relies on a run-time rewrite of portions of the memory image of the application (either the import table for functions in dynamically-linked libraries (DLLs) or the headers of arbitrary functions) to redirect API requests originating from the application to appropriate functions in the middleware layer. This paper describes how this basic mechanism augmented with support for handle translation, buffering, and flow control can be used to provide network connectivity across migration of application components. An additional advantage of our approach is that it can *adapt* transparently to changes in the underlying network configuration. For example, given a situation where the application components have a choice of multiple networking substrates to communicate over (e.g., both Ethernet and Myrinet), the middleware layer can automatically redirect application interactions to the network (and accompanying underlying messaging layer) that delivers the higher performance. Note that this switch between networks and messaging layers is accomplished completely transparent to the application.

3 Persistent Network Connections: Design

To make a network connection transparently migratable and capable of adapting itself to underlying resource characteristics, the communication layer *virtualizes* the physical socket connection. Virtualization, achieved using API interception, comprises of two parts: (1) *association of a global identity* (GID) with the connection independent of the physical location of the end-point processes, and (2) *rerouting of application requests* that use the socket to appropriate handler routines, which complete the requests using available physical resources. Figure 1 shows these two virtualization components.

The GID-to-physical socket translation and the handlers of redirected requests together constitute the *agent* activity of the layer. The agent creates virtual sockets by allocating appropriate physical resources and associates a GID with it. Application requests use this GID and are handled by realizing them using semantics-preserving operations on the underlying physical network resources. The GID persists across migrations of application components: the agent allocates physical resources on the new location and reassociates the GID with them. Agents on the two nodes involved in the migration coordinate with each other to ensure that application components remain unaware of the migration. In addition to performing GID translations and physical data transfer, the agent handles flow control and management of resources at the two ends of the connection.

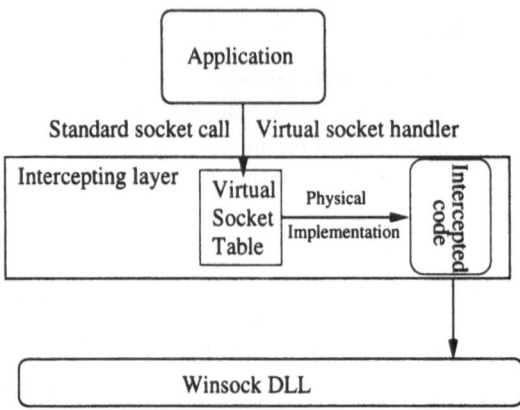

Fig. 1. Virtualizing the socket layer using API interception.

This section describes two implementations of this design. The two implementations, referred to as the *thick agent* and *thin agent* implementations in the rest of the paper, differ in how the agent activity is integrated with the application and represent different tradeoffs between extensibility and performance. In the thick agent implementation, described in Section 3.1, the agent is realized as a separate process that interacts with the application components using a pair of FIFO buffers. In the thin agent implementation, described in Section 3.2, a subset of the agent functionality that is on the critical path is injected into the application itself (again using API interception). The rest of the agent functionality remains in a separate process that is only used to coordinate actions at startup and upon migration and interacts with the application components using a shared buffer.

In both cases, we assume that the actual migration of the application components themselves is accomplished through orthogonal mechanisms not discussed here. These mechanisms can be simple such as restarting an application component on a new node with different parameters (a common strategy for stateless servers), or more elaborate involving process checkpoint and restart.

3.1   Thick Agent Implementation

The thick agent implementation is illustrated in Figure 2. The basic idea is that each end of a socket connection (in general, any interprocess communication (IPC) mechanism) can be abstracted in terms of a pair of FIFO buffers between the application component and the agent process. The IPC mechanisms inject data into and extract data from these buffers; physical data transfer is realized by the agent processes. The agent processes are also responsible for buffer management and maintaining data stream continuity upon migration.

Buffer Management. The FIFO buffers between the application component and the agent processes are of fixed size. The agent processes remove messages from

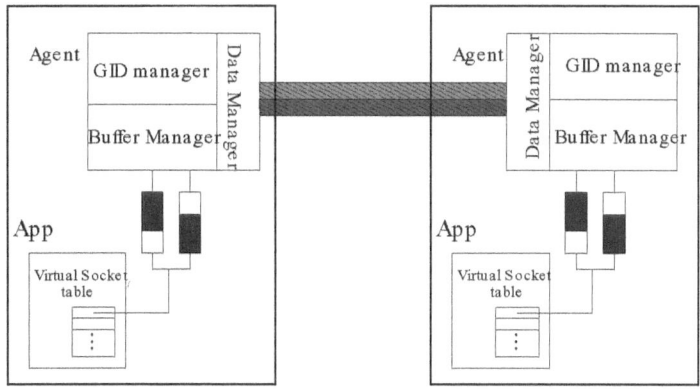

Fig. 2. Overall structure of the thick agent implementation.

the application out-buffer and inject them into the network, and extract messages from the network and insert them into the application in-buffer. To handle situations where the application is not responsive in consuming messages in the in-buffer, the agent processes divert received messages into dynamically allocated overflow buffers prior to transferring them to the in-buffer.

Data Stream Continuity. To maintain data stream continuity across migrations, both the data stored in the FIFO buffers on the original site as well as any messages in transit must be flushed to the new site. The agent processes coordinate to achieve this using the following eight steps (Figure 3) shows these steps for the migration of a connection end-point from node B to node C; the other end-point stays fixed on node A):

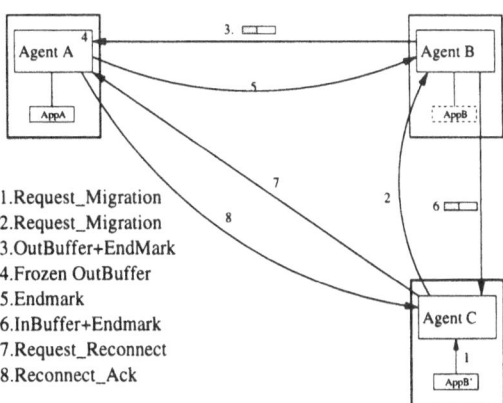

Fig. 3. Migration protocol in the thick agent implementation.

1. Upon realizing that it has migrated, the application component sends a REQUEST-MIGRATION message with the connection GID as a parameter to the local agent (on node C).
2. The agent on node C forwards the message to the agent at the old site (node B).
3. Upon receiving the REQUEST-MIGRATION message, the agent on node B flushes its out-buffer to the other end of the connection (node A) and sends an END-MARK message. It then waits for Step 5, extracting in-transit messages into its in-buffer.
4. When the agent on node A receives the END-MARK message, it freezes the out-buffer for the connection.
5. The agent on node A then injects an END-MARK message into the network.
6. Receipt of this END-MARK message on node B implies that no more data will be sent from node A on this connection. The agent then forwards all of the messages in its in-buffer to node C.[1]
7. When the agent on node C receives all of these messages, it recreates its data structures and sends out a REQUEST-RECONNECT message to the agent on node A.
8. Upon receiving the REQUEST-RECONNECT message, the agent on node A reactivates the send buffer for the connection, and sends back an ack message to node C.

The primary advantage of the thick agent implementation is its extensibility. Support for new IPC mechanisms can be easily incorporated with minimal code modifications to capture its semantics. Another advantage is the complete decoupling between application-agent and agent-agent interactions. This decoupling permits the agents to appropriately adapt to the underlying communication substrate without affecting the rest of the implementation in any way. For instance, the agents can use a faster networking layer/substrate (e.g., FastMessages on Myrinet) when available, or introduce codecs to minimize bandwidth requirements on a wireless connection.

The primary disadvantage of this implementation is its performance penalty. Each data transmission between data components will introduce two extra context switches between the application and agent processes and two extra data copies. To improve on this, in the thin agent implementation described next, we move the agent data transfer functionality into the application itself. This reduces the overhead to a single data copy on the send side.

3.2   Thin Agent Implementation

The basic idea of the thin agent implementation, illustrated in Figure 4, is to move the critical part of the agent functionality into the application component itself. *Note that the application binary remains unmodified; this functionality is injected at load-time using the API interception technique described earlier.*

---

[1] The message forwarding actually proceeds concurrently with steps 4 and 5, but is stated this way for clarity.

The injected functionality permits applications to communicate with each other directly, maintain necessary state of data connections, and adapt themselves to underlying resources. Application components detect migration by detecting that the existing connection has broken. To re-establish a connection, they rely on GID tables of active local connections maintained in the separate agent process at each site. Agents coordinate upon migration to determine the two connection end-points; application components reconnect to these points by replaying the original (logged) API request.

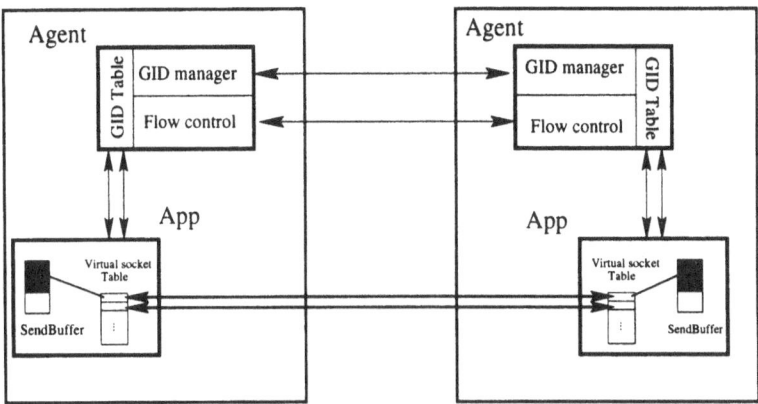

Fig. 4. Overall structure of the thin agent implementation.

Buffer Management. Each end of the connection, besides storing necessary state information, also maintains a send-side buffer. This buffer stores copies of messages that have been transmitted but not yet acknowledged. Send-side buffering suffices because data is directly routed into application buffers on the receive side. Management of these buffers uses a straightforward window-based flow control scheme. These buffers are expanded dynamically as required by application communication patterns; space is freed upon acknowledgement of the receipt of the corresponding message(s) on the receiver. For efficiency, acknowledgements are batched together and piggy-backed on data messages. Explicit flow control messages are used whenever the unacknowledged data for a communication endpoint exceeds a threshold. For improved locality and better small message performance, messages below a threshold size are copied inline into the send buffer; all other messages are allocated out-of-line (with explicit freeing of storage upon acknowledgment of receipt). When an application component exits, its send-side buffer is saved into the agent's pool (if non-empty). This permits the agent to retransmit the data, in case the component termination overlaps with the migration of the component at the other end of the connection.

Data Stream Continuity. To maintain data stream continuity, the application components need to reconnect after migration. The send buffers associated with the virtual socket connection at each end point contain sufficient state to handle any retransmissions as necessary. Note that migration of an application component is assumed to also migrate the corresponding send buffer(s).

Reconnection of application components is achieved using the following five-step migration procedure (Figure 5 shows these steps for the migration of a connection end-point from node B to node C):

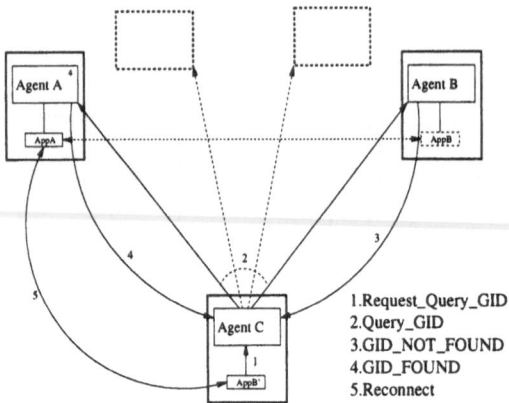

Fig. 5. Migration protocol in the thin agent implementation.

1. The migrated application component, upon detecting a broken connection, sends a REQUEST-QUERY message with its GID as a parameter to the local agent (on node C). The other end-point of the connection (on node A) also performs a similar action (with its local agent).
2. The agent on node C coordinates with other agents (e.g., using multicast) to determine the other end-point of the connection.
3. The agent on the old site (from where the component migrated) will no longer find the process corresponding to the GID, hence will not respond.
4. The agents on nodes A and C will receive information about the location of each other's end-points (node C and A respectively).
5. The application components on nodes A and C (a) reconnect with each other, (b) exchange state information (about messages sent and acknowledged), (c) retransmit any lost messages using the send buffers, and (d) resume operation.

The primary advantage of the thin agent implementation is its efficiency; the only overheads that remain are for the send-side buffering. However, this advantage comes at the cost of increased complexity: the agent functionality injected into the application must be aware of the underlying resource characteristics and explicitly adapt to them. As mentioned earlier, this complexity does not affect the user application.

3.3 Using Other Transport Layers

Although we have discussed the thick and thin agent implementations on top of reliable connection-based transport protocols, they can be as conveniently implemented on top of other transports. We briefly sketch the differences for two interesting transports. For *unreliable connectionless layers* (e.g., UDP), the agent activity must also handle retransmission and removal of duplicates. In addition, the agents need to coordinate to locate the end-points of the connection, similar to what was described above for the thin agent implementation. For *active message layers* (e.g., FM), in addition to the above, the agent activity needs to handle the extraction of messages that belong to other application streams. An efficient implementation minimizes the amount of buffering that needs to be provided, directly rerouting received messages into posted buffers when the latter are available.

4 Persistent Network Connections: Performance

To assess the run-time overheads of the network connectivity layer, we measured the performance of the thick and thin agent implementations in two environments—a 100 Mbps Ethernet LAN on top of TCP/IP, and a 1.28 Gbps Myrinet LAN on top of Illinois Fast Messages (FM). All of the experiments were run on Pentium Pro 200 MHz machines with 64 MB memory. The FM experiments used the HPVM 1.2 release of the messaging layer.

4.1 Overheads of Transparent Connectivity

Figure 6 shows the impact on round-trip time and bandwidth of maintaining a transparent migratable connection. Table 1 show the raw data for these plots.

Message bytes	128	256	512	1024	2048	4096	8192	16384	32768
Round Trip Time(microsecond)									
Unintercepted	265	294	362	470	753	1104	2013	3804	7569
Thin agent	316	318	449	563	808	1152	2094	3958	8081
Thick agent	538	577	655	773	1066	1603	2424	4458	8459
Bandwidth(MBytes/sec)									
Unintercepted	1.58	2.97	5.94	9.24	9.46	9.95	9.89	9.92	9.30
Thin agent	1.48	2.77	6.23	8.46	9.42	9.89	9.89	9.94	9.52
Thick agent	0.81	1.49	2.59	3.95	5.74	8.63	9.81	9.96	9.30

Table 1. Round-trip time and Bandwidth vs. message size for the thick and thin agent implementations in the Ethernet/TCP environment.

The plots show that the thick agent implementation has measurable impact on both round-trip time and bandwidth (increasing the former by up to 24%

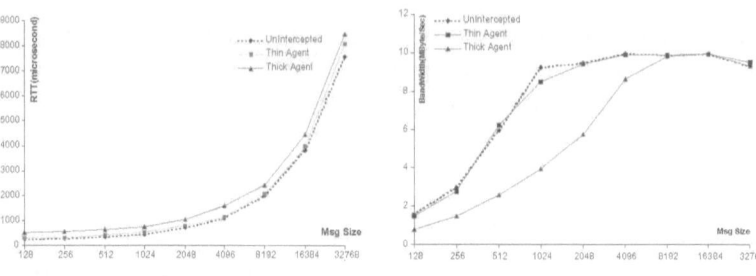

(a) Round-trip time vs. message size

(b) Bandwidth vs. message size

Fig. 6. Round-trip time and bandwidth achieved by the thick and thin agent implementations in the Ethernet/TCP environment.

and decreasing the latter by up to 50%), primarily because of additional context switches and data copies. On the other hand, the thin agent implementation incurs no noticeable overheads as compared to the unintercepted (and hence not-migratable) TCP/IP implementation. Both round-trip time and bandwidth are within 5% of the unintercepted version, demonstrating that our connectivity layer can efficiently maintain data stream continuity over migrations.

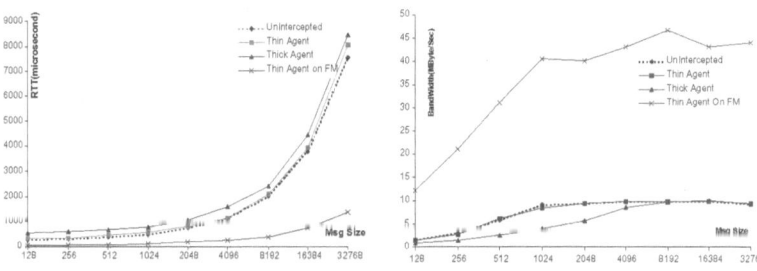

(a) Round-trip time vs. message size

(b) Bandwidth vs. message size

Fig. 7. Round-trip time and bandwidth achieved by the thin agent implementation in the Myrinet/FM environment.

Message bytes	128	256	512	1024	2048	4096	8192	16384	32768
Round Trip Time(microsecond)									
Unintercepted	265	294	362	470	753	1104	2013	3804	7569
FM-thin-agent	37	47	65	100	181	250	373	738	1367
Bandwidth(MBytes/sec)									
Unintercepted	1.58	2.97	5.94	9.24	9.46	9.95	9.89	9.92	9.30
FM-thin-agent	12.20	21.02	31.06	40.60	40.07	43.14	46.67	43.07	44.05

Table 2. Round-Trip time and Bandwidth vs. message size for the thin agent implementation in the Myrinet/FM compared with Unintercepted socket interface in the Ethernet/TCP environment.

4.2   Adaptation to Networking Substrate

As mentioned earlier, our communication layer can transparently adapt to the characteristics of the underlying networking susbtrate. To assess the gains possible by such adaptation, we compared the round-trip time and bandwidth of the thin agent implementation in the Myrinet/FM environment with the corresponding implementation in the Ethernet/TCP environment.

In both cases, the applications used the unmodified traditional socket interface; the interception layer decides which of the underlying communication mechanisms to use. The purpose of this experiment is to show the performance benefit which an application can gain by adaptation. As mentioned earlier in Section 2, using API interception, such adaptation is accomplished completely transparent to the application. To enable the applications to adapt to the networking substrate, a negotiation phase is required during connection setup. Each endpoint of the communication sends out a connection request which includes information about the local communication configuration (which substrates are available, and (optionally) any user preferences). The server-side agent decides the substrate/transport layer that will be used for the connection, based on the application parameters and current system load.

Figure 7 and Table 2 show these costs. The plots show that the mismatch between application-level WinSock semantics and transport-level FM semantics results in higher overheads in the communication layer as compared to the Ethernet/LAN environment. To put our implementation in context, base FM has a minimum round-trip time and maximum bandwidth of $21\mu s$ and 65 MB/s on our experiment testbed. In contrast, our layer achieves a minimum latency of $35\mu s$ and a maximum bandwidth of 46 MB/s. While these numbers by themselves are quite good, we expect them to improve further with additional tuning of our implementation.

More importantly, the plots show the advantages of our layer automatically adapting itself to the underlying substrate. The thin agent implementation on Myrinet/FM improves round-trip time by up to 8x, and bandwidth by up to 5x as compared to the Ethernet/TCP environment. These improvements become transparently available to the application components.

5   Interfacing with General Applications

Although our work began in the context of process migration, the transparent network connectivity functionality can be packaged into a stand-alone software module for use by general applications. The interfaces to this module permit applications to explicitly dump and restore individual connection state using files, enabling its use by applications that perform migration using checkpoint/restart techniques. The connection dump/restore API is as follows:

makePersistent(SOCKET s [, File * dumpFile])
    dumps the connection state into a dumpfile.
resetup(SOCKET s [, File * dumpFile])
    restores the connection state associated with previous SOCKET handler s from the dumpfile.

Additionally, when the application component is stateless (i.e., it does not require any state to be stored other than that of the connection), the application does not require *any* modification. Our package supports a scenario where there is one original server process residing on the site where the server process is supposed to be, with a number of backup servers distributed across the network. Any connection can be migrated among these servers (e.g., for load-balancing or fault-tolerance purposes), which by default listen to a publicly advertised port for new incoming connections. By intercepting the corresponding API call, the agent processes on the original and backup server sites can negotiate to divert connections as desired. The migration is totally transparent to applications, requiring only that environment variable on the backup server sites convey information about the original server site (IP address and port number).

6   Discussion

Although we have limited our attention here to providing data stream continuity across migrations, our approach of transparently rerouting application requests to a middleware layer can also be used to address several related concerns. We briefly discuss some of these issues below.

Separation from the Underlying OS Interfaces. The layer can be used to decouple an application from the interfaces provided by the underlying operating system. The implementation of our communication layer on top of the FM interface demonstrates this capability; application-level WinSock requests are translated to semantically equivalent sets of FM operations.

Adaptation to Changing Resource Characteristics. The middleware layer provides a natural place for incorporating different policies for customizing application use of underlying resources. This provides a powerful infrastructure for allowing the application to become aware of changes in network conditions and adapt to them. These adaptation policies can be either application-independent (e.g., interfacing with different transport layers or inserting compression/decompression operations at the end-points), or application-aware (e.g., selective dropping of packets in a video stream based on its encoding to reduce overall bandwidth requirements).

7   Conclusion

We have described the design of a communication layer that maintains network connectivity across migrations of application components in a distributed system. This layer is transparently inserted between unmodified applications and commodity operating systems using API interception techniques. Results based on implementations of the layer in two environments—Ethernet on top of TCP/IP and Myrinet on top of FM—show that the layer introduces negligible overheads during normal operation (when the components do not migrate), and can additionally seamlessly choose the best among available networking substrates.

Acknowledgments

This research was sponsored by the Defense Advanced Research Projects Agency and Rome Laboratory, Air Force Materiel Command, USAF, under agreement numbers F30602-96-1-0320 and F30602-99-1-0517; by the National Science Foundation under CAREER award number CCR-9876128; and Microsoft. The U.S. Government is authorized to reproduce and distribute reprints for Government purposes notwithstanding any copyright annotation thereon. The views and conclusions contained herein are those of the authors and should not be interpreted as necessarily representing the official policies or endorsements, either expressed or implied, of the Defense Advanced Research Projects Agency, Rome Laboratory, or the U.S. Government.

References

1. Balzer, R. Mediating Connectors. In *Proc. of ICDCS Middleware Workshop*, 1999.
2. Baratloo, A., Dasgupta, A., and Kedem, Z. Calypso: A novel software system for fault-tolerant parallel processing on distributed platforms. In *Proc. of 4th IEEE Intl. Symp. on High Performance Distributed Computing*, 1995.
3. Birman, K. Replication and fault-tolerance in the ISIS system. In *Proc. of 10th ACM Symp. on Operating System Principle*, pages 79–86, 1985.
4. Blumofe, R., Joerg, C., Kuszmaul, B., Leiserson, C., Randall, K., and Zhou, Y. Cilk: An efficient multithreaded runtime system. In *5th ACM SIGPLAN Symp. on Principles and Practice of Parallel Programming*, pages 207–216, 1995.
5. Dasgupta, P., Karamcheti, V., and Kedem, Z. Transparent distribution middleware for general purpose computations. In *Proc. of Intl. Conf. on Parallel and Distributed Processing Techniques and Applications (PDPTA'99)*, June 1999.

6. Douglis, F. and Ousterhout, J. Process migration in the sprite operating system. In *Proc. of 7th Intl. Conf. on Distributed Computing Systems*, pages 18–25, 1987.
7. Hayden, M. The Ensemble System. Technical Report TR98-1662, Cornell University, 1998.
8. Hunt, G. and Brubacher, D. Detours: Binary interception of Win32 functions. Technical Report MSR-TR-98-33, Microsoft Research, 1999.
9. Lauria, M., Pakin, S., and Chien, A.A. Efficient layering for high speed communication: Fast Message 2.x. In *Proc. of the 7th High Performance Distributed Computing (HPDC7) conf.*, 1998.
10. Milojicic, D., Zint, W., Dangel, A., and Giese, P. Task migration on the top of the mach microkernel. In *Proc. of the 3rd USENIX Mach Symp.*, pages 273–289, 1993.
11. Pakin, S., Karamcheti, V., and Chien, A. Fast message (FM): efficient, portable communication for workstation clusters and massively-parallel processors. *IEEE Concurrency*, Vol.5:60–73, 1997.
12. Paoli, D. and Goscinski, A. The RHODOS Migration Facility. Technical Report TR C95/36, School of Computing and Mathematics, Deakin University, 1995.
13. Rozier, M., Abrossimov, V., Gien, M., Guillemont, M., Hermann, F., and Kaiser, C. Chorus (Overview of the Chorus distributed operating system). In *Proc. of USENIX Workshop on Micro-Kernels and Other Kernel Architectures*, pages 39–70, 1992.

A New Methodology to Compute Deadlock-Free Routing Tables for Irregular Networks*

José Carlos Sancho, Antonio Robles, and José Duato

Departamento de Informática de Sistemas y Computadores
Universidad Politécnica de Valencia
P.O.B. 22012,46071 - Valencia, Spain
{jcsancho,arobles,jduato}@gap.upv.es

Abstract. Networks of workstations (NOWs) are being considered as a cost-effective alternative to parallel computers. Many NOWs are arranged as a switch-based network with irregular topology, which makes routing and deadlock avoidance quite complicated. Current proposals use the $up^*/down^*$ routing algorithm to remove cyclic dependencies between channels and avoid deadlock. However, routing is considerably restricted and most messages must follow non-minimal paths, increasing latency and wasting resources. In this paper, we propose a new methodology to compute deadlock-free routing tables for NOWs. The methodology tries to minimize the limitations of the current proposals in order to improve network performance. It is based on generating an underlying acyclic connected graph from the network graph and assigning a sequence number to each switch, which is used to remove cyclic dependencies. Evaluation results show that the routing algorithm based on the new methodology increases throughput by a factor of up to 2 in large networks, also reducing latency significantly.

1 Introduction

Networks of workstations are being considered as a cost-effective alternative to parallel computers, since they meet the needs of a great variety of parallel applications at a lower cost [3]. NOWs offer a wide range of advantages when implemented on a building-wide scale of hundreds of machines. The pool of resources include memory, disk, and processors. Using switch-based interconnects provides the wiring flexibility, scalability, and incremental expansion capability required in this environment. In order to achieve high bandwidth and low latencies, NOWs are often connected using gigabit local area network technologies. There are recent proposals for NOW interconnects like Autonet [13], Myrinet [4], Servernet II [10], and Gigabit Ethernet [14].

The three most important issues in network design are the network topology, the switching technique, and the routing algorithm [7]. In current NOWs the topology is defined by the customer. Switch designs must be flexible enough to

---

* This work was supported by the Spanish CICYT under Grant TIC97-0897-C04-01.

B. Falsafi and M. Lauria (Eds.): CANPC 2000, LNCS 1797, pp. 45–60, 2000.
© Springer-Verlag Berlin Heidelberg 2000

support any topology with degree bounded by the number of switch ports. In many cases, the connections between switches do not follow any regular pattern. The resulting topologies are referred to as irregular topologies. Different switching techniques, like wormhole [8] or virtual cut-through [11], are suitable for being implemented in NOWs. For example, Myrinet and Servernet II use wormhole switching. Routing in irregular topologies can be based on source routing or distributed routing. In the former case, the message header contains the sequence of ports to be used at intermediate switches to reach the destination. Routing tables are used at each host to obtain the port sequence for each message. In the latter case, switches require routing tables. When a message arrives at a switch, the destination address stored in its header is used, concatenated with the incoming port number, to address the routing table of the switch. This table returns the outgoing port number the message must be routed through. In both routing strategies, the routing tables must be filled before messages can be routed.

Several deadlock-free routing schemes have been proposed for NOWs, like $up^*/down^*$ routing [13], adaptive-trail routing [12], minimal adaptive routing [15], and smart-routing [6]. In $up^*/down^*$ routing [13], a breadth-first search spanning tree (BFS) is computed. This algorithm is quite simple, and has the property that all the switches in the network will eventually agree on a unique spanning tree. However, in most cases $up^*/down^*$ routing does not always supply minimal paths between non-adjacent switches, becoming more frequent as network size increases. On the other hand, minimal adaptive routing [15] provides minimal paths in most cases. However, this algorithm requires the use of virtual channels, which are not implemented in current commercial switches. The smart-routing algorithm [6] is impractical due to its high computation overhead, since it computes a linear programming solver to balance the traffic while it tries to break the deadlock cycles. The adaptive-trail routing algorithm [12] is based on an Eulerian trail, which establishes a dependency order for all the channels to avoid deadlocks. The main drawback of adaptive-trail routing is that it is quite complex to find heuristics to form the Eulerian trail and to remove cycles when shortcuts are added. In addition, an Eulerian trail may be hard to find in some irregular topologies, since all the switches must have even degree or exactly two switches must have odd degree. This is a serious limitation when the network changes its topology, which is quite frequent in a LAN environment because some links may fail or some components may be added/removed.

In this paper we propose and evaluate a new methodology to compute deadlock-free routing tables for irregular networks. The routing algorithm resulting from this methodology increases throughput by a factor of up to 2 in large networks, also reducing latency significantly. The rest of the paper is organized as follows. In Section 2, the $up^*/down^*$ routing scheme and its main drawbacks are described. Section 3 presents some terminology and definitions. Section 4 describes the proposed methodology, also discussing the applied heuristic. Section 5 shows performance evaluation results for the routing algorithm based on the new methodology. Finally, in Section 6 some conclusions are drawn.

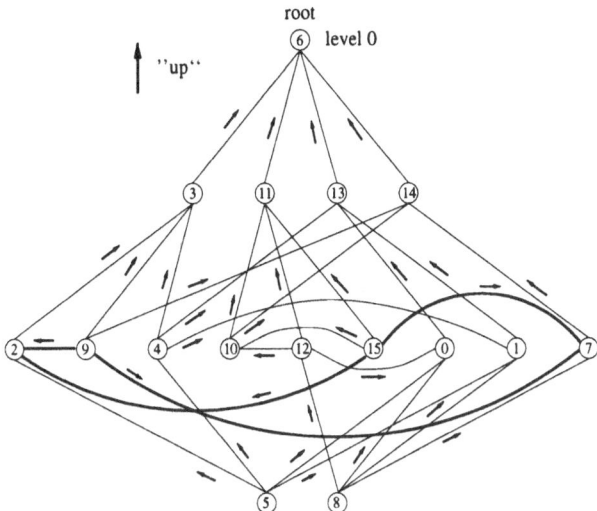

Fig. 1. Link direction assignment for a 16-switch network.

2   Up*/Down* Routing

$Up^*/down^*$ routing is the most popular routing scheme currently used in commercial networks, such us Myrinet [4] or Autonet [13]. It is a generic routing algorithm valid for being applied to any network with regular or irregular topology. The $up^*/down^*$ routing scheme is deadlock-free and, when implemented in a distributed way, provides partially adaptive routing. Routing is based on a methodology to compute routing tables which makes an assignment of direction to the operational links in the network by building a BFS spanning tree. The "up" end of each link is defined as: 1) the end whose switch is closer to the root in the spanning tree; 2) the end whose switch has the lower identifier, if both ends are at switches at the same tree level. The result of this assignment is that each cycle in the network has at least one link in the "up" direction and one link in the "down" direction. To avoid deadlocks while still allowing all links to be used, this routing scheme uses the following up*/down* rule: a legal route must traverse zero or more links in "up" direction followed by zero or more links in "down" direction. Thus, cyclic channel dependencies [1] [8] are avoided because a message cannot traverse a link along the "up" direction after having traversed one in "down" direction.

Unfortunately, $up^*/down^*$ routing has several drawbacks that limit its performance. Before constructing the routing tables, a breadth-first search spanning tree (BFS) is computed. In order to avoid deadlocks, a direction is assigned to all the network links. However, this assignment depends on the structure of the BFS spanning tree. Moreover, given that the label of the links connecting nodes

---

[1] There is a channel dependency from a channel c_i to a channel c_j if a message can hold c_i and request c_j. In other words, the routing algorithm allows the use of c_j after reserving c_i.

at the same tree level is based on their node identifiers, which are assigned randomly, it follows that $up^*/down^*$ routing also removes channel dependencies randomly. Therefore, no optimization can be applied and most minimal paths will be forbidden.

On the other hand, the $up^*/down^*$ routing scheme does not guarantee that the removal of cyclic dependencies is done by imposing the lowest number of routing restrictions, as is shown in [1]. Moreover, in [2] it is shown by means of genetic algorithms that for large networks it is usually possible to find a better assignment of direction to the operational links in the network than the one provided by current methodologies.

As an example, Figure 1 shows the link direction assignment for a 16-switch network using $up^*/down^*$ routing. Switches at the same tree level are at the same vertical position. A cycle between nodes at the same tree level is shown in bold lines in the figure. This cycle is broken at two points (nodes 9 and 15), since the transition from "down" to "up" channels is not allowed by $up^*/down^*$ routing. A better direction assignment would reverse the direction of the channel that links nodes 15 and 2. The cycle will still be broken at node 9, and the change will increase the number of minimal paths. For example, the path length from node 2 to node 7 will decrease from 4 to 2 hops.

Additionally, $up^*/down^*$ routing prevents routing across the leaf nodes since the direction of their outgoing channels are usually "up", and the $up^*/down^*$ rule does not allow the transition from "down" to "up" channels. As shown in Figure 1, nodes 5, 8, 9, and 15 do not allow routing across them. In a BFS spanning tree the number of leaf nodes increases as network size increases. Thus, the number of routing restrictions will increase with network size, preventing most messages from following minimal paths.

Moreover, the number of different BFS spanning trees that can be computed on a network graph is limited by the number of switches in the network. This is an important limitation for finding more efficient heuristics to improve network performance. Thus, we suggest that a new underlying graph, more general than the BFS spanning tree, should be better used. In particular, we wonder if it will be possible to find another method to compute routing tables that introduce less routing restrictions than the one based on a BFS spanning tree.

3   Preliminaries

Graphs will be used to model the underlying network topology. We will closely follow the graph theoretical terminology and notation in [5]. Let $G(V, E)$ denote a graph with node set V and edge set E. The interconnection topology of a switch-based network is modeled by a graph $G(V, E)$, where each node v in V corresponds to a switch, and each edge in E corresponds to a bidirectional physical link (channel).

A *trail* is a finite sequence of edges of the form $v_0 \rightarrow v_1 \rightarrow \ldots, v_{m-1} \rightarrow v_m$, in which all the edges are distinct. If the nodes $v_0, v_1, \ldots v_{m-1}, v_m$ are also distinct, it is called a *path*. When $v_0 = v_m$, it is called a *cycle*. A graph is said

---

procedure Depthfirst(v_k)
begin
while all nodes have not been visited yet *do*
   for i := 1 to *links(v_k)* *do*
      select output channel in node v_k: $v_k \rightarrow v_q$
      according to heuristic.
      if node v_q has not been visited yet *then*
         add the channel $v_k \rightarrow v_q$ to the tree.
         add the node v_q to the tree.
         mark v_q as visited.
         call to Depthfirst(v_q).
      endif.
   endfor.
endwhile.
endprocedure.

Fig. 2. DFS spanning tree computation algorithm.

to be *connected* if every pair of its nodes are joined by a path. A graph is said to be acyclic if it is not possible to form a cycle. A *spanning tree* is an acyclic and connected graph containing all the nodes in the network. However, it may contain only a subset of the links. The *average distance* is the average number of links in the shortest paths between any two nodes. When paths are computed by assuming that there are no routing restrictions then the average distance is called *average topological distance*. Every non-acyclic graph contains a basic set of independent cycles. An *independent cycle* is a cycle in the graph such that it has at least one edge that does not belong to any other independent cycle.

4 A New Methodology to Compute Deadlock-Free Routing Tables

In this section, we propose a new methodology to compute deadlock-free routing tables, which is applicable to any network with regular or irregular topology. The routing algorithm based on the proposed methodology is valid for NOWs using any switching technique, including wormhole and virtual cut-through, and can be implemented using source or distributed routing. Like $up^*/down^*$ routing, the proposed routing scheme is suitable for networks without virtual channels, which is the case for most commercial interconnects. In this case, the only practical way of avoiding deadlock consists of restricting routing in such a way that cyclic channel dependencies are avoided [8]. Nevertheless, the new methodology can also be applied to networks with virtual channels by combining it with the design methodology proposed in [9] and adapted to NOWs in [15].

    The new methodology is based on obtaining a spanning tree on the network graph. Starting from this spanning tree, the remaining links are added and routing tables can be computed. Deadlock-free routing is guaranteed by restricting

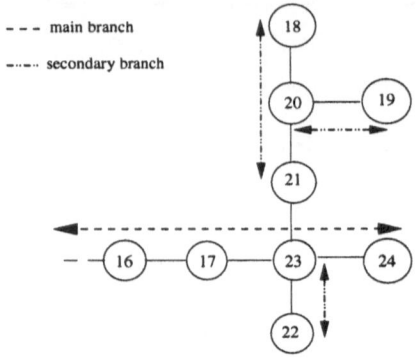

Fig. 3. Labeling the main and secondary branches.

routing on the added links in such a way that cyclic channel dependencies are avoided.

First, we describe how the spanning tree is computed, later we explain how the cyclic dependencies between channels are removed, and finally, we propose a heuristic required to compute the spanning tree.

4.1   Obtaining the Spanning Tree

Spanning trees are suitable to achieve deadlock-free routing since they form an acyclic connected graph. Our methodology to compute routing tables is based on computing a *depth-first search* spanning tree (DFS). A recursive procedure used to compute the DFS spanning tree is shown in Figure 2. The number of links connected to other switches for switch v_k will be referred to as *links(v_k)*. Initially, all the nodes are marked as not visited. An initial node, v_i, must be chosen and marked as visited before starting the computation of the DFS spanning tree. The selection of the node v_i is made by using heuristics. We will address this issue later. The recursive procedure builds a path (*main branch*) that begins at node v_i and ends at the node where the recursive procedure returned the first time. As the main branch may not contain all the nodes in the network graph, new paths (*secondary branches*) must be found to connect the remaining nodes.

Unlike BFS spanning trees, DFS spanning trees allow more flexibility in the definition of heuristic rules, possibly leading to improved performance.

As a DFS spanning tree is acyclic, when routing is based on it no deadlock is possible. However, when the remaining channels are added to the spanning tree, cyclic dependencies may arise. Thus, a method is needed to break the cycles. The following section addresses this goal.

4.2   Removing Cyclic Dependencies

The method for removing cycles is based on labeling the nodes in the network graph with positive integer numbers and then breaking the cycles using this

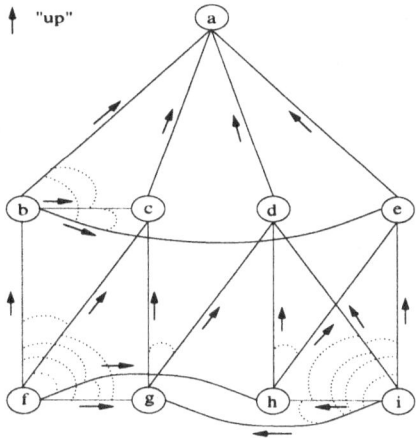

Fig. 4. $Up^*/down^*$ scheme.

labeling. A different label is assigned to each node. Next, the routing tables are filled with all the possible shortest paths between every pair of nodes.

In a network with N nodes and M edges, the number of independent cycles will be $M - N + 1$ [5]. This is the minimum number of channel dependencies that must be removed in order to break all the cycles. These channel dependencies arise between channels belonging to the DFS spanning tree and channels that do not belong to it. Additionally, there may exist cycles formed by channels that do not belong to the DFS spanning tree, and they also have to be removed.

Let $L(x)$ be a function that returns the label assigned to node x. In order to reduce the number of routing restrictions, the DFS spanning tree is labeled in two ways, one for the main branch and another one for the secondary branches. The main branch is labeled by using increasing integers in the order nodes were visited while building the DFS spanning tree. Every secondary branch is labeled in reverse order, that is, the lower label is assigned to the leaf node of the branch. Additionally, the labels for secondary branches are interleaved between those for the branch they are connected to. Figure 3 shows an example of how to label the nodes in the DFS spanning tree.

In order to remove cyclic channel dependencies the following rule is applied: Remove the channel dependency between channels (x,y) and (x,z), x, y, $z \in V$, if $L(y) > L(x) < L(z)$.

It is easy to prove that if a different label is assigned to each node, every cycle will have a single node that satisfies the above condition. This is a general method to break cycles in a graph. Note that there is no danger of breaking the DFS spanning tree, since nodes along branches are labeled in decreasing or increasing order.

Once all the cyclic channel dependencies have been removed by breaking each cycle as indicated above, the remaining channel dependencies define the routing algorithm. Note that the resulting routing algorithm follows the same

$up^*/down^*$ rule (see Section 3) as the $up^*/down^*$ routing algorithm. However, link direction assignment is different from the one used in $up^*/down^*$ routing because it is based on DFS instead of BFS spanning tree. Thus, the proposed routing scheme can be considered as an $up^*/down^*$ routing algorithm, although based on DFS instead of BFS spanning tree, that is, it is based on a different methodology to compute routing tables.

In general, the greater the number of links connecting nodes at the same tree level in the BFS spanning tree, the greater the difference in the number of channel dependencies that have to be removed in a BFS spanning tree with respect to DFS spanning tree. The reason is that the assignment of direction to these links in the BFS spanning tree depends on the identification numbers of the nodes at the same tree level. Obviously, it strongly depends on network topology.

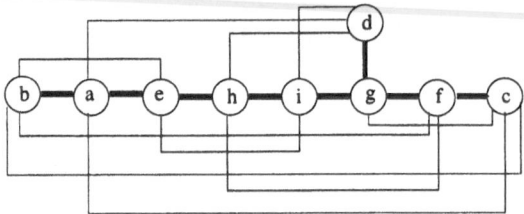

Fig. 5. Generated DFS spanning tree.

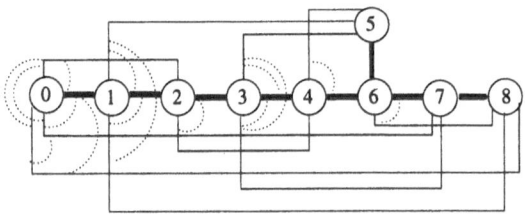

Fig. 6. Label assigned to each node and removed channel dependencies.

To illustrate the new methodology, we present an example for the 9-switch network depicted in Figure 4. The channel dependencies that must be removed according to the original $up^*/down^*$ routing algorithm are shown in dotted lines in Figure 4. As can be seen, the number of routing restrictions is equal to 34 (17 bidirectional restrictions). The DFS spanning tree obtained by using the algorithm in Figure 2 is shown in bold lines in Figure 5, whereas the remaining channels in the network are shown in thin lines. Then, the nodes in the DFS spanning tree are labeled according to the procedure described above. Figure 6 shows the label assigned to each node. Finally, cyclic channel dependencies are removed by applying the rule proposed above. As can be observed, the number of routing restrictions is now equal to 30 (15 bidirectional restrictions), which is

Table 1. Behavioral routing metrics.

Network size	Average distance		Restrictions per node		Long paths		Diameter		Crossing paths	
	BFS	DFS	BFS	DFS	BFS	DFS	BFS	DFS	BFS	DFS
9	1.583	1.556	3.774	3.552	5 %	3.7 %	3	3	12	6
16	2.208	2.108	3.375	3.125	9 %	4 %	4	4	37	23
32	3.102	2.792	3.562	2.821	21 %	9 %	7	6	173	73
64	4.013	3.634	3.281	2.687	26 %	14 %	8	7	593	204

smaller than that imposed by the $up^*/down^*$ scheme based on a BFS spanning tree.

Table 1 shows the values of some behavioral routing metrics that have been computed for several network sizes when using the $up^*/down^*$ routing algorithm based on two methodologies to compute routing tables, that is, the original methodology that makes use of a BFS spanning tree and the new methodology based on a DFS spanning tree. Topologies have been randomly generated. We assume that switches have 8 ports, using 4 of them to connect to hosts [2].

The computed metrics are: (1) *average distance*; (2) average number of routing *restrictions per node*; (3) percentage of paths whose length exceeds the topological path length or minimal path, referred to as *long paths*; (4) *diameter* and (5) the maximum number of routing paths crossing through any network channel, referred to as *crossing paths*.

As can be seen, the values achieved by the routing scheme based on a DFS spanning tree improve over the ones achieved by the original $up^*/down^*$ routing scheme. Moreover, improvement increases with network size. From these results, we conclude that messages follow minimal paths more frequently under the new methodology than under the original methodology based on a BFS spanning tree. The new methodology also achieves a higher adaptivity degree (less routing restrictions) and a better traffic balance (lower value for crossing paths). This is mainly due to the smaller number of channels dependencies that have to be removed in the routing scheme based on DFS spanning tree in order to break cycles in the network.

4.3   Heuristic

Unlike BFS spanning tree, DFS spanning tree allows us to apply more flexible heuristic rules while computing it. We wonder if it will be possible to compute a DFS spanning tree that allows us to achieve the highest network performance. We have analyzed many different networks and concluded that the highest network performance is usually achieved when the average distance and the crossing paths metrics are low. In this way, the following heuristic is used to compute the DFS

---

[2] For further details on topology generation see Section 5.1.

spanning tree. Actually, we compute the DFS spanning tree starting from every node in the network. Also, for each tree, when selecting an output channel (see Figure 2) the link to the node with higher average topological distance to the rest of the nodes will be selected first. Finally, the DFS spanning tree with lower average distance will be chosen.

5   Performance Evaluation

In this section, we evaluate by simulation the performance of the routing scheme based on the methodology proposed in Section 4 for some network configurations. We will refer to it as UD_DFS because it is an $up^*/down^*$ routing scheme based on a DFS spanning tree. For comparison purposes, we have also evaluated the original $up^*/down^*$ routing, based on a BFS spanning tree, which will be referred to as UD_BFS. In the BFS spanning tree the root switch is chosen as the switch whose average distance to rest of the switches is the smallest one [15]. Note that the proposed routing scheme is indeed identical to the original $up^*/down^*$ routing except that link direction assignment is different. We have selected the UD_BFS algorithm for comparison because it is the one currently used in commercial networks. The remaining algorithms mentioned in Section 1 have not been considered due to their computational cost or their limited applicability.

We assume that the network topology is irregular because this is frequently the case in NOW environments, and regular topologies can be considered a particular case of the former. In order to obtain realistic simulation results, we have used timing parameters for the switches taken from a commercial network. We have selected Myrinet because it is becoming increasingly popular due to having very good performance/cost ratio. Also, we have chosen wormhole switching and deterministic source routing because they are implemented in Myrinet.

5.1   Network Model

Network topology is completely irregular and has been generated randomly. We have evaluated networks with size of 9, 16, 32, and 64 switches. We have generated ten different topologies for each network size analyzed. The maximum variation in throughput improvement of UD_DFS routing with respect to UD_BFS routing is not larger than 18% . Results plotted in this paper correspond to the topologies that achieve the average behavior for each network size. We assume that every switch in the network has 8 ports, using 4 ports to connect to workstations and leaving 4 ports to connect to other switches. For message length, 32-flit and 512-flit-messages were considered. Different message destination distributions have been used like uniform, bit-reversal, perfect shuffle and matrix transpose.

5.2 Switch Model

The path followed by each message is obtained using table-lookup at the source host, very much like in Myrinet networks. Therefore, deterministic source routing is assumed. Wormhole switching is used. Each switch has a crossbar arbiter that processes one message header at a time to select the outgoing channel. It is assigned to waiting messages in a demand-slotted round-robin fashion. If the output channel is busy, the message must wait in the input buffer until its next turn. A crossbar inside the switch allows multiple messages to be transmitted simultaneously without interference. We take the values for temporal parameters from Myrinet switches, that is, the latency through the switch for the first flit is 150 ns, and after transmitting the first flit, the switch transfers at the link rate of 6.25 ns per flit. The clock cycle is 6.25 ns. Flits are one byte wide and the physical channel is one flit wide.

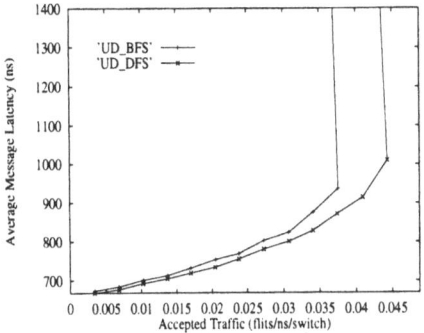
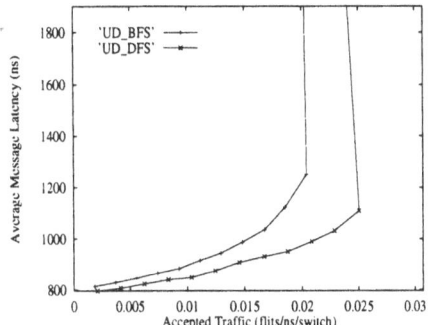

Fig. 7. Average message latency vs accepted traffic. Network size is 9 switches. Message length is 32 flits. Uniform distribution.

Fig. 8. Average message latency vs accepted traffic. Network size is 16 switches. Message length is 32 flits. Uniform distribution.

5.3 Simulation Results

Figures 7, 8, 11, and 12 show the average message latency versus accepted traffic for networks with 9, 16, 32, and 64 switches, respectively. Message size is 32 flits and uniform destination distribution is used. In particular, Figure 7 shows the behavior of the 9-switch network shown in Figure 4. As can be seen, UD_DFS routing reduces latency and increases throughput with respect to UD_BFS routing. In large networks, the improvement is more noticeable. Throughput improvement ranges from a factor of 1.17 in the 9-switch network up to a factor of 2 in the 64-switch network. The reason is that when the network size increases the

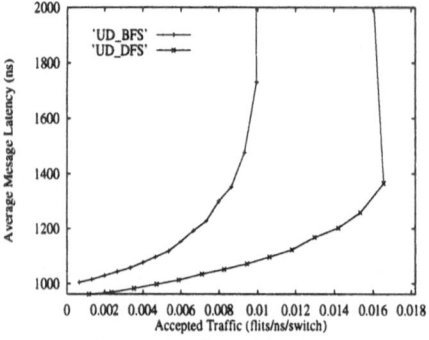

Fig. 9. Average message latency vs accepted traffic. Network size is 32 switches. Message length is 32 flits. Uniform distribution.

Fig. 10. Average message latency vs accepted traffic. Network size is 64 switches. Message length is 32 flits. Uniform distribution.

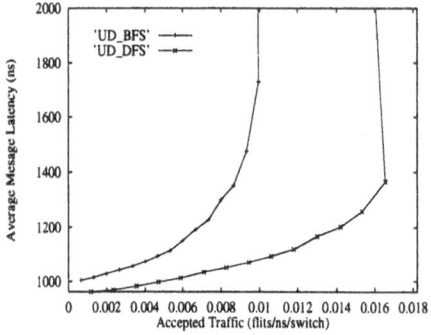
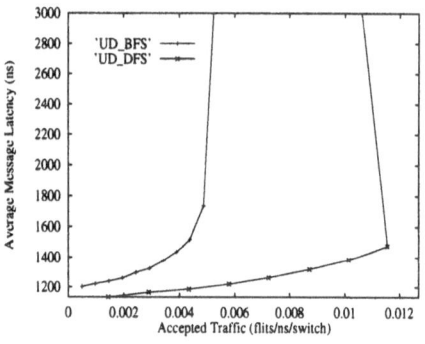

Fig. 11. Average message latency vs accepted traffic. Network size is 32 switches. Message length is 32 flits. Uniform distribution.

Fig. 12. Average message latency vs accepted traffic. Network size is 64 switches. Message length is 32 flits. Uniform distribution.

number of routing restrictions per node for UD_BFS routing increases significantly, reducing the number of minimal paths followed by messages, and increasing latency. Also, UD_BFS routing concentrates traffic near the root switch of the spanning tree, leading to a premature saturation of the network. However, the proposed routing strategy spreads traffic more evenly across different links, thus achieving a higher throughput.

Figures 13, 14, 15, and 16 show the results for networks with 9, 16, 32, and 64 switches, respectively, when long messages are used (512 flits), for the same destination distribution. We can observe that the improvement in performance decreases slightly with respect to the one achieved with short messages, due to

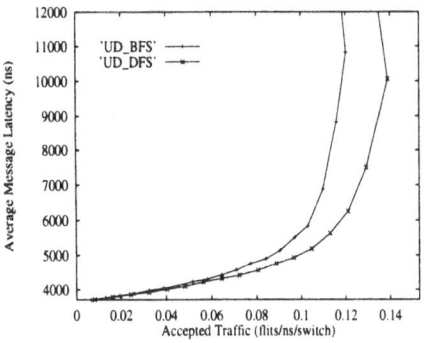

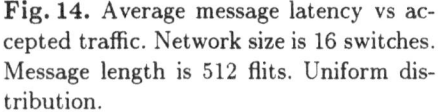

Fig. 13. Average message latency vs accepted traffic. Network size is 9 switches. Message length is 512 flits. Uniform distribution.

Fig. 14. Average message latency vs accepted traffic. Network size is 16 switches. Message length is 512 flits. Uniform distribution.

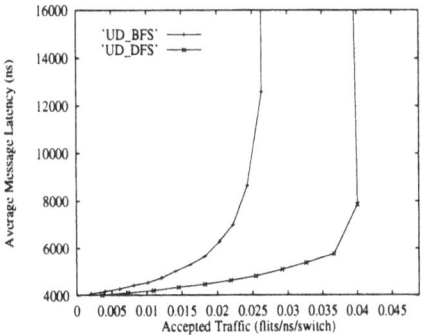

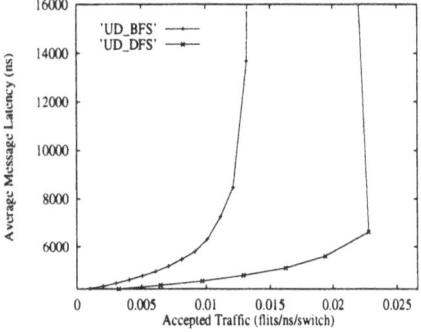

Fig. 15. Average message latency vs accepted traffic. Network size is 32 switches. Message length is 512 flits. Uniform distribution.

Fig. 16. Average message latency vs accepted traffic. Network size is 64 switches. Message length is 512 flits. Uniform distribution.

the fact that the latency of long messages is less sensitive to the distance between hosts. As a consequence, the benefits of following shorter paths decrease.

Figure 17 shows the results under bimodal traffic, which is formed by 25% of long messages and 75% of short messages. As can be observed, the improvement in performance slightly decreases when a small percentage of long messages is introduced.

On the other hand, when message distributions showing temporal locality, such as bit-reversal, matrix transpose, and perfect shuffle are used, the improvement in performance of UD_DFS with respect to UD_BFS is noticeably larger, as can be observed in Figures 18, 19, and 20. The best improvement

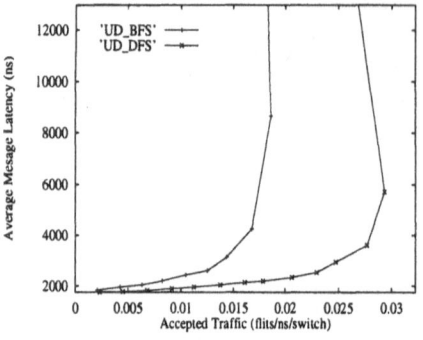
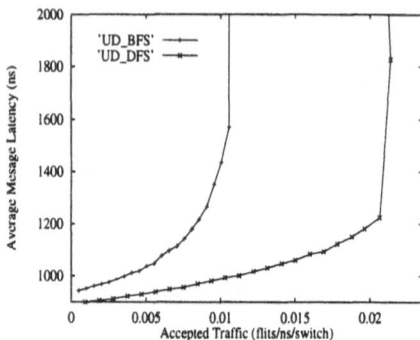

Fig. 17. Average message latency vs accepted traffic. Network size is 32 switches. Message length is 75% of 32 flits and 25% of 512 flits. Uniform distribution.

Fig. 18. Average message latency vs accepted traffic. Network size is 32 switches. Message length is 32 flits. Bit-reversal distribution.

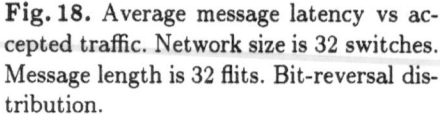
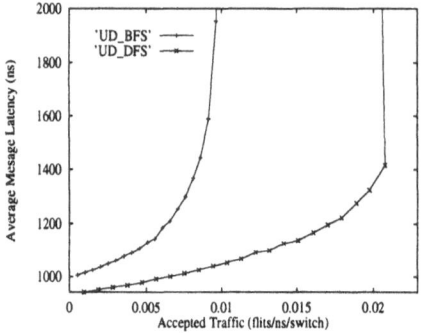
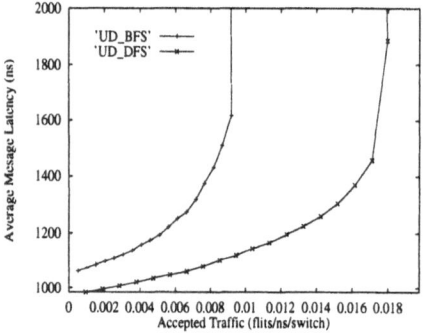

Fig. 19. Average message latency vs accepted traffic. Network size is 32 switches. Message length is 32 flits. Matrix transpose distribution.

Fig. 20. Average message latency vs accepted traffic. Network size is 32 switches. Message length is 32 flits. Perfect shuffle distribution.

(a factor of 2.1) is achieved when matrix transpose distribution is used. Factors of 1.8 and a 2 are achieved for perfect shuffle and bit-reversal distributions, respectively. The reason for the larger improvement is that these message distributions are more sensitive to short paths because all the messages from a given host are sent to the same destination.

However, when message distributions showing spatial locality are used, the improvement in performance of UD_DFS with respect to UD_BFS decreases. In particular, for a 32-switch topology and 32-flits messages we have used a local message distribution in which 60% of messages are uniformly distributed inside a sphere centered in their source host, with radius equal to 5 links (messages have to traverse up to 5 links to reach the destination host). We have observed that the improvement in throughput of UD_DFS with respect to UD_BFS decreases from 65% for uniform message distribution down to 15% when local message distribution is used. The reason is that when traffic has spatial locality, the average distance traversed by message decreases, increasing the probability that most messages follow minimal paths.

6   Conclusions

In this paper, we have proposed a new methodology to compute deadlock-free routing tables that is simple and can be applied to both regular and irregular topologies, source and distributed routing, and is valid for every switching technique. The proposed methodology is based on a depth-first search spanning tree (DFS). DFS spanning tree has been chosen because it simplifies the assignment of an ordering to the nodes in the network in order to remove cyclic channel dependencies. Routing tables are built by considering all the possible shortest paths between every pair of nodes (or just one of them if deterministic routing is preferred). The routing algorithm based on the proposed methodology can be also considered as an $up^*/down^*$ routing algorithm, although based on DFS instead of BFS spanning tree.

The main contribution of the proposed methodology is that it is able to improve network performance without adding resources to the network that would increase its cost. Simply, routing tables must be updated. The simulation results modeling a Myrinet network show that throughput is doubled in large networks with respect to the $up^*/down^*$ routing algorithm based on BFS spanning tree. For smaller networks, performance improvement is also smaller but the proposed routing scheme always improves latency and throughput.

As future work, we plan to implement the proposed routing scheme on the GM software from Myrinet.

References

1. Abali, B.: A Deadlock Avoidance Method for Computer Networks, in Proc. of CANPC'97, (1997).
2. Alfaro, F. J., et al.: On the Performance of Up*/Down* Routing, in Proc. of CANPC'00, (2000).
3. Arpaci-Duseau, A. C., et al.: High Performance sorting on networks of workstations, in Proc. of ACM SIGMOD'97, (1997).
4. Boden, N. J., et al.: Myrinet - A gigabit per second local area network, IEEE Micro, vol. 15, (1995).
5. Bollobas, B.: Graph Theory, Springer-Verlarg New York Inc, (1979).
6. Cherkasova, L., Kotov, and Rockicki, T.: Fibre channel fabrics: Evaluation and design, 29th Hawaii International Conference on System Sciences, (1995).
7. Dally, W. J.: Network and Processor Architecture for Message-Driven Computing, in VLSI and Parallel Processing, R. Suaya and G. Birtwistle, Eds., Morgan Kaufmann, (1990).

8. Dally, W. J., and Seitz, C. L.: Deadlock-free message routing in multiprocessors interconnection networks, IEEE Transactions on Computers, vol. C-36, no. 5, pp. 547-553, (1987).
9. Duato, J.: A new theory of deadlock-free adaptive routing in wormhole networks, *IEEE Transactions on Parallel and Distributed Systems*, vol. 4, no. 12, pp. 1320-1331, (1993).
10. Garcia, D., and Watson, W.: Servernet II, in Proceedings of the 1997 Parallel Computer, Routing, and Communication Workshop, (1997).
11. Kermani, P., and Kleinrock, L.: Virtual cut-through: A new computer communication switching technique, Computer Networks, vol. 3, pp. 267-286, (1979).
12. Qiao, W., and Ni., L. M.: Adaptive routing in irregular networks using cut-trough switches, in Proc. of the 1996 Int. Conf. on Parallel Processing, (1996).
13. Schroeder, M. D., et al.: Autonet: A high-speed, self-configuring local area network using point-to-point links, SRC research report 59, DEC, (1990).
14. Sheifert, P.: Gigabit Ethernet, Addison-Wesley, (1998).
15. Silla, F., and Duato, J.: Improving the Efficiency of Adaptive Routing in Networks with Irregular Topology, in Int. Conference on High Performance Computing (1997).

On the Performance of Up*/Down* Routing*

Francisco J. Alfaro[1], Aurelio Bermúdez[2], Rafael Casado[2], José Duato[3],
Francisco J. Quiles[2], and José L. Sánchez[2]

[1] Department of Computer Engineering and Technology
University of Murcia, 30071- Murcia, Spain
falfaro@ditec.um.es

[2] Department of Computer Science, University of Castilla-La Mancha
02071- Albacete, Spain
{abermu,rcasado,paco,jsanchez}@info-ab.uclm.es

[3] Department of Information Systems and Computer Architecture
Technical University of Valencia
46071- Valencia, Spain
jduato@gap.upv.es

Abstract. Networks of Workstations (*NOWs*) are usually arranged as
a set of interconnected switches with hosts connected to switch ports
through interface cards. Several commercial interconnects for high-speed
NOWs use up*/down* routing. Every time the network is powered on
or the topology is changed, a configuration algorithm is executed, which
provides information about the topology and generates a directed graph.
Routing tables are computed from this directed graph. There are several ways to obtain the directed graph. The most frequent way is by
means of algorithms based on minimum-depth spanning-trees (*MDST*)
or propagation-order spanning-trees (*POST*). This paper shows that, for
most networks, graphs obtained by means of these methods can be improved in order to achieve higher network performance.

1 Introduction

High-speed NOWs, like Autonet [14], Myrinet [1] and Servernet [9], provide an
inexpensive alternative for building parallel computers with high communication bandwidth and reduced latency. These networks usually consist of a set
of switches connected by point-to-point links, and of hosts linked to switches
through a network interface card (NIC).

Up*/down* routing is broadly used for routing in high-speed NOWs [14, 1].
However, it is well known that the performance of up*/down* routing is strongly
dependent on the network topology [10]. The generation of up*/down* routing
tables requires the construction of a directed graph by assigning directions to the
operational links in the network. As we will see later, this direction assignment
has a strong impact on network throughput.

---

* This work was partly supported by the Spanish CICYT under Grant TIC97-0897-
C04, and Caja Castilla-La Mancha

B. Falsafi and M. Lauria (Eds.): CANPC 2000, LNCS 1797, pp. 61–72, 2000.

There are several ways of assigning link direction through the construction of a directed graph: minimum-depth spanning-tree (MDST) [14], propagation-order spanning-tree (POST) [12], etc. This paper shows that these methods do not produce the best graph, and that it is possible to find a link direction assignment that makes the network achieve a higher throughput.

Our main goal is to compare the behavior of directed graphs generated by traditional methods with the behavior of the best directed graph that we can obtain.

In Section 2 we describe the up*/down* routing algorithm used by Autonet and Myrinet as well as two methods used by Autonet to obtain the directed graph: MDST and POST. Section 3 presents an example that shows how performance can be improved and presents a genetic algorithm that searches for the best possible directed graph for a given network. Section 4 compares the performance of the network when using the traditional approach and when using the optimized directed graph.

2   Background

2.1   Up*/Down* Routing and Correct Graphs

Up*/down* routing [14] is a partially adaptive deadlock-free routing algorithm suitable for regular and irregular topologies [7]. Up*/down* routing requires assigning a direction to all the links of the network. In every link, a direction is named *up* and the opposite one is named *down*. Legal routes never use a link in up direction after having used one in down direction, in order to avoid deadlocks. Messages can cross zero or more links in up direction, followed by zero or more links in down direction. By doing so, cycles in the channel dependency graph [5] are eliminated and deadlock is avoided.

In order to use up*/down* routing, the directed graph which represents the link direction assignment must satisfy some properties [3, 2]. A graph satisfying those properties will be referred to as a *correct graph*. Those properties are the following:

1. A *root node* is a node in a directed graph that is not the source of any arc. The up*/down* routing algorithm requires the existence of a single root node in the graph. The reason is that there are no up*/down* legal routes between two root nodes, since each possible route requires down to up transitions. This restriction is required for the routing algorithm to provide paths between any pair of nodes.
2. The graph must be acyclic to avoid deadlock.

Thus, every link direction assignment leading to an acyclic directed graph that contains a single root node is a *correct graph*. It is important to remark that no more restrictions are imposed on the directed graph. Therefore, several correct directed graphs can be obtained starting from the same topology.

2.2   MDST and POST Directed Graphs

As mentioned above, the generation of up*/down* routing tables requires the construction of a correct directed graph of the network in which nodes are the active network switches and arcs are the links among switches. Two of the methods used for obtaining this directed graph are minimum-depth spanning-tree (MDST) [14] and propagation-order spanning-tree (POST) [12].

Both methods are based on the execution of a distributed algorithm that builds a spanning-tree from the network graph. Starting from this spanning-tree, the algorithm assigns directions to all the links of the network. In particular, the "up" end of each link is defined as: 1) the end whose switch is closer to the root in the spanning-tree; 2) the end whose switch has the lower identifier (id), if both ends are at switches at the same tree level. The MDST and POST methodologies are based on a breadth-first searching methodology [12].

On the one hand, MDST produces the minimum-depth spanning-tree of the network, where the root node is the switch with the lowest id and the rest of switches are assigned positions in the tree that provide the shortest distance to the root. If there are several positions that provide the shortest distance to the root, then the one provided by the switch with the lowest id is selected. Thus, it is possible to guarantee that there is only one possible minimum-depth spanning-tree for a network topology and an accompanying identifier assignment.

Figure 1 shows a network topology and the id for each switch. The resulting directed graph using MDST is shown in Figure 2. Note that the link between Node 14 and Node 10 is the only one that does not belong to the spanning-tree.

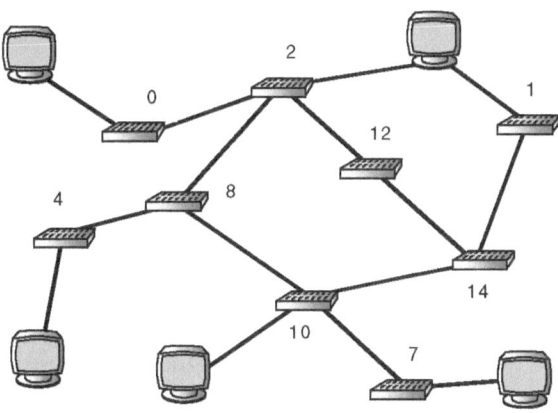

Fig. 1. An example of irregular network

On the other hand, POST chooses as the root node of the spanning-tree the switch that detects the change in the topology and starts the reconfiguration process. This node is called the *initiator*. The initiator sends messages to its neighboring switches. When a switch receives a control message, it join the tree

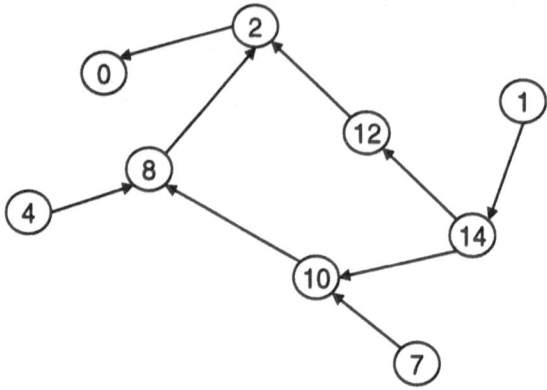

Fig. 2. Directed graph for the network in Figure 1 obtained by using MDST method

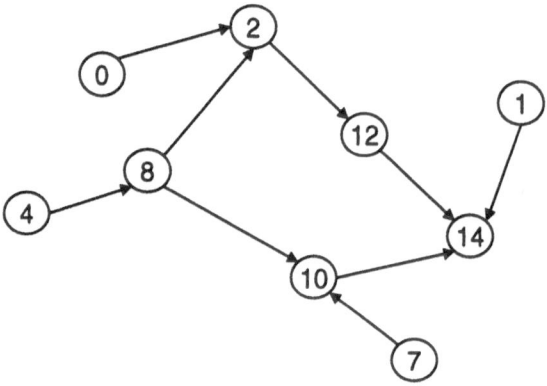

Fig. 3. Directed graph for the network in Figure 1 obtained by using POST method

and propagates new control messages to its own neighboring switches (the switch that sent it the incoming message is omitted). In this way, the switches will join the tree as soon as they receive messages from other switches.

Note that the resulting spanning-tree depends on the initiator switch, but also on the propagation order of the reconfiguration process through the network.

Figure 3 shows a possible directed graph for the network shown in Figure 1 using POST and assuming that the initiator is Node 14.

3 Improving Network Performance

As we will see in Section 4, network throughput has a direct relationship with the directed graph used to build the up*/down* routing tables. In other words, network throughput will be determined by the direction assigned to the network links.

Figure 4a shows a network with a link direction assignment provided by the MDST method. The up*/down* routing rules lead to a bottleneck at Node 0 (the root node of the tree), because messages are not allowed to cross Node 3 in order to move from the right subtree to the left one, and vice versa. If we change the direction of link 1 (see Figure 4b), we might achieve an improvement in network throughput of about 100%. The reason is that now messages can also cross from one subnetwork to the other through Node 3.

If we study the directed graph generated by Autonet, we will see that in most cases it is not the one that achieves the highest network throughput. Our purpose is to determine how suboptimal the directed graph obtained by MDST and POST is, comparing the resulting network performance with that obtained by using the best possible directed graph.

Each possible graph can be obtained from another graph by changing the direction of some links of the network. Therefore, the number of possible variations for a certain network is $N_g = 2^{links}$, where *links* is the number of links in the network and the number of correct graphs is $N_c = 2^{links}$ - {incorrect graphs}. The number of incorrect graphs is much smaller than the number of correct ones. Thus, even for a relatively small network with a few links, the number of directed graphs to study is too high to recommend the use of an exhaustive search method.

3.1   Genetic Algorithms

Genetic Algorithms (GAs) [8] are adaptive methods used to solve search and optimization problems in wide or complex spaces. They are based on the genetic behavior of the living beings and the natural evolution and the adaptation of these beings alongside successive generations. We will make use of GAs to search for the best (or near-optimal) possible directed graph.

GAs work with a population of t individuals, where each one represents a feasible solution to the given problem. An adaptation value is associated to each individual, which indicates its capacity to survive. The individuals of a generation that better adapt to the requirements of the problem will have a higher probability of surviving and reproducing in the following generation than the worse adapted individuals. This reproduction leads to the perpetuation of their genes in substitution for the genes of the weakest individuals. Thus, the individuals of next generations will be better and better adapted to the conditions of the problem.

Each individual is represented by means of a chain of values, or *chromosome*, which contains the necessary information to encode the values for the important problem parameters. When the reproduction of the best adapted individuals for a generation takes place, a series of genetic operators are applied to their chromosomes. The most usual genetic operators are: *cross*, which picks up two parents and mixes their chromosomes starting from a randomly generated gene

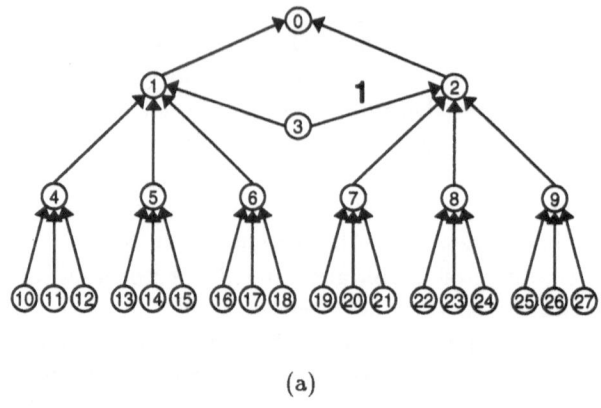

(a)

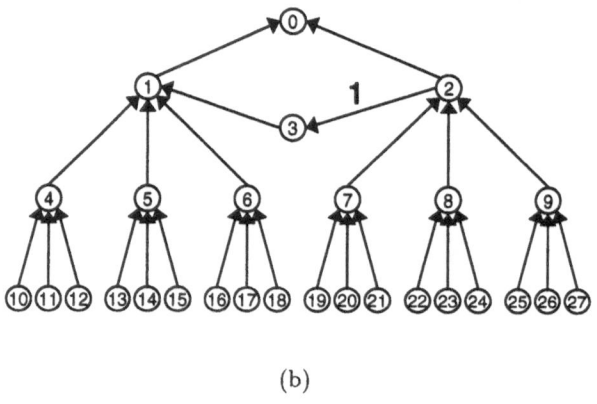

(b)

Fig. 4. An example of throughput improvement by changing only the direction of link 1

or position, and *mutation*, which consists of randomly altering some of the parent's genes. The individuals that are born in generation i are evaluated together with the survivors of generation $i-1$ and, amongst them, the best adapted ones will reproduce to give rise to generation $i+1$.

3.2   GAs and NOWs

In our research, we will consider each possible correct directed graph as individuals belonging to the same population. Individuals of the same population will then be distinguished from each other according to the direction of their links.

The form in which a directed graph is encoded in the chromosome for its later treatment has a great importance, and it must be unique. We represent a link between nodes i and j ($i < j$) with a gene in the chromosome, being equal to 1 if the link from node i to node j is in the up direction, and equal to 0 if it is in the down direction. The place that each link occupies in the chromosome is called a *locus* and it is defined by assigning a number to the links, beginning from port 0 of Node 0 and continuing in increasing order. Note that links are numbered only the first time they are evaluated. Therefore, their locus is fixed. Figure 5 shows an example of link numbering and the associated chromosome.

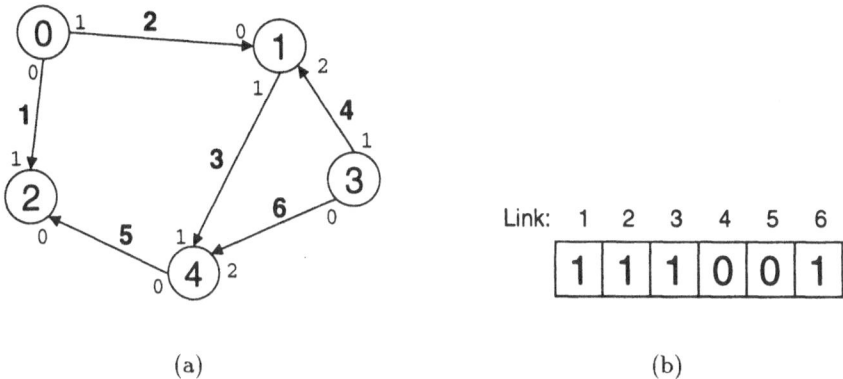

(a)   (b)

Fig. 5. An example encoding of the network (a) in the chromosome (b). Small numbers next to each node represent port numbers

The way in which we measure the adaptation of the individuals of a generation is by using the throughput achieved by the routing algorithm that they represent. Throughput is defined as the maximum amount of information that the network is able to transmit per unit of time. We obtain this value by simulation.

Two important parameters for the GA are the number of individuals in a generation, and how many of them die in order to give way to the following generation. We have seen that the best results are obtained by considering a population of 12 individuals in which the four worst adapted die. Four new individuals will be born in the next generation by applying the genetic operators cross and mutation to the two best individuals of the current generation. Obviously, these new individuals must represent correct graphs.

4   Performance Evaluation

In this section, we show the results of our comparison. We have evaluated the performance of MDST and POST directed graphs and the performance of the directed graph obtained using the GA described in the previous section through the evaluation of the associated up*/down* routing algorithm.

GAs have an inherent non-determinism. For this reason, we have evaluated how stable the results provided by them are. To achieve it, we have obtained the entire set of possible correct directed graphs for several small networks (with 8 switches). For each topology, the directed graph provided by the GA obtained the best throughput.

Simulation was used to evaluate network performance. Our simulators model the network at the phit[1] level. The evaluation methodology used is based on the one proposed in [6].

4.1 Network Model

The network consists of a set of switches as well as hosts connected to them. We used a set of irregular randomly generated topologies. Also, we have evaluated hierarchical topologies like the example in Figure 4. We have evaluated networks with 8, 16, 24, 32, 48, and 64 switches.

4.2 Packet Generation

We have considered uniform traffic. Message destination is randomly chosen amongst all the hosts in the network, and the average generation rate is constant and the same for all the hosts. For packet length, 16-byte and 64-byte packets were considered. Nevertheless, we have found that packet length does not significantly affect the relative performance of the routing algorithms computed from different directed graphs. Thus, we will only show the results for short packets.

4.3 Simulation Results

As indicated above, we use network throughput to evaluate the optimality of the directed graph. Tables 1a, 1b, 1c, and 1d show the throughput achieved by several networks of size 8, 16, 24, and 32 switches, respectively. First, we can see that the throughput obtained when using our GA is always equal to or greater than that obtained by using the other methods. For networks with 8 switches, there is no difference. However, for larger networks, we can observe increments of 50%, 60%, and even 80% in network throughput. For networks with 48 switches we have obtained increments of up to 24% with respect to MDST and up to 80% with respect to POST, and for networks with 64 switches the increment reaches 58% with respect to MDST and 78% with respect to POST.

We have also evaluated the average message latency versus traffic for some networks with 24, 32, and 64 switches. Figures 6, 7, and 8 show the results. As can be observed, in all the cases the routing algorithm obtained using GAs reduces latency and increases throughput with respect to the MDST and POST methods.

---

[1] Unit of information that can be transferred across a physical channel in a single step or cycle.

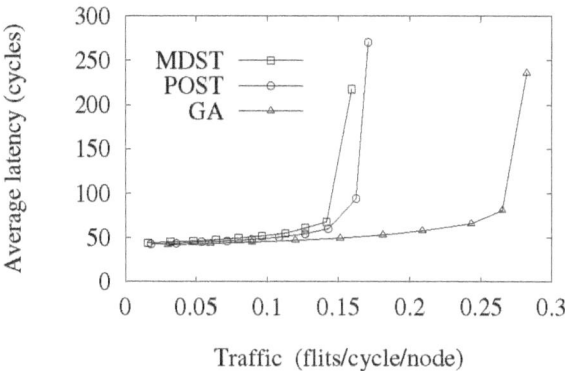

Fig. 6. Average message latency versus traffic for an irregular network with 24 switches

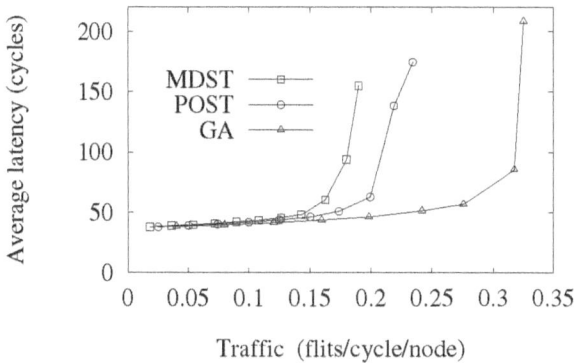

Fig. 7. Average message latency versus traffic for an irregular network with 32 switches

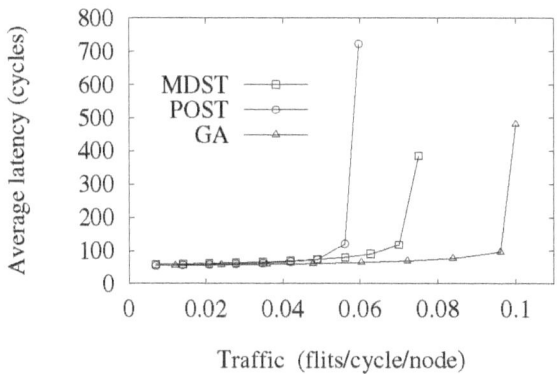

Fig. 8. Average message latency versus traffic for an irregular network with 64 switches

We have analyzed the directed graphs obtained by MDST, POST and GAs. The performance improvement obtained by using GAs comes from a reduction in the number of routing restrictions required to avoid deadlock. In those cases that does not exist any better set of routing restrictions, all the strategies obtained the same results.

5 Related Work

Two approaches that improve performance by obtaining a better directed graph are proposed in [10, 13]. The former is suitable for regular topologies and is based on a previous appropriate assignment of switch identifiers (*id*). The latter is suitable for general topologies including irregular ones. In this case, the directed graph requires the previous generation of a deep-first tree (DFT), instead of a breadth-first spanning-tree, like MDST or POST.

Another deadlock-free routing schemes have been proposed for NOWs, like the adaptive-trail routing algorithm [11], the minimal adaptive routing [15], and the smart-routing [4].

Table 1. Throughput for several irregular networks with 8, 16, 24, and 32 switches

Network	MDST	POST	GA
A	0.469	0.468	0.469
B	0.469	0.468	0.469
C	0.469	0.468	0.469
D	0.328	0.328	0.328
E	0.328	0.328	0.328

(a) 8 switches

Network	MDST	POST	GA
A	0.180	0.183	0.203
B	0.180	0.175	0.180
C	0.469	0.412	0.469
D	0.406	0.329	0.469
E	0.328	0.295	0.359
F	0.203	0.223	0.328
G	0.203	0.199	0.234

(b) 16 switches

Network	MDST	POST	GA
A	0.164	0.185	0.297
B	0.148	0.148	0.234
C	0.180	0.161	0.203
D	0.164	0.141	0.164
E	0.117	0.117	0.133
F	0.133	0.122	0.133
G	0.117	0.117	0.117
H	0.203	0.157	0.234
I	0.133	0.151	0.203

(c) 24 switches

Network	MDST	POST	GA
A	0.102	0.096	0.102
B	0.102	0.102	0.133
C	0.102	0.100	0.102
D	0.148	0.190	0.328
E	0.234	0.228	0.469
F	0.180	0.245	0.406
G	0.180	0.226	0.359
H	0.297	0.249	0.406
I	0.234	0.252	0.406
J	0.203	0.237	0.359

(d) 32 switches

6 Conclusions

In this paper we have shown that changing the direction of some links in the directed graph used for up*/down* routing has a significant impact on the throughput achieved by the network. We conclude that there are correct graphs that offer a higher network throughput than the graphs generated by usual methods, such as MDST and POST, which are used in Autonet and Myrinet. Also, differences in network performance for GA, MDST and POST increase with network size.

In order to obtain the best possible directed graph, we have used a search and optimization tool based on genetic algorithms, which are a very good choice when the search space is wide and complex. We have defined a representation of the NOWs for the GA. Also, we have used throughput as the adaptation metric.

7 Future Work

Obviously, GAs are not suitable for computing routing tables during a reconfiguration process due to the very high computational cost. As future work, we plan to study the best networks obtained, and try to characterize them. We will attempt to propose an efficient design methodology that obtains the best graph when a reconfiguration takes place, thus maximizing network throughput.

Acknowledgements

The authors thank *Timothy M. Pinkston*, at the University of Southern California, for his suggestions and comments on drafts of this paper. We also thank *Juan Luis García-Navarro* and *José A. Gámez-Martín* for their collaboration with genetic algorithm simulations.

References

1. N.J. Boden, D. Cohen, R.E. Felderman: Myrinet – a gigabit per second local area network. IEEE Micro, pages 29–36, February 1995.
2. R. Casado, A. Bermúdez, F.J. Quiles, J.L. Sánchez, J. Duato: Performance evaluation of dynamic reconfiguration in high-speed local area networks. In Proceedings of the sixth Symposium on High Performance Computer Architecture (HPCA-6), January 2000.
3. R. Casado, F.J. Quiles, J.L. Sánchez, J. Duato: Deadlock-free routing in irregular networks with dynamic reconfiguration. In Lecture Notes in Computer Science, vol. 1602, pp. 165–180. Springer, January 1999, Proceedings of the CANPC'99.
4. L. Cherkasova, V. Kotov, T. Rockicki: Fibre channel fabrics: evaluation and design. In Proceedings of 29th Hawaii International Conference on System Sciences, February 1995.
5. W.J. Dally, C.L. Seitz: Deadlock-free message routing in multiprocessor interconnection networks. IEEE Transactions on Computers, C-36(5), May 1987.

6. J. Duato, A. Robles, F. Silla, R. Beivide: A comparison of router architectures for virtual cut-through and wormhole switching in a NOW environment. In Proceedings of the 13th International Parallel Processing Symposium and 10th Symposium on Parallel and Distributed Processing (IPPS/SPDP'99), April 1999.
7. J. Duato, S. Yalamanchili, L. Ni: Interconnection networks. An engineering approach. IEEE Computer Society, 1997.
8. D. E. Goldberg: Genetic Algorithms in search, optimization and machine learning. Addison-Wesley, 1989.
9. R. W. Horst: Tnet: A reliable system area network. IEEE Micro, February 1995.
10. S. Owicki, A. R. Karlin: Factors in the performance of the AN1 computer network. Technical Report 88, Digital Equipment Corporation Systems Research Center, Palo Alto, CA, June 1992.
11. W. Qiao, L.M. Ni: Adaptive routing in irregular networks using cut-through switches. In Proceedings of the 1996 International Conference on Parallel Processing (ICPP'96), August 1996.
12. T.L. Rodeheffer, M.D. Schroeder: Automatic reconfiguration in Autonet. Technical Report 77, Systems Research Center of Digital Equipment Corporation, September 1991.
13. J.C. Sancho, A. Robles, J. Duato: A new methodoly to compute deadlock-free routing tables for irregular networks. In Proceedings of the WorkShop on Communication and Architectural Support for Network-Parallel Computing'00 (CANPC'00), January 2000.
14. M.D. Schroeder, A.D. Birrell, M. Burrows, H. Murray, R.M.Needham, T.L. Rodeheffer, E.H.Satterthwate, C.P.Thacker: Autonet: a high-speed, self-configuring local area network using point-to-point links. Technical Report 59, Systems Research Center of Digital Equipment Corporation, 1990.
15. F. Silla, J. Duato: Improving the efficiency of adaptive routing in networks with irregular topology. In Proceedings of the 1997 Int. Conference on High Performance Computing (HiPC'97), December 1997.

Extending Dynamic Reconfiguration to NOWs with Adaptive Routing*

Aurelio Bermúdez[2], Francisco J. Alfaro[1], Rafael Casado[2], José Duato[3], Francisco J. Quiles[2], and José L. Sánchez[2]

[1] Department of Computer Engineering and Technology
University of Murcia, 30071- Murcia, Spain
falfaro@ditec.um.es
[2] Department of Computer Science
University of Castilla-La Mancha
02071- Albacete, Spain
{abermu,rcasado,paco,jsanchez}@info-ab.uclm.es
[3] Department of Information Systems and Computer Architecture
Technical University of Valencia
46071- Valencia, Spain
jduato@gap.upv.es

Abstract. Many distributed applications executed on networks of workstations (*NOWs*) require the interconnection network to provide some quality of service (QoS) support. These networks must be able to support topology changes (due to component failures, hot replacement, hot expansion, etc.) without stopping traffic, in order to satisfy QoS requirements. Traditional network reconfiguration methods do not take this into account, causing a serious performance degradation while the network is being reconfigured.

In [1, 2], we proposed a new dynamic network reconfiguration protocol, called *Partial Progressive Reconfiguration*. It significantly reduces the negative effects produced by traditional methods. For this reason, it is especially suitable for applications requiring QoS. This reconfiguration protocol requires that messages are routed using up*/down* routing.

In this paper, we extend this dynamic reconfiguration technique to support adaptive routing, based on the design methodology for adaptive algorithms proposed in [3,4]. We also present performance evaluation results, clearly showing the benefits of using dynamic reconfiguration combined with adaptive routing.

1 Introduction

NOWs are usually composed of several hosts interconnected by means of switches and point-to-point links in an arbitrary topology. Network topology may change

---

* This work was partly supported by the Spanish CICYT under Grant TIC97-0897-C04, and Caja Castilla-La Mancha

B. Falsafi and M. Lauria (Eds.). CANPC 2000, LNCS 1797, pp. 73–83, 2000.

due to switches and hosts being turned on/off, link remapping, component failures, hot replacement, hot expansion, etc. In these cases, a reconfiguration process must update the routing tables to guarantee network connectivity. Several current reconfiguration algorithms need to stop user traffic during reconfiguration to prevent deadlock. For this reason, this methodology is called *static reconfiguration*. Autonet [5] and Myrinet [6] are two representative examples.

Several distributed real-time applications have strict communications requirements [7, 8], with rigorous limitations on CDV (cell delay variation), CTD (maximum cell transfer delay) and CLR (cell loss ratio) parameters. Distributed multimedia applications have similar, although less strict, quality of service (QoS) requirements. Nowadays, many distributed multimedia applications such as real-time video compression and decompression, video-on-demand servers, distributed databases, etc., require computing power beyond that available in current uniprocessors. These applications require very high network bandwidth, which can be provided by means of a high-speed LAN.

When multimedia applications are executed on a local area switch-based network, topology changes may affect their behavior. If static reconfiguration is used, user traffic is stopped and the average packet latency increases dramatically during the reconfiguration. It should be noted that traffic is stopped in the entire network, even if topology changes only affect a small region of the network. Thus, it will not be possible to guarantee the required QoS [9] during reconfiguration. Moreover, messages buffered in their source nodes during reconfiguration will be transmitted immediately after finishing the reconfiguration, possibly leading to network saturation and preventing QoS from being guaranteed for even longer. Stopping user traffic has even worse effects on distributed real-time applications due to the more strict timing constraints required for them.

A different approach to solve this problem is *dynamic reconfiguration*. Unlike static reconfiguration protocols, dynamic protocols do not require stopping network traffic during the reconfiguration in order to guarantee the absence of deadlock. This fact leads to shorter packet delays and reduced packet loss rates even during the reconfiguration. This approach is applicable to networks that attempt to provide delivery guarantees and QoS. Note that dynamic reconfiguration by itself does not guarantee QoS. However, it is not possible to guarantee QoS without dynamic reconfiguration when the topology changes.

A dynamic reconfiguration protocol, called *Partial Progressive Reconfiguration* (PPR), was proposed in [1, 2]. This approach avoids deadlock during reconfiguration by applying a sequence of partial routing table updates. PPR was designed for virtual cut-through networks without virtual channels and distributed up*/down* routing. On the other hand, networks with virtual channels can support adaptive routing, which is much more efficient than up*/down* routing. In fact, adaptive routing can use up*/down* routing to escape from deadlock [3, 4]. This work focuses on extending dynamic reconfiguration to NOWs that support virtual channels and adaptive routing.

The next section presents up*/down* routing and describes a methodology to extend it to adaptive routing. Also, both static and dynamic reconfiguration schemes are described in an informal way. The third section describes the strategy used to update the routing tables during dynamic reconfiguration. In the fourth section we present simulation results. Finally, there are some conclusions and future work.

2 Background

2.1 Up*/Down* versus Adaptive Routing

Up*/down* is a partially adaptive deadlock-free routing algorithm suitable for regular as well as irregular topologies [10]. This algorithm avoids deadlock by preventing cyclic dependencies between network links [11].

Up*/Down* routing is based on a cycle-free assignment of *direction* to the operational links in the network. This assignment is always possible, regardless of network topology [5]. Therefore, the network is configured as an acyclic directed graph with one (and only one) root node. A graph satisfying those properties will be referred to as a correct graph. For each link, a direction is named *up* and the opposite one is named *down*. Legal routes never use a link in the up direction after having used one in the down direction, in order to avoid deadlocks. In other words, messages can cross zero or more links in the up direction, followed by zero or more links in the down direction. By doing this, cycles in the channel dependency graph [11] are avoided, thus preventing deadlock.

Up*/down* routing is not always able to provide a minimal path between every pair of nodes due to the restrictions imposed by the up*/down* rule. As the network size increases, this effect becomes more wide-spread.

In order to increase the adaptivity of this routing scheme, we apply the general methodology for the design of deadlock-free adaptive routing algorithms for networks with irregular topology proposed in [3, 4]. We split each physical link into two virtual channels, called *original* and *new* channels. New channels are used for fully adaptive minimal routing. The new routing scheme gives a higher priority to the new channels. Original channels are used as escape channels to avoid deadlock when all the minimal routes are busy, using in this case up*/down* routing.

In the wormhole version of this routing scheme, once a message reserves an original channel, it must be routed using only original channels until it is delivered, in order to prevent deadlock situations. However, as we use virtual-cut through switching, this restriction is not necessary [12] and so, a message that is using an up*/down* channel can use an adaptive channel in the next link.

Another issue is that a reconfiguration process that updates up*/down* routing tables requires information about the entire topology and a correct directed graph computed from it. However, a reconfiguration process that updates minimal routing tables only requires the topologic information. In this case, no correct directed graph is required because minimal adaptive routing allows cyclic dependencies between channels.

2.2   Static versus Dynamic Reconfiguration

After the topology has changed, a static reconfiguration protocol computes the direction assignment for every link in the network starting from scratch, i.e., it discards the previous configuration.

For example, in Autonet each switch is responsible for monitoring the state of the links to its neighbors. A switch that detects any change and triggers a topology acquisition is called the *initiator*. A topology acquisition is a diffusing computation that spreads from its point of initiation over the entire network. It contains three phases: propagation, collection, and distribution. The collection phase ends at the point of initiation, so the initiator knows when the collection phase has ended. A data structure used in this process is called *propagation-order spanning-tree* (POST) [13]. At this point the initiator knows the complete network topology. Distribution then proceeds until all switches know the complete topology.

Every switch clears its old routing table during the propagation phase and then computes its new routing table after it gets the new network topology during the distribution phase. Since the initiator detects the end of the collection phase before starting the distribution phase, it assumes that all switches have a cleared routing table and all old user packets have been flushed from the network. Flushing all old user packets avoids deadlocks between user packets routed according to the old routing table and user packets routed according to the new routing table.

On the other hand, a dynamic reconfiguration protocol such as PPR propagates the new configuration across the network while it remains operational. To achieve it, when a switch is activated, it is added as a leaf to the graph, in order to avoid cyclic dependencies between channels. Moreover, if the new switch connects two subnetworks that were initially isolated, then both subnetworks remain disconnected because the up*/down* routing algorithm does not allow traffic through leaf switches. Similarly, when the root switch of a graph is removed, two or more root nodes may appear. Again, the up*/down* routing algorithm does not allow traffic between root nodes, which become logically isolated. If there is no network connectivity, certain packets should will be discarded.

To restore network connectivity, the PPR protocol progressively changes the direction of some links, until it reaches a correct graph according to the new topology. For this reason we call this data structure an *adaptive directed graph* (ADG). The PPR protocol consists of five steps: first, it generates the *correct regions* of the graph. A correct region is a maximal subgraph of an incorrect graph that it is correct. Second, a *virtual inter-region graph* is obtained. It is an abstraction of every correct region in the graph. Third, its necessary to modify this virtual graph to make it correct by changing the direction of some virtual links. Fourth, virtual link direction changes are propagated to physical links. And fifth, although this is not a separate step, routing tables are updated through a sequence of partial table updates that are embedded in steps 1 and 4. A detailed description of PPR is beyond of the scope of this paper and can be found in [1].

3   Updating Routing Tables

Every time a change in the network topology is detected, a reconfiguration process should update all the routing tables. The original static and dynamic protocols analyzed in [1] only support up*/down* routing tables. When we add support for adaptive routing, these reconfiguration protocols should support up*/down* routing tables and minimal adaptive routing tables. Obviously, both tables should be updated during the reconfiguration process.

In static reconfiguration schemes, a *Propagation-Order Spanning Tree* (POST) could be used in order to gather information about the topology. This methodology is suitable for update both up*/down* and minimal adaptive routing tables.

On the other hand, in our dynamic reconfiguration protocol, instead of initially starting the PPR process, we have opted for triggering a different distributed process to obtain the entire network topology. This process is called *Topology Task* (TT) and is based on the construction of a *Propagation-Order Spanning Tree* (POST) from the topology. The main difference between TT and POST data structures is that the former only contains topologic information used to generate the minimal adaptive routing tables. The latter also contains a direction for each link, required to generate up*/down* routing tables. In our dynamic approach, up*/down* routing tables are generated by a PPR process.

When the root node of this tree has acquired the entire topology, it is ready to trigger a PPR process, which will update up*/down* routing tables as described in [1]. At the same time, it sends the topologic information to every switch in the network. In this way, when switches have acquired the new topology, they are ready to update their minimal adaptive routing tables. The up*/down* routing tables will be updated later.

Figures 1 and 2 show how the two processes (TT and PPR) are overlapped in time. Figure 1 represents a network supporting up*/down* routing running a PPR process. Figure 2 represents the same topology supporting adaptive routing and running the two overlapped processes, TT and PPR.

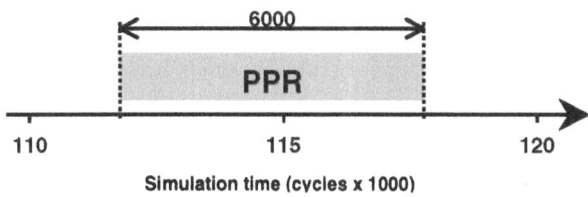

Fig. 1. A representation of dynamic reconfiguration process using up*/down* routing

The TT distribution phase is overlapped with the PPR propagation phase. Observe that, in the latter case, the PPR process takes longer to complete than

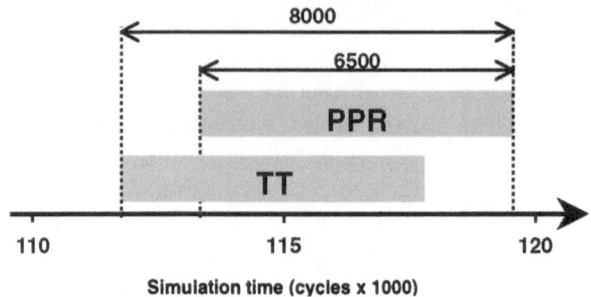

Fig. 2. A representation of dynamic reconfiguration process using adaptive routing

in the former. The reason is that PPR control messages must coexist with TT messages distributing the entire topology through the network.

4   Performance Evaluation

In this section, we present performance evaluation results, comparing the behavior of static and dynamic reconfiguration when the network uses fully adaptive routing. Static reconfiguration is based on the generation of the propagation-order spanning-tree (POST), similar to the technique implemented in Autonet network [13]. Dynamic reconfiguration combines TT and PPR tasks as described in Section 3. Simulation is used to evaluate the performance. Our simulators model the network at the phit[1] level. The evaluation methodology used is based on the one proposed in [12].

4.1   Network Model

Networks consist of a set of switches as well as hosts connected to them. We have used a set of randomly generated irregular topologies. We have evaluated networks with 8, 16, 24, 32, 48, and 64 switches.

4.2   Switch Model

The switch model used is shown in Figure 3. This architecture is identical to the one described in [1], except that virtual channels have been added to support adaptive routing. Virtual channels are implemented by replicating each packet buffer corresponding to a physical link, and maintaining the control buffer. Also, all packet buffers are directly connected to the crossbar. Thus, several packets stored in different packet buffers of the same physical link can simultaneously use the crossbar toward different output links. The resulting architecture is similar to the virtual cut-through router with partially multiplexed crossbar proposed in [12], but including control buffers.

---

[1] Unit of information that can be transferred across a physical channel in a single step or cycle.

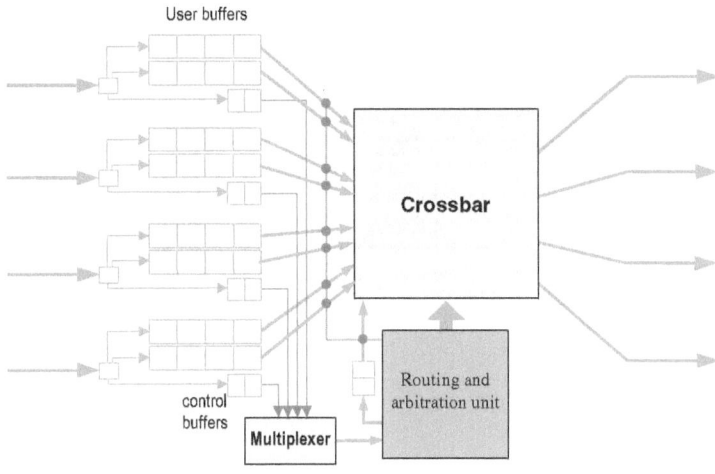

Fig. 3. Switch architecture

4.3 Packet Generation

We have considered uniform traffic. Message destination is randomly chosen among all the hosts in the network, and the average generation rate is constant and the same for all the hosts. For packet length, 16-byte and 64-byte packets were considered. Nevertheless, we have found that packet length does not significantly affect the relative performance of the reconfiguration techniques. Thus, we will only show the results for short packets.

4.4 Simulation Results

In order to implement adaptive routing, we have used two virtual channels. The first one is used for fully adaptive minimal routing and the other one is an escape channel. Therefore, it uses up*/down* routing.

First, we compare the effect of the reconfiguration process on user traffic. Figures 4 and 5 show instantaneous latency versus simulation time for an irregular network composed of 32 and 48 switches, respectively. In both cases, the root node (switch 0) is disabled after 150×10^3 simulation cycles, and enabled again after 200×10^3 simulation cycles.

The behavior of static reconfiguration is independent of which switch is enabled or disabled [13]. When we apply our dynamic reconfiguration strategy, we must distinguish between switch enabling and disabling. For a switch activation the algorithm is also independent on which switch is enabled. However, a switch deactivation is very dependent on which switch is disabled. The worst case occurs when the root node is disabled, because several false root nodes can arise [1,2]. Figures 4 and 5 show the latency when the root node (switch 0) is disabled and enabled again.

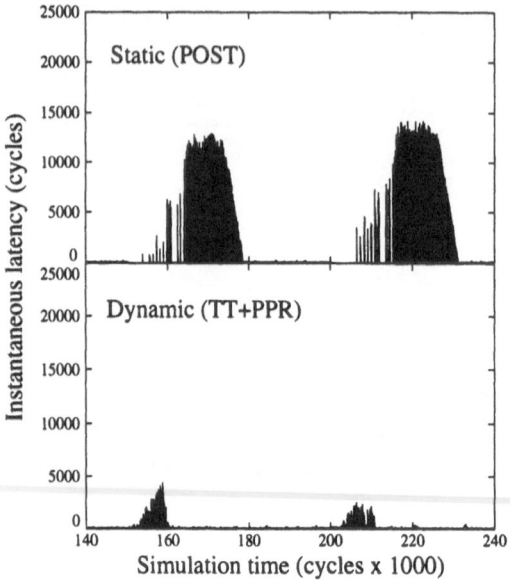

Fig. 4. Instantaneous latency versus simulation time for an irregular network composed of 32 switches. Packet length is 16 bytes

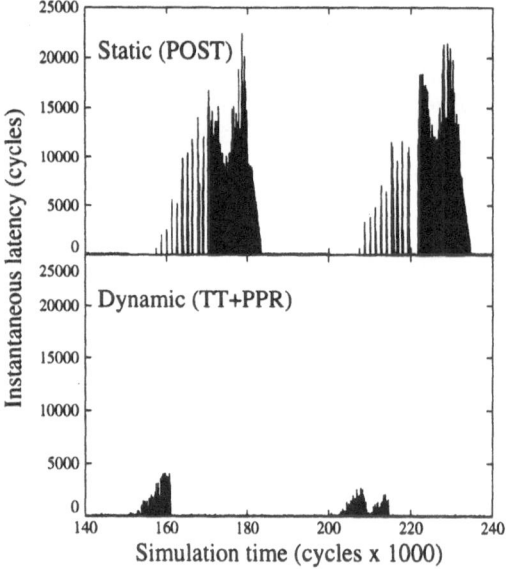

Fig. 5. Instantaneous latency versus simulation time for an irregular network composed of 48 switches. Packet length is 16 bytes

For both network sizes, results are qualitatively similar. For a static reconfig-uration, there is a time interval of several thousands of cycles in which messages are not transmitted into the network. The absence of messages is due to stopping user traffic during the reconfiguration. After reconfiguration, messages waiting to be injected produce an important increase in injection rate, saturating the network and drastically increasing packet latency.

For dynamic reconfiguration, user traffic is only slightly affected during the reconfiguration process. The network does not stop its activity, and packet la-tency slightly increases during a short period of time.

Figure 6 shows the amount of packets discarded when the reconfiguration process starts. The figure corresponds to the worst case of dynamic reconfigura-tion (the deactivation of the root node). In case of static reconfiguration, these packets come from emptying the virtual channel buffers when the reconfigura-tion process starts. For that reason, the number of discarded packets increases when the network size increases. However, the amount of packets discarded dur-ing the dynamic reconfiguration depends on the network size only in an indirect way. The figure shows that the number of discarded packets is much lower when dynamic reconfiguration is applied.

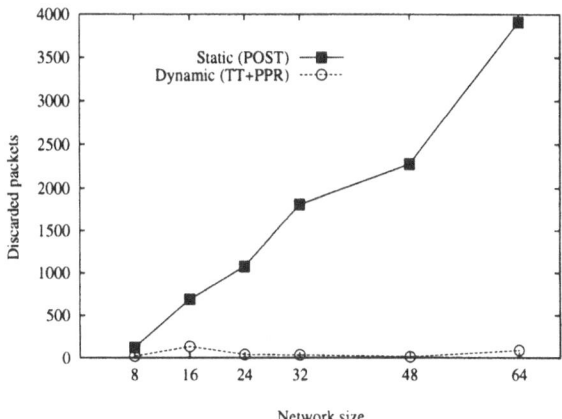

Fig. 6. Discarded packets versus network size for a switch deactivation on irregular networks with random traffic

Finally, Figure 7 shows reconfiguration time versus network size. We can see that our dynamic protocol requires less time than static reconfiguration. The reason is that TT and PPR processes are shorter than a POST process, and they are partially overlapped in time. This behavior remains as network size increases.

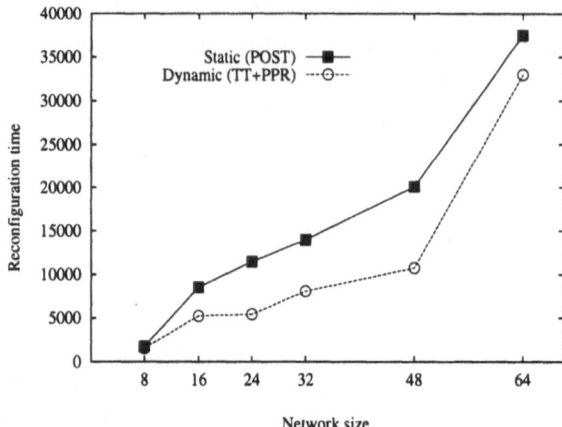

Fig. 7. Reconfiguration time versus network size for a switch deactivation on irregular networks with random traffic

5   Conclusions and Future Work

In [1] we compared the performance of our dynamic reconfiguration process (PPR) with the performance of the traditional static reconfiguration techniques, using up*/down* routing. In that work, we showed that this new reconfiguration technique outperforms traditional methods, because it does not require stopping user traffic during the reconfiguration.

In this work, we have shown that we can easily extend this technique to networks using adaptive routing, obtaining similar results. Our approach consists of having two separated and overlapped processes to update both minimal and up*/down* routing tables. One of them (Topology Task) obtains the new complete network topology and then builds minimal adaptive routing tables. The other process (Partial Progressive Reconfiguration) dynamically updates up*/down* routing tables. Therefore, we believe that PPR can be simplified if it starts from the complete topology (obtained by Topology Task). By combining TT and PPR, we hope to reduce reconfiguration time, the number of reconfiguration messages and discarded messages, while maintaining the benefits provided by adaptive routing.

Acknowledgements

The authors thank *Tom Rodeheffer* at Digital Equipment Corporation for his explanations and discussions of the Autonet reconfiguration algorithm. We also thank *Timothy M. Pinkston* at the University of Southern California for his comments and suggestions on drafts of this paper.

References

1. R. Casado, A. Bermúdez, F.J. Quiles, J.L. Sánchez, J. Duato: Performance evaluation of dynamic reconfiguration in high-speed local area networks. in Proceedings of the sixth Symposium on High Performance Computer Architecture (HPCA-6), January 2000.
2. R. Casado, F.J. Quiles, J.L. Sánchez, J. Duato: Deadlock-free routing in irregular networks with dynamic reconfiguration. In Lecture Notes in Computer Science, vol. 1602, pp. 165–180. Springer, January 1999, Proceedings of the CANPC'99.
3. F. Silla, M.P. Malumbres, A. Robles, P. López, J. Duato: Efficient adaptive routing in networks of workstations with irregular topology. in Proceedings of the WorkShop on Communication and Architectural Support for Network-Parallel Computing'97 Workshop (CANPC'97), February 1997.
4. F. Silla, J. Duato: Improving the efficiency of adaptive routing in networks with irregular topology. in Proceedings of the 1997 Int. Conference on High Performance Computing (HiPC'97), December 1997.
5. M.D. Schroeder, A.D. Birrell, M. Burrows, H. Murray, R.M.Needham, T.L. Rodeheffer, E.H.Satterthwate, and C.P.Thacker: Autonet: a high-speed, self-configuring local area network using point-to-point links. Tech. Rep. 59, Systems Research Center of Digital Equipment Corporation, 1990.
6. Myricom GM documentation. http://www.myri.com:80/GM/doc.
7. ATM Forum. ATM Forum traffic management specification. Version 4.0, May 1995.
8. G. Karlsson: Asynchronous transfer of video. IEEE communication Magazine, vol. 24, no. 8, pp. 118–126, August 1996.
9. E.W. Knightly, H. Zhang: D-BIND: An accurate traffic model for providing QoS guarantees to VBR traffic. IEEE Trans. on Networking, vol. 5, no. 2, April 1995.
10. J. Duato, S. Yalamanchili, L. Ni: Interconnection networks. An engineering approach. IEEE Computer Society, 1997.
11. W.J. Dally, C.L. Seitz: Deadlock-free message routing in multiprocessor interconnection networks. IEEE Transactions on Computers, vol. C-36, no. 5, May 1987.
12. J. Duato, A. Robles, F. Silla, R. Beivide: A comparison of router architectures for virtual cut-through and wormhole switching in an NOW environment. in Proceedings of the 13th International Parallel Processing Symposium and 10th Symposium on Parallel and Distributed Processing (IPPS/SPDP'99), April 1999.
13. T.L. Rodeheffer, M.D. Schroeder: Automatic reconfiguration in Autonet. Tech. Rep. 77, Systems Research Center of Digital Equipment Corporation, September 1991.

MPI Derived Data Types Support in VIRTUS

Rosario Cristaldi and Giulio Iannello

Dipartimento di Informatica e Sistemistica
Università di Napoli Federico II
v. Claudio, 21 – 80125 Napoli
rcristal@grid.unina.it, iannello@unina.it

Abstract. The VIRTUal System (VIRTUS) project is focused on providing advanced features for high performance communication and I/O
in cluster environments. In this paper we report our experience in porting MPICH 1.1.x atop the Fast Messages library and how we used the
features of FM to provide efficient communication for non-contiguous
data structures. The porting concerned two different internal interfaces
of MPICH 1.1.x called *channel* and *ADI-2*, respectively. The ADI-2 interface offers a rich set of primitives that allow the implementation of
communication support to MPI derived data types. We present extensive
experimental data gathered on Solaris, Linux and WinNT platforms that
show how the ADI-2 interface achieves the same performance levels of
FM for contiguous and non-contiguous data. These results confirm the
effectiveness of FM's interface and implementation in delivering the raw
hardware performance of the communication subsystem to the applications.

1 Introduction

The availability of new technologies for Gigabit LANs offers comparable latency
and bandwidth to the proprietary interconnect traditionally found in massively
parallel processors. This has made increasingly attractive building large parallel
systems from commodity off-the-shelf components that can be used as a single,
unified computing resource (clusters).

The commodity nature of clusters' components, however, makes challenging
to achieve the single system image mentioned above. This motivated an in-
tense research activity in the area of system software to improve the integration
between the basic components of clusters. A first step in this regard was the
development of low-level communication libraries capable to deliver to the applications the performance of modern Gigabit LANs: Active Messages (AM) [5],
Fast Messages (FM) [12], U-Net [6], VMMC-2 [4], PM [14]. A second step was to
integrate low-level libraries into higher level, standard communication interfaces
to provide programming environments on clusters similar to those available on
commercial MPP machines. For instance, in the HPVM project the full bandwidth of the low-level library FM was made available to a range of high level
interfaces [3]. In particular, HPVM includes MPI-FM [11], an high performance
implementation of the Message Passing Interface 1.0 (MPI) standard [13], based
on the MPICH library [8].

B. Falsafi and M. Lauria (Eds.): CANPC 2000, LNCS 1797, pp. 84–99, 2000.
© Springer-Verlag Berlin Heidelberg 2000

In the VIRTUal System (VIRTUS) project, following an approach similar to HPVM and relying on the same low-level library FM, we focused on advanced features for high performance communication, such as support for non-contiguous data structures and collective communications, and on tight integration between high performance communication and parallel I/O.

The core of VIRTUS is the MPI 1.1 standard and we used the MPICH 1.1.x implementation of this interface to develop our prototype. This version of MPICH includes many features that were not present in the one used in HPVM, including a richer internal layered structure and the parallel I/O features recently defined in the MPI-2 standard.

In this paper we report our experience in porting MPICH 1.1.x atop the Fast Messages library and how we used the features of FM to provide efficient communication for non-contiguous data structures in our VIRTUS prototype. In particular, we discuss the porting atop FM of two different internal interfaces of MPICH 1.1.x called *Channel* and *ADI-2*, respectively. The ADI-2 interface substitutes the former ADI, used to develop MPI-FM, and offers a richer set of primitives. Our prototype is highly portable and we present extensive experimental data gathered on Solaris, Linux and WinNT platforms that show how the new ADI-2 interface achieves the same performance of the former ADI for both contiguous and noncontiguous data. The results also confirm the effectiveness of FM's interface and implementation in delivering the raw hardware performance of the communication subsystem to the applications.

The paper is organized as follows. In section 2 we briefly discuss the Myrinet network used in our experiments, the Fast Messages and the MPICH libraries. In section 3 we discuss the porting on FM of the ADI-2 and channel interfaces and present its basic performance on three platforms: Solaris-SPARC, Linux-Pentium and WinNT-Pentium. In section 4 we discuss the integration of derived datatype support into VIRTUS and present the corresponding performance data. In section 5 we report about related work, and in section 6 we conclude the paper.

2 Background

2.1 Myrinet and Fast Messages

Myrinet [1] is a high speed LAN composed of network adapters connected to crossbar switches by point-to-point links. The network adapter includes fast SRAM and a custom VLSI chip (the *LANai*), which contains link interfaces, a processor and three DMA engines (one each for the incoming channel, outgoing channel, and the I/O bus). The physical peak bandwidth of the links is of nearly 160 MB/s in each direction and the latency of the switches is of about half a microsecond.

Data transfers between the host and the LANai can be performed through DMA, using pinned-down buffers in the kernel address space. This implies that general purpose communication libraries must introduce a memory copy between these buffers and user-provided buffers. Alternatively, host-LANai interaction can be performed by mapping the interface memory into the user address space

Table 1. FM layer calls.

Function	Operation
FM_begin_message(dest,len,handler)	Start of a message to be sent, returns a *stream*
FM_send_piece(stream,buffer,len)	Send a piece of the message
FM_end_message(stream)	End of a message to be sent
FM_receive(buffer,stream,len)	Get a piece of data from the message
FM_extract()	Process received messages

and by using programmed I/O to read/write the interface memory. While this method implies the processor is busy during the whole transfer, on modern I/O buses (PCI) it may achieve the same bandwidth and lower latency than DMA. As an additional advantage it does not require data to be stored in a pinned-down buffer, leading to true 0-copy protocols.

Fast Messages (FM) [12] is a low-level, high performance communication library characterized by an accurate choice of the services to be provided at the library interface. By providing a few key services – buffer management, reliable and in-order delivery – the FM programming interface allows for a leaner, more efficient implementation of the higher level communication layers.

According to the Fast Messages programming model, the parallel system consists of n nodes. Messages can be sent to any process and they have an associated *handler* function, which is invoked on message reception as in the Active Messages model [5]. Message reception is performed through the **FM_extract** primitive which implements a flexible polling mechanism. Messages are sent and received as *streams* of bytes and primitives are provided for the piecewise manipulation of data, both on the send and on the receive side (see table 1). Hence, messages can be gathered and scattered on-the-fly so that their size and content can be decided dynamically during message transmission.

Internally the library segments messages into packets of fixed size. The sender host uses programmed I/O to inject the packets into the network. At the receiver side, incoming packets are DMAed to a properly allocated (pinned-down) region into the host kernel memory. Data have to be copied at least once to be made accessible to the application. Note that segmentation and reassembly of messages allows the overlapping of the send, network, and receiver protocol processing during the transfer of a message. These operations are completely transparent and independent of the piecewise manipulation of the data stream possibly performed by the user. In particular, handlers execute asynchronously with respect to the application program and can interleave their execution according to the arrival order of incoming packets.

2.2   The Internal Structure of MPICH 1.1.x

The software architecture of MPICH has been designed to support the conflicting goals of portability and high performance. This was achieved by maximizing the amount of code that can be shared without compromising performance. As a result, a large amount of the code is system independent. For instance, implementation of most of the MPI opaque objects, including datatypes, groups, attributes, and even communicators, is platform-independent. Many of the complex communication operations can then be expressed portably in terms of lower-level ones. After a working implementation of the library is available, the porting may be gradually tuned for a specific platform by replacing parts of the shared code with platform-specific code.

The central mechanism for achieving the goals of portability and performance is a specification called the *Abstract Device Interface* (ADI) [8]. All MPI functions are implemented in terms of the macros and functions that make up this interface. All such code is portable. Hence, MPICH may contain many implementations of the ADI, which provide portability, ease of implementation, and an incremental approach to trading portability for performance.

One implementation of the ADI is in terms of a lower level (yet still portable) interface called the *Channel interface* [9]. The Channel interface can be extremely small (five functions at minimum) and provides the quickest way to port MPICH to a new environment. Such a port can then be expanded gradually to include specialized implementation of more of the ADI functionality.

MPICH 1.1.x is implemented in terms of a *second generation* ADI (ADI-2) [10], designed after the experience gathered from a former ADI used to implement previous versions of MPICH. The goals of the ADI-2 design were: lower latency in special cases, support for non-contiguous messages, simpler management of heterogeneity, and better error handling.

The main difference with respect to the previous design is a specialization of the point-to-point communication routines, including operations for general datatypes, to reduce overhead in special cases and increase bandwidth in non-contiguous data transfers. The interface and implementation of ADI-2 routines have been changed to facilitate the development of multi-device (i.e. heterogeneous) implementations and to allow a more efficient error handling. Internally, the ADI-2 routines carry out most of their work by calling other routines designed to hide heterogeneity. Calls to these routines are performed through function pointers stored in a *device* descriptor. This enables the library to use different descriptors to manage multiple heterogeneous communication subsystems. Efficient error handling has been achieved by placing error checks nearest to the first use of data so to limit the number of redundant memory operations.

3   Porting MPICH 1.1.x on Fast Messages

3.1   The Channel Layer

We carried out the porting of MPICH 1.1.x into two steps. We first implemented a minimal Channel interface leading quickly to a working version of VIRTUS that will be referred to in the following as VIRTUS 1.0. The minimal Channel interface consists of only five required functions. Three routines (**MPID_SendControl**, **MPID_RecvAnyControl**, and **MPID_ControlMsgAvail**) send and receive envelope (or control) information; two routines (**MPID_SendChannel** and **MPID_RecvFromChannel**) send and receive data.

The Channel interface can be used to implement different data exchange mechanisms. At the moment, the MPICH implementation uses the *eager* and the *rendezvous* protocols. In the eager protocol, data is sent to the destination immediately. If the destination is not expecting the data (e.g., no receive buffer has yet been posted for it by the application), the receiver must allocate some space to store the data locally (*unexpected* messages). This mechanism often offers the highest performance, but it can cause problems when large amounts of data are sent before their matching receives are posted. In the rendezvous protocol, the control information describing the message is always sent, while data is sent to the destination only when requested (i.e. when a receive buffer that matches the message is posted). When this happens the destination sends the source a request for the data. This mechanism is the most robust but, depending on the underlying system software, may be less efficient than the eager protocol.

At compilation time it is possible to set the message length at which the rendezvous protocol replaces the eager protocol. The rendezvous protocol is always used to implement the synchronous mode of communication defined in the MPI standard. Since typical modern host configurations can tolerate the eager protocol even for quite long messages, we enabled the rendezvous protocol only for very large messages. Since in this case there are no notable differences in performance, all measures reported in this paper refer to tests using the eager protocol.

The semantics of the Channel interface requires that the implementation performs the necessary buffer management and flow control. Unfortunately, even though FM includes flow control, its internal buffer management is not sufficient to satisfy the requirements of the Channel receive functions. In particular, since there is no way to post in advance the final receive buffer, data extracted by handlers must be copied into a temporary buffer managed internally by the Channel layer. We therefore implemented a buffering system, where handlers can copy control and data information extracted from the network. Since one copy on the receive side is always performed when data are extracted from the DMA region (see section 2.1), this solution implies that two copies are performed on message reception if messages are expected. An additional copy into a temporary buffer managed by the layers above the Channel interface is required for unexpected messages.

Conversely, on the send side, a transmission with no copies is easily implemented by mapping the **MPID_SendControl** and **MPID_SendChannel** primitives to distinct **FM_send_piece** calls. For very short messages (less than 512 bytes in our tests), however, the data part of the message is copied in a space contiguous to the control part, in order to reduce latency by avoiding the second **FM_send_piece** call.

The effort to port the Channel interface on top of FM was very limited. Basically no changes were required to the ADI-2 implementation. In table 2 the number of code lines modified or added are reported for all these files.

Table 2. Coding effort needed to implement VIRTUS 1.0.

File	# code lines modified/added
packets.h	39
mpiddev.h	69
mpid_time.h	40
chdef.h	70
chconfig.h	10
fmqueue.h	43
fmqueue.c	127
fmpriv.c	484

3.2   The Second Generation ADI Layer

The porting of the ADI-2 interface atop FM was twofold motivated. On the one hand we wanted to avoid the additional copy on the receive side that we had to introduce in the implementation of the Channel interface. On the other hand, we wanted to exploit the management of non-contiguous data provided at ADI-2 level, to implement efficient communication for MPI derived data types. We briefly discuss here the former issue, while the latter one will be treated in the next section.

Starting from VIRTUS 1.0, we rewrote part of the send and receive routines. This work led to a new version of VIRTUS that will be referred in the following as VIRTUS 2.0. On the send side, VIRTUS 2.0 retains the Channel implementation of the ADI-2 since our porting already provided a 0-copy protocol. Conversely, some work was needed on the receive side. We eliminated the queuing system introduced into the Channel layer and redesigned the FM handler so that it could directly access the data structures used by the ADI-2 receive routines to enqueue buffers for expected and unexpected messages.

A potential problem of this solution was the presence of race conditions between the receive routines called by the application via the MPI interface, and the handler's instances, which are asynchronously invoked when the FM packets are extracted from the network. The problem was solved by using special flags to synchronize concurrent accesses to the message descriptors. The result was a receive protocol which requires, for expected messages, just the copy from the DMA region to the receive buffer provided by the application. For unexpected messages, the use of a temporary buffer cannot be avoided, which leads to a 2-copy protocol.

The effort to port the ADI-2 interface on top of FM was again very limited. The original ADI-2 implementation included: 33 files (**adi2xxx.c** and **chxxx.c**) implementing ADI-2 routines, 18 header files, and a few more files implementing auxiliary routines. In table 3 the number of code lines modified or added are reported for all files involved in the porting. For files already included in table 2, the total line count (i.e. including VIRTUS 1.0 code) is reported.

Table 3. Coding effort needed to implement VIRTUS 2.0.

File	# code lines modified/added
packets.h	39
mpiddev.h	72
mpid_time.h	40
chdef.h	87
chconfig.h	10
chinit.c	40
chshort.c	23
chbeager.c	38
chbrndv.c	45
chchkdev.c	20
fminit.c	160
fmpriv.c	614

Table 4. Setup configurations.

Platform	clock (Mhz)	2L cache (Kbytes)	I/O bus (Mhz)	Myrinet adapter	FM release	FM packet size (bytes)
SPARC/Solaris	167	512	SBus (25)	M2F-SBus 32C	2.0	1024
Pentium II/Linux	450	512	PCI (33)	M2F-PCI 32C	2.0	1024
Pentium II/WinNT	450	512	PCI (33)	M2F-PCI 32C	2.1	1536

3.3   Microbenchmarks and Experimental Setup

In order to assess the VIRTUS performance, we used two microbenchmarks to measure the one-way latency and the sustained bandwidth. Repeating those measures on different platforms and comparing them with the performance of FM and MPI-FM, we can evaluate the overhead introduced in the each version of VIRTUS we developed, including the one supporting derived data types (section 4).

The one-way latency is measured using a simple ping-pong program. The time needed to complete N round trips between two machines is taken and divided by $2N$. The bandwidth is measured sending a continuous sequence of N messages and stopping the timer when the last message is acknowledged. The measured time is then divided by the number of bytes sent (figure 1-a). In this way we are sure that all sent data have been received and no bottlenecks in the communication subsystem can be hidden by intermediate buffering. Even though this test can underestimate the actual bandwidth, the error introduced is small for large N.

For our experiments, we used three different platforms: a Myrinet cluster of SUN Ultra 1 running Solaris 2.6, and a Myrinet cluster of dual-Pentium running Linux and Windows NT 4 (WinNT). The hardware and software characteristics of the platforms are reported in table 4.

The main differences among the platforms affecting the results presented in the next sections, concern the I/O bus and the implementation of the FM library.

The SBus of the SPARC/Solaris platform has a DMA and Programmed I/O peak bandwidths of approximately 80 and 40 Mbytes/s, respectively. The only version of FM available on this platform is the release 2.0 of the library, which does not support multiple processes on the same host.

The PCI bus of the Pentium-based cluster has a measured peak bandwidth larger than 100 Mbytes/s for both DMA and Programmed I/O. In the latter case, however, this limit can be attained only if the adapter's memory is mapped to virtual addresses for which the Write Combine (WC) facility of the Pentium processor is enabled. The FM distribution for WinNT we used includes a special Myrinet driver which enables this feature, which implies that the full potential of the PCI can be exploited. This version has also an FM packet size larger than the other ones. In the Linux case, since the distribution of FM that includes write combine support does not run on our Linux installation, we used a version of FM we derived from the version running under Solaris. This version does not contain WC support, and this limits the peak bandwidth of the I/O bus at about 45 Mbytes/s. Comparing the measures carried out on the Linux and WinNT platforms can therefore give insight on the role of the I/O bus speed on overall performance.

Another important characteristics of all FM implementations we used is that they do not use a thread package to implement the handler semantics (as it is the case for more recent distributions for WinNT), but execution interleaving is made possible by a special transformation of the handler's code. While highly portable, this solution nevertheless introduces limitations on the handler code that will be discussed in more detail in section 4.1.

3.4   Basic VIRTUS Performance

Since VIRTUS has been developed on the SPARC/Solaris platform we used the latency and bandwidth measurements gathered on this platform to contrast the performance of the two versions of VIRTUS and of MPI-FM, which is based on a former ADI interface (release 1.0.8 of MPICH). We then present data gathered on all platforms to evaluate the overhead introduced in VIRTUS 2.0 (VIRTUS 1.0 has not been ported on the Pentium platforms) with respect to the underlying FM library.

From figure 1-b, we observe that the additional layer introduced in MPICH 1.1.x affects VIRTUS 1.0 latency. The penalty, however, is relevant only for relatively short messages and it can be almost entirely attributed to the allocation of the temporary buffer managed by the Channel implementation on the receive side. Things improve considerably when we consider VIRTUS 2.0. In this case the penalty is reduced to a few microseconds only for very short messages.

Coherently with this observations, the bandwidth of VIRTUS 1.0 is slightly worse than the one of MPI-FM up to 4K messages (figure 1-c). For middle sized messages, VIRTUS 1.0 and MPI-FM exhibit the same performance. For large messages, the additional copy on the receive side limits the bandwidth of VIRTUS 1.0. The penalty increases with the message size since, in the bandwidth test, the two copies are partially overlapped with the DMA of the next message.

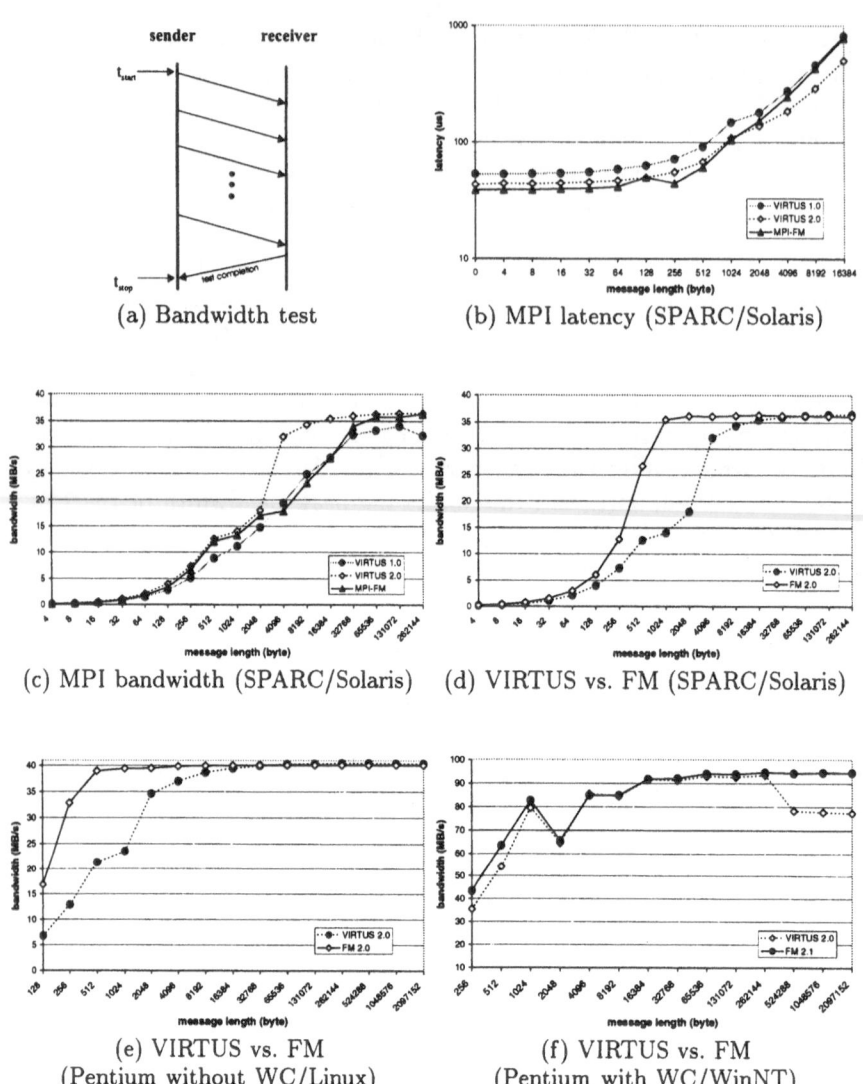

Fig. 1. Basic VIRTUS performance.

Cache effects cause an increase in the memory access time which explain the typical shape of the VIRTUS 1.0 curve.

In VIRTUS 2.0, the bandwidth of middle sized messages is notably better than in MPI-FM (figure 1-c). Data not reported here show that this difference disappears on other platforms were MPI-FM exhibit the same bandwidth as VIRTUS 2.0. We have not a clear explanation for this effect which is in some way related to the interplay between the different ADI implementations and I/O bus speeds in the three platforms.

Table 5. 0-byte latency (all platforms).

Platform	FM	VIRTUS
SPARC/Solaris	35.4	42.8
Pentium II/Linux	14.0	17.0
Pentium II/WinNT	8.9	16.9

Figures 1-d, 1-e, and 1-f compare the bandwidth of VIRTUS 2.0 and FM on the three platforms. Peak performance of VIRTUS and FM are the same on all platforms.

On the SPARC/Solaris and Pentium II/Linux platforms, the bandwidth of VIRTUS for middle sized messages (up to 32 Kbytes) is notably lower than the one of FM. This is mainly due to the presence of a 16 byte header that requires the transmission of an additional (almost empty) packet in the VIRTUS case when payload length is a multiple of the FM packet size. Note that the additional packet, besides wasting bandwidth, also increases the overhead due to the flow control protocol. As expected the effect is limited to small multiples of the packet size. The slope change observed in the VIRTUS curve at 512 bytes is due to the protocol change at the sender mentioned above.

On the WinNT platform, cache effects limit the VIRTUS performance for very large messages. We have not a certain explanation for this behavior, but the same bandwidth drop can be observed also in the MPI-FM implementation on WinNT (not shown here). The drop probably depends on cache effects depending on the greater locality of the handler's code and data structures in the FM case (see also the comment on latency). Also the bandwidth loss for 2 Kbytes messages is typical of FM on the WinNT platform; it is due to a steep bandwidth decrease at the first packet boundary. Note that the bandwidth decrease due to the 16 byte header is not apparent in these curves because on the one hand it is partially hidden by the previous effect, and on the other hand the points of the plot do not coincide with multiples of the FM packet length.

As to latency (table 5), we first note that the relatively high latencies measured on the Solaris and Linux platforms are due to the FM packet length which is large with respect to the I/O bus speed. We then observe that on all platforms the difference between VIRTUS and FM is limited. It can be explained with the higher level of the VIRTUS library, which introduces more protocol overhead, and with the presence of a message header in VIRTUS. The cause of the larger difference observed in the WinNT case can be explained again by the greater locality of the handler's code and data structures in the FM case.

4   Adding Derived Data Types Support

4.1   Implementation Details

In MPICH a derived data type (ddt) consists of a descriptor containing all the information needed to manage the type. If the ddt is not a primitive type, the descriptor is a linked structure containing pointers to the component types' descriptors.

In the ADI-2 layer, there are specialized operations for sending and receiving ddts. Their default implementation uses an additional temporary buffer where the ddt is linearized by traversing its descriptor through a recursive algorithm. This leads to a 1-copy protocol on the send side, and a 2 or 3-copy protocol on the receive side, depending if messages are expected or unexpected, respectively.

To avoid these additional copies, we modified the ADI-2 implementation of the specialized operations leading to version 3.0 of VIRTUS.

On the send side, we added a modified version of the recursive traversing algorithm which calls the **FM_send_piece** primitive, in place of a copy routine, each time it finds the descriptor of a contiguous piece of data to be sent. In this way, data are directly copied from the noncontiguous send buffer provided by the application to the adapter's send queue through the I/O bus.

To achieve a similar behavior on the receive side, a modified version of the traversing algorithm has to be embedded into the FM handler. When the control part of a message containing a ddt is extracted from the network and the receive buffer has been already posted (i.e. the message is expected), the handler traverses the ddt descriptor and it calls the **FM_receive** primitive each time it finds the descriptor of a contiguous piece of data to be received. In this way, data are directly extracted and copied to the noncontiguous receive buffer provided by the application.

This solution, however, presents a technical problem due to the versions of FM we used. The technique used in both versions to implement the handler semantics forbids calling any subprogram which calls in turn the **FM_receive** primitive. Since this would be the case if a recursive version of the traversing algorithm were used, the only way to implement the solution outlined above is to use an iterative version of the algorithm, whose code can be embedded in the handler code without any subprogram calls.

We therefore rewrote the traversing algorithm in iterative form, using a dynamically allocated linked list of activation records to implement the recursion stack. The corresponding code, is executed by the handler on receiving expected messages containing a ddt.

In case the message containing a ddt is unexpected, a temporary contiguous buffer must be allocated and data can be extracted from the network with a single call to the **FM_receive** primitive. When the noncontiguous buffer is eventually posted by the application, data are copied using the original recursive version of the traversing algorithm.

Once more, the effort to add non-contiguous data support was very limited. The new code is contained almost entirely in the **fmpriv.c** file (487 additional code lines basically implementing the traversal algorithms for sending and receiving general datatypes) and in a new file called **fmddt.c** (280 code lines). We also slightly modified four ADI-2 files (**adi2init.c**, **adi2hsend.c**, **adi2hrecv.c**, **chinit.c**) to retain the possibility of using multiple devices on heterogeneous systems.

4.2 Performance Analysis

VIRTUS 3.0 was initially developed, as previous versions, on the SPARC/Solaris platform and then ported on the Pentium II/Linux and Pentium II/WinNT platforms. Since the behavior of the library on the SPARC/Solaris and on the Pentium II/Linux is very similar and the absolute performance on the latter platform is slightly better, for the sake of brevity, we limit discussion here to the results gathered on the two Pentium-based platforms, which differ mainly for the I/O bus speed on the send side (see section 3.3).

In all cases we discuss only the results of the bandwidth test, which seems by far the most interesting. The tests were carried out by using a 2D strided array as a ddt. The array stride was twice the inner blocksize which was varied from 128 bytes to several Kbytes. In each graph we report for comparison the bandwidth of the contiguous case and of the ddt case with inner blocksize of 128, 1024 and 8192 bytes, respectively. Moreover, in order to analyze the behavior of either communication side, we instrumented the library so that ddt support can be disabled selectively.

The bandwidth of VIRTUS on the Linux platform when ddt support is disabled on both communication sides is reported in figure 2-a. In these conditions, the original MPICH protocol is used. The graphs show that additional copies on both communication sides remarkably affect the peak bandwidth, even though, on this platform, the low speed of the I/O bus on the send side. For messages larger than 120 Kbytes, bandwidth drops due to cache effects on the 2-copy protocol, which causes the receiver host to become the bottleneck. Figure 2-a also show that the overhead introduced by traversing of the ddt descriptor affects bandwidth for small inner blocksizes.

The situation changes when ddt support is enabled (2-b). Peak bandwidth in the ddt case is virtually the same as in the continuous case. Tests with ddt support enabled on just one side confirm that both sides are potential bottlenecks. Again, a small inner blocksize introduces some overhead which slightly reduces the peak bandwidth.

Comparing the shapes of the ddt curves in figures 2-a and 2-b, it is worth noting the absence of a bandwidth drop for long messages. Since the handler extracts packets from the pinned-down area in parallel with the network transfers, when ddt support is enabled, the copy of received data to the final noncontiguous buffer is completely hidden by the relatively low speed at which data are injected into the network on the send side.

The latter observation induced us to port VIRTUS 3.0 on the WinNT platform where the bottleneck on the send side is removed. The results of this experiment are reported in figures 2-c and 2-d.

The introduction of ddt support has essentially the same final effect as in the Linux case, leading to the same bandwidth for the ddt and the contiguous case.

This time, however, the relative weights of the several potential bottlenecks are different. First, the performance penalty of the original MPICH protocol is much higher (2-c). Second, the main bottleneck is always the protocol on the receive side, which is responsible also of the poor performance of the ddt support

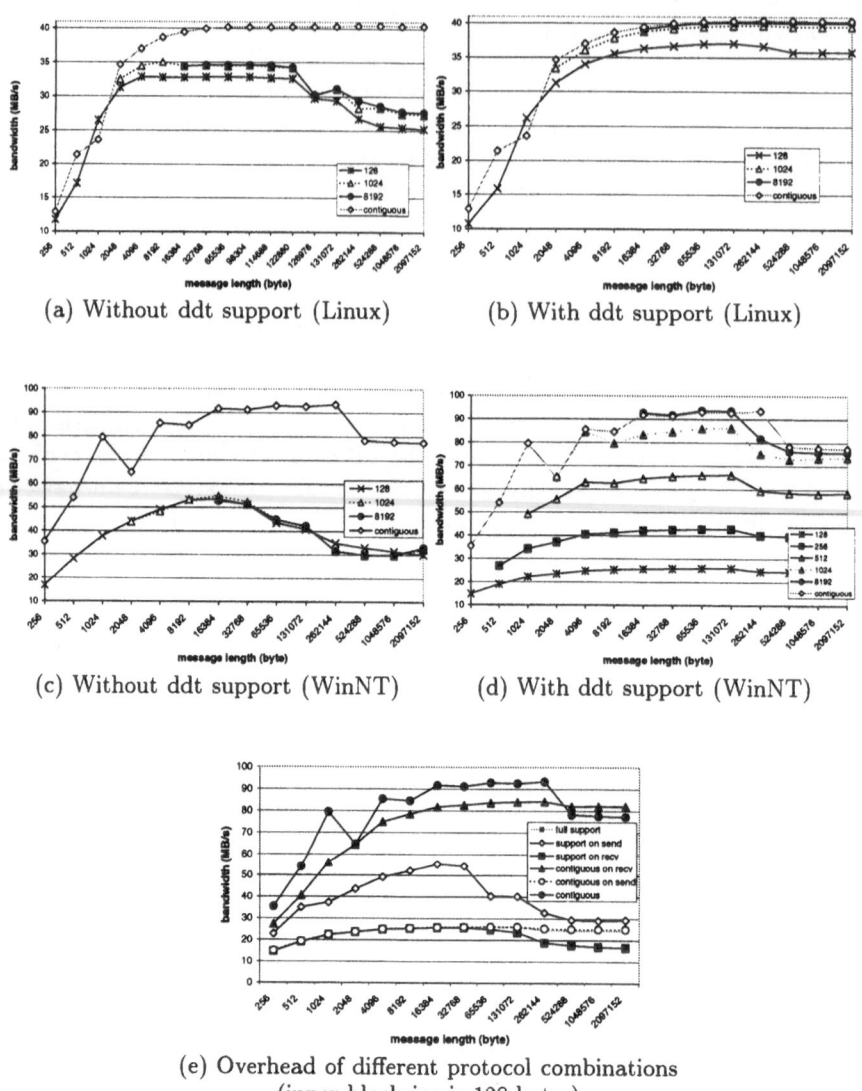

(a) Without ddt support (Linux)

(b) With ddt support (Linux)

(c) Without ddt support (WinNT)

(d) With ddt support (WinNT)

(e) Overhead of different protocol combinations
(inner blocksize is 128 bytes)

Fig. 2. Derived data types communication performance (bandwidth).

for inner blocksizes smaller than 1 Kbytes (2-d). This conclusion is confirmed by
the results reported in figure 2-e, where six different protocol combinations are
contrasted (fixing the inner blocksize to 128 bytes).

The first curve corresponds to enabling ddt support on both sides (*full support*) and it is the same reported in figure 2-d. The second and third curves
correspond to enabling ddt support only on either the send (*support on send*) or
the receive side (*support on receive*), respectively. They expose the overhead of
the additional copies on the other side. The fourth and fifth curves correspond

to using a non contiguous buffer with ddt support only on either the send (*contiguous on recv*) or the receive (*contiguous on send*) side, respectively, whereas a contiguous buffer (i.e. a primitive data type) is used on the other side. They expose the overhead of the protocol used to support efficient ddt communication. The last curve (*contiguous*) corresponds to use contiguous data on both sides and it is reported as a reference.

When a contiguous buffer is used on the receive side the overhead of the recursive traversing algorithm executed on the send side is minimal (curve labeled *contiguous on recv*). This result seems to indicate that the main cause of the poor performance attainable when the blocksize is small is the overhead introduced by the iterative implementation of the traversing algorithm. Indeed, there are at least two sources of overhead that we could not eliminate for lack of time. The first source is the absence of an optimization for regular non-contiguous data structures (i.e. data structures with fixed stride, such as those used for our tests) which is present in the recursive version of the algorithm, but it is not straightforward to introduce in the iterative version. The second source is dynamic allocation of activation records to emulate the recursion stack which makes expensive the treatment of small blocks. We believe that both sources of overhead can be easily removed. Alternatively, we can employ the recursive version of the algorithm on the receive side also, by using the most recent implementation of FM under WinNT which allows the handler to call subprograms without limitations. The latter solution, however, would not be easily portable to other platforms.

5 Discussion and Related Work

Several efficient implementations of MPI exist on both MPPs [7] and clusters [11], including some that use recent versions of the MPICH library [2]. All these implementations achieve remarkable performance and demonstrate that the design of the MPI standard and of its probably most popular public domain implementation, MPICH, succeeded in attaining both high efficiency and wide portability. Our own porting of MPICH on the FM platform attain at least the same performance levels on a variety of software/hardware platforms.

To our knowledge however, most of these implementations do not deal with the issue of efficient communication of noncontiguous data structures. As a matter of fact, the only reported experience on this issue we are aware concern the proprietary IBM implementation of MPI for the SP platform [7]. Our work demonstrates that the same qualitative behavior (same performance for contiguous and noncontiguous data structures) can be obtained in a less expensive cluster environment. This result is important because general datatypes can be profitably exploited in MPI applications to improve the readability and manageability of the code, and the flexibility of the implementation. The use of non-contiguous data would be clearly discouraged if it introduced a significant bandwidth penalty. Two other examples of the need to send/receive a large amount of non-contiguous data are some collective communication algorithms and global exchanges used in parallel I/O libaries, including MPI-2. Finally, communication of non-contiguous data seem increasingly important in distributed, object-based, platform-independent programming environments, where data are commonly represented by data structures even more general than MPI ddts. Although the work reported in this paper does not directly address the latter issue, our experience and performance data we reported can help in providing efficient communication support to these environments.

We also explored two more issues not explicitly covered and/or supported with extensive quantitative data by previous work. First, we have confirmed in a different context the results of [11], namely that the distinctive features of the Fast Messages library offer a very flexible basis for efficient implementation of higher level interfaces. Second, we have reported experience on using the different alternatives offered by the MPICH internal structure for porting the library to new platforms. Our experimental results show that even a quick porting to the channel interface can attain a performance comparable with more sophisticated implementations.

6 Conclusions

In this paper we have reported our experience in developing the core of VIRTUS, a platform for high performance computing on workstation clusters. We focused on the communication part of the system which uses the MPI standard and provides support for efficient communication of noncontiguous data structures. The system runs on three different platforms exhibiting high portability and competitive performance in a variety of conditions. The extensive experimental data we reported in the paper help in analyzing and understanding potential sources of overhead in the communication software and confirm the effectiveness of the approach followed.

Future work include further development of VIRTUS, especially for what is concerned with parallel I/O on clusters, and its interaction with high performance communication so that full available I/O bandwidth can be made accessible to all computing nodes.

Acknowledgements

This work has been carried out partially under the financial support of the Ministero dell'Università e della Ricerca Scientifica e Tecnologica (MURST) in the framework of the Project "Design Methodologies and Tools of High Performance Systems for Distributed Applications (MOSAICO)", of the Consiglio Nazionale delle Ricerce (CNR) in the framework of the project "ADESSO", and of the University of Napoli Federico II in the framework of the Short-Term Mobility Programme.

The authors wish to acknowledge the contribution of all the people that made possible this work. We especially thank Sonia Iannone and Luciano Fenizia for their contribution in developing the VIRTUS code, and Andrew Chien for making available the FM and MPI-FM sources to a few selected groups outside the University of Illinois.

References

1. N.J. Boden, D. Cohen, R.E. Felderman, A.E. Kalawik, C.L. Seitz, J.N. Seizovic, and W.-K. Su, "Myrinet–a gigabit-per-second local-area network", *IEEE Micro*, 15(1), February 1995.
2. F. O'Carroll, H. Tezuka, A. Hori, and Y. Ishikawa, "The design and implementation of zero copy MPI using commodity hardware with a high performance network", *Procs. of International Conference on Supercomputing*, Melbourne, Australia, July 13-17, 1997, pp. 243–250.
3. A.A. Chien, S. Pakin, M. Lauria, M. Buchanan, K. Hane, L. Giannini, and J. Prusakova, "High Performance Virtual Machines (HPVM): Clusters with Super-computing APIs and Performance", *Procs. of 8th SIAM Conference on Parallel Processing for Scientific Computing (PP97)*, March, 1997.
4. C. Dubnicki, L. Iftode, E. Felten, and K. Li, "Software support for virtual memory-mapped communication", *Procs. of the 1996 International Parallel Processing Symposium*, Aug. 1996.
5. T. von Eicken, D. Culler, S. Goldstein, and K. Schauser, "Active Messages: a mechanism for integrated communication and computation", *Procs. of the International Symposium on Computer Architecture*, May 1992.
6. T. von Eicken, A. Basu, V. Buch, and W. Vogels, "U-Net: a user-level network interface for parallel and distributed computing", *Procs. of the 15th ACM Symposium on Operating System Principles*, Dec. 1995.
7. H. Franke, C.E. Wu, M. Riviere, P. Prattnaik, and M. Snir, "MPI Programming Environment for IBM SP1/SP2", *Procs. of 15th International Conference on Distributed Computing Systems*, Vancouver, Canada, May 30-June 2, 1995.
8. W. Gropp and E. Lusk, N. Doss, and A. Skjellum, "A High-Performance Portable Implementation of the MPI Message Passing Interface Standard", Tech. Rep. Preprint MCS-P567-0296, Argonne National Laboratory, Available from: ftp://ftp.mcs.anl.gov/pub/mpi/workingnote/mpicharticle.ps.
9. W. Gropp and E. Lusk, "MPICH Working Note: The Secon Generation ADI for the MPICH Implementation of MPI", Tech. Rep., Argonne National Laboratory, Available from: ftp://ftp.mcs.anl.gov/pub/mpi/workingnote/nextgen.ps.
10. W. Gropp and E. Lusk, "MPICH Working Note: Creating a new MPICH device using the Channel interface", Technical Report, Argonne National Laboratory, Available from: ftp://ftp.mcs.anl.gov/pub/mpi/workingnote/newadi.ps.
11. M. Lauria, and A.A. Chien, "MPI-FM: High performance MPI on workstation clusters", *Journal of Parallel and Distributed Computing*, vol. 40(1), January 1997, pp. 4–18.
12. M. Lauria, S. Pakin, and A.A. Chien, "Efficient Layering for High Speed Communication: Fast Messages 2.x", *Procs. of the 7th High Performance Distributed Computing Conference (HPDC7)*, Chicago, Illinois, July 28-31, 1998.
13. Message Passing Interface Forum, "Document for standard message-passing interface", Tech. Rep. CS-93-214, Univ. of Tennessee, November 1993.
14. H. Tezuka, A. Hori, Y. Ishikawa, M. Sato, "PM: An Operating System Coordinated High Performance Communication Library", *Procs. HPCN'97*, P. Sloot, B. Hertzberger, (eds.), Lecture Notes in computer Science, n. 1225, April 1997.

Fast Collective Communication Algorithms for Reflective Memory Network Clusters[1]

Vijay Moorthy, Dhabaleswar K. Panda, and P. Sadayappan

Network Based Computing Laboratory
Department of Computer and Information Science
The Ohio State University, Columbus, OH 43210
Phone: (614) 292-5911, Fax: (614) 292-2911
{moorthy,panda,saday}@cis.ohio-state.edu

Abstract. In this paper, we present algorithms for efficiently implementing three collective communication operations on reflective memory network clusters: Broadcast, Barrier Synchronization and All-Reduce. These algorithms have been implemented as an extension to the Bill-Board Protocol, a low-latency communication protocol for reflective memory networks that we previously developed [6,7]. Simulated performance results are presented for these algorithms. The performance of the algorithms is evaluated in detail. A comparative study with Myrinet, a popular point-to-point switched interconnect for clusters is also presented.

1   Introduction

In recent years, clusters of workstations have become a popular platform for high-performance computing [1,2]. Clusters typically use commodity networks for intra-cluster communication. Performance of applications running on these clusters directly depends upon the performance of the interconnecting network. Point-to-Point networks such as Myrinet [3], switched Ethernet, and ATM have become popular interconnects for clusters. Though these networks provide high bandwidth, delivering low latencies and providing good communication and computation overlap is a non-trivial problem. Consequently, a lot of research has been done on finding solutions for these problems [4,5,16,17].

Recently, there has been interest in the research community in applying other types of networks to cluster computing, such as reflective memory networks [8]. Reflective memory networks provide a limited amount of shared memory across a cluster of workstations. Each workstation is equipped with a network interface card

---

[1]This research is supported in part by an NSF Career Award MPI-9502294, NSF Grant CCR-9704512, an Ameritech Faculty Fellowship award, and grants from the Ohio Board of Regents.

B. Falsafi and M. Lauria (Eds.): CANPC 2000, LNCS 1797, pp. 100–114, 2000.

(NIC) which possesses a memory bank. Memory on the NICs is not physically shared but updates to a location on any one of the NICs are transmitted to the other NICs on the network. This causes the memory at each NIC in each workstation to be a reflection of the memory on the other NICs.

Reflective memory networks have some unique features. The most important feature is that communication is abstracted to memory reads and writes. No operating system intervention is required for communication. Once a message is written to the NIC, the host processor can resume computation. In addition, latencies are predictable. This is especially important for some applications, such as real-time applications. Finally, the inherent broadcast nature of reflective memory networks makes them ideal for implementing some frequently used collective operations, which are useful in many parallel and distributed applications.

In this paper, we develop algorithms for efficiently implementing three collective communication operations on reflective memory networks: Broadcast, Barrier Synchronization, and All-Reduce. These algorithms have been implemented as extensions to the BillBoard protocol (BBP) [6,7], a low latency communication protocol for reflective memory networks that we have previously developed. We have developed an analytical model of reflective memory networks, which is used to evaluate these algorithms.

The paper is organized as follows: The next section gives a broad overview of reflective memory networks. Section 3 describes the algorithms. Section 4 describes the analytical modeling of the algorithms for reflective memory networks. Section 5 presents performance evaluation results. Section 6 presents our conclusions.

2   An Overview of Reflective Memory Systems

A Reflective Memory (RM) network provides a limited amount of shared memory across a cluster. There are many reflective memory networks available today. SCRAMNet [11] from Systran, RTNet [12] from VMIC and DEC MemoryChannel [13] are popular reflective memory products. VMMC [14] from Princeton and Merlin and Sesame [15] from Sandia Labs and SUNY, Stony Brook, are research projects involving reflective memory. A detailed survey of existing RM networks is presented in [8].

The most common application of RM networks has been for Real time Systems. They have been used in aircraft simulators, telemetry, and robotics. They have also been applied to distributed applications such as on-line transaction processing (OLTP) and client-server computing, as well as parallel computing applications.

The basic operation of any reflective memory network is as follows. Each node on the network has a memory bank (normally residing on the NIC). The memory bank is mapped to the address space of the processes using the reflective memory. When a process writes to a location in its virtual address space that maps to the reflective memory bank, the RM system propagates that write to every other node in the network. The propagation of the update happens asynchronously, and without intervention of the application process. When a process reads from a location in the shared area of memory, no communication is required to the other nodes, because any updates to that location by other nodes would have been automatically sent when writes occur.

There is no software protocol overhead for communication in RM networks as it is handled by the hardware. Consequently, communication latencies are very low. Since communication is abstracted to memory loads and stores, the host processor is freed from communication processing overhead, and applications can achieve good overlap between computation and communication. However, the performance of any RM network is limited by the amount of memory on each NIC, and the bandwidth of the underlying interconnect. The greater the amount of memory on each NIC, and greater the bandwidth of the network, the better its performance delivered by the system.

The Bill-Board Protocol (BBP) is a low-latency message passing protocol for RM networks that we have previously developed. With a little software overhead, it provides basic message passing functionality over an RM network. The BBP is described in detail in [6]. A brief description is given below.

The BBP is a lock-free protocol providing basic send/receive and multicast services. In the BBP, the shared memory on the RM network is split into two areas: a control area and a message area. Each area is equally divided into N partitions for N nodes on the network. Each node's message partition is used for message buffers. Each node's control partition contains flags, which control the actual transfer of messages. For each source, a node has as many "Message" flags as there are buffers in the message partition of the source. For each destination, a node has as many "Ack" flags as it has buffers. There exists a unique message flag and a unique ack flag for every (source, destination, buffer) triple.

To send a message, a node allocates a buffer in its message partition, writes the message to the buffer and then toggles the message flag for that buffer and destination. Every node polls its set of message flags to check for incoming messages. A change in state in a message flag indicates the arrival of a new message. To receive this message, the destination node reads the message from the source's message partition. It then and toggles the ack flag corresponding to the message buffer in the control partition of the source. This indicates that the buffer is now free for further use by the source. In order to multicast a message, the sender simply sets message flags for multiple receivers. In the BBP, all writes to shared memory by a node appear in the same order at other nodes as they were written. Since the message is always written before the flags are set, there is no danger of a node noticing a change in flag state before the corresponding message has been written to its copy of the shared memory.

In this paper, we present performance of the proposed algorithms over one particular network, i.e. SCRAMNet, as implemented in the BBP. In addition, we develop an analytical model of RM networks, which is representative of current day technology. Performance of the proposed algorithms has been evaluated for the modeled RM network.

3   Collective Communication Algorithms for Reflective Memory Networks

Algorithms for three collective communication operations are described here: Broadcast, Barrier Synchronization, and All-Reduce. These operations were chosen because a broadcast of information occurs in each one of these, and therefore they are good candidates for using the inherent broadcast nature of reflective memory networks.

3.1   Broadcast

In a broadcast, one process sends the same message to more than one node. Many algorithms have been proposed for accomplishing a broadcast. These solutions typically involve a number of point-to-point messages. Such solutions, if used over a broadcast network, involve the same message being broadcast multiple times. An efficient solution for a broadcast network should make use of the broadcast nature of the network.

One such solution is the single copy algorithm in the original BBP implementation [6]. The sender copies the message once, to a buffer in the reflective memory. Then, the sender sets message flags for all the receivers. The receivers poll on their flags. When a flag changes state, indicating a newly arrived message, receivers read the message from the shared memory. The advantage of this approach is that a message can be sent to more than one recipient and the overhead for multiple receivers is independent of the message length. However, as the number of recipients increases, the overhead for setting flags increases linearly.

Solutions with $O(log(N))$ time complexity exist for broadcast on point-to-point networks. The Binomial tree algorithm is an $O(log(N))$ broadcast algorithm [18]. This algorithm requires $log_2(N)$ steps for N participating nodes. In each step, a node that has already received the message forwards it to a node that has not received it yet. Initially, only the sender has the message. The sender sends it to one other node, starting the broadcast. In the next step, two nodes have the message and they send it to two more. In this manner, at each step the number of nodes which have received the message doubles. The binomial tree algorithm has been shown to be optimal for point-to-point networks of homogenous nodes [18]. However, the entire message is transmitted multiple times in this algorithm. Therefore, it is not the best suited for RM networks.

We propose a new broadcast algorithm for RM networks, which combines the advantages of both the single copy algorithm as well as the binomial tree algorithm. In this algorithm, message arrival notifications (change in flag state) are distributed hierarchically. The sender writes the message to a location in shared memory only once. Then it sets message flags for the first r recipients. Each of these r recipients sets flags for r more recipients. In this way, a tree of depth $log_r(N)$ is built for setting message flags, with the sender at the root. In $log_r(N)$ steps, all the recipients are notified of the arrival of the broadcast message.

This algorithm allows better concurrency in the setting of flags than the single copy algorithm. Since the same number of flags is being set, there is no increase in network usage. As in the single copy scheme, for a fixed system size, the time taken to complete the broadcast increases linearly with message size. In addition, the overhead for setting flags increases logarithmically with system size. Therefore, for a fixed message length, the time taken to complete the broadcast increases $O(log(N))$ with the number of nodes. It is to be noted that the time taken not only depends on N, the number of nodes, but also r, the ordinality of the tree used for distributing the notifications. For a specific system, this parameter has to be tuned, in order to determine the value of r that will give the best performance. We study the impact of r on broadcast time in section 5.

3.2   Barrier Synchronization

In Barrier Synchronization, N processes synchronize at a point called the barrier. When a process crosses that point, it is guaranteed that every other process has reached that point. It is a special case of phase synchronization as defined in [10].

The original implementation of BBP [6,7] used a naive algorithm. In this implementation, there is one designated process, called the root. Each process sends a message to the root on arriving at the barrier. The root, on reaching the barrier, waits for messages from every other node, and then broadcasts a message to all nodes notifying them that the barrier has been completed. This algorithm does not make efficient use of the broadcast nature of the network. The time required to complete the barrier grows linearly with the number of participating nodes.

Consider the following scheme, which is similar to the solution in [10]. Each process sets a unique flag on the shared memory and then polls on the entire set of flags to see if all of them are set. For small system sizes, this method is extremely fast. However, as the system size increases, the number of flags to be polled increases linearly.

For better scalability, we use a hierarchical scheme. Given below is a hierarchical algorithm for barrier synchronization on RM networks. The N nodes are split into groups of r each where $r \leq N$. Each group synchronizes itself by the above method. Then, one node is selected from each group, and a barrier is performed on this set of nodes. This process is repeated recursively until there are r or fewer nodes left. When these nodes synchronize, the barrier is complete. When the final round of synchronization completes, one node is selected to set a flag, which marks the completion of the barrier. All other nodes poll on this flag while waiting for the barrier to complete.

This algorithm takes $log_r(N)$ steps to complete. At any step, the maximum number of flags to be polled is r. Again, as in the case of the hierarchical broadcast algorithm, the performance of the algorithm depends on the value of r. The impact or r on the barrier time is studied in section 5.

3.3   All-Reduce

In an All-Reduce operation, each process has an array of elements. The result required is an associative operation on all the arrays. Each process should have the result array at the end of the all-reduce.

Several algorithms have been suggested for the all-reduce operation on point-to-point networks, such as the ring algorithm and the hypercube algorithm proposed in [19].

In the ring algorithm, nodes are arranged in a logical ring. In N successive steps, each node receives an array from the node logically to its left and sends an array to the node logically to its right. In the first step, each node sends its own array to the node on its right. In subsequent steps, it forwards arrays from other nodes that were received in previous steps from the node on the left. At the end of N such steps, each node has all the arrays and can independently compute the result. The ring algorithm is essentially an all-to-all broadcast, followed by computation of the result.

In the hypercube algorithm, there are $log_2(N)$ steps. In the first step, pairs of nodes exchange their respective arrays and compute partial results. The partial results are exchanged in the following step. In each step, a node exchanges its partial results with a different node and at the end of $log_2(N)$ steps, each has the complete result.

The ring and hypercube algorithms move $O(MN^2)$ and $O(MNlog(N))$ data if used over a point-to-point network, where M is the size of one array. An all-reduce can also be accomplished by a reduce operation to one node (using an inverted binomial tree) followed by a binomial tree broadcast of the computed result. In this case, only $O(MN)$ data need be moved. However, this advantage is lost when used over a broadcast network. Our initial implementation of the reduce-broadcast algorithm over RM networks showed poor results.

Presented below is a better solution for RM networks. Each node simultaneously broadcasts its array to all others; waits for the arrays from the others and then independently computes the result. The broadcast itself can be done using the hierarchical broadcast algorithm or the single copy algorithm described in section 3.1. In either case, the number of flags that each node sets is the same. To reduce contention on the network during the setting of message flags, each node sets them in a different order. A node takes its destination set (which is all the nodes except itself) and starts from the node logically next to it in rank order, that is, node i will first send to node $(i+1)$ mod N. This also means that it will receive notifications in reverse rank order starting from $(i-1)$ mod N.

4 Modeling Collective Communication Algorithms for Reflective Memory Networks

The algorithms presented in this paper were implemented and tested on a 4-node SCRAMNet cluster of Pentium PCs.[2] We developed an analytical model of a reflective memory network in which we could choose parameters such as network bandwidth, I/O bus read and write times which are representative of current RM networks and systems. The model has been evaluated for correctness, by comparing timings measured for the algorithms presented in this paper on the testbed with timing values generated using the model. Section 5 presents a comparison of measured and modeled timings. It can be observed that modeled timings track our measurements closely.

Since considerable variation exists in RM networks available today, we have attempted to pick some common features of RM networks for use in the model. We have chosen the register insertion ring topology [9] and serial links used in SCRAMNet and RTNet. We have modeled a non-coherent RM network. The granularity of sharing was chosen to be one word. This modeled network will be referred to as the "RM model network".

A register insertion ring [9] is a more sophisticated form of a slotted ring. In a register insertion ring, NICs have two shift registers: a ring shift register and an input shift register. Traffic from the ring enters the ring shift register. Updates from the host enter the input shift register. The NIC switches between the two shift registers to transmit data onto the ring. If there is data in the ring shift register, it is always transmitted before any data in the input register. Data in the input register is queued in a FIFO, so that the host can make multiple writes even if there is traffic on the network. The host blocks on writes to shared memory if the FIFO is full.

It is important to model performance of the I/O Bus as well as the underlying network because access times to the shared memory depend on the performance of the I/O bus. In order to model the I/O bus, we measured the performance of the PCI bus on a 300 MHz Pentium II PC with the Intel 440 FX PCI chipset. Access times for reads and writes tend to be asymmetric on the PCI bus, so we measured read times as well as write times. We have chosen to model the PCI bus as it is widely used.

The following are the major parameters in the model that can be tuned according to the characteristics of the network being modeled: ring slot time, I/O bus read latency, and I/O bus write latency. The ring slot time is the time that elapses between two successive transmission slots on the ring. It depends on the network bandwidth and link width. The read and write latencies are the times required for a minimum size read or a write.

---

[2] Our experimental testbed was originally configured with 8 nodes. However, four of the NICs are not currently functional, and we were unable to obtain replacements by the time this paper went to print. We will be generating experimental results for an 8-node system as soon as replacements arrive and we will make these results available on the web.

The slot time for SCRAMNet was measured to be 571 ns in our cluster, corresponding to a network bandwidth of 7 MB/s. We use a slot time of 58 ns for the RM model network, assuming serial links, which corresponds to a network bandwidth of 70 MB/s. This bandwidth was chosen because it is representative of current RM networks. VMIC RTNet, for instance, uses a serial link and has a bandwidth of 69.5 MB/s [12]. PCI read and write latencies measured for the Intel 440 FX chipset with the SCRAMNet NIC were used in the model. These were measured to be 950 ns and 330 ns respectively.

The time taken for any communication operation can be split into message-length independent processing overhead time and message length dependent message copying and transmission time. From the implementation of that operation, it is possible to determine how these individual components overlap. A message can be viewed as going through a number of pipelined stages such as copy from sender host memory to sender NIC, transmission from sender NIC to receiver NIC, and transmission from receiver NIC to receiver host memory. The time taken for any pipelined process is determined by the slowest pipeline stage. The time taken for a communication operation through a pipeline is given by the time spent by the sum of the time spent by entire message in the longest pipeline stage and the latencies of the other pipeline stages. For SCRAMNet, the transmission over the network turns out to be the slowest pipeline stage. In the RM model network, the I/O bus is the slowest pipeline stage

For each algorithm presented in this paper, we have determined the time spent in individual stages and derived a mathematical equation to estimate time for each operation. The model is simplistic. No background traffic has been modeled, and all times are for best case scenarios.

Given below are the equations used to estimate times for the RM model network. Equation (4.1) gives the time taken by the hierarchical broadcast algorithm. It measures the time taken from the source node initiating the broadcast to the last node receiving the message.

$$
\begin{aligned}
T_{broadcast} =& \lfloor \log_r (N-1) \rfloor * T_{flag\_read} \\
&+ (r-1)*T_{flag\_write} \\
&+ (\left\lceil \frac{N-1}{r^{\lfloor \log_r(N-1)\rfloor}} \right\rceil - 1)*(T_{flag\_write}) \\
&+ (W + (N_{ring} - 1)*T_s) \\
&+ T_{PCI\_write} \\
&+ T_{PCI\_read}(W) \\
&+ T_{overhead}
\end{aligned}
\tag{4.1}
$$

where T_{flag_read} is the time taken to read a flag from the NIC, T_{flag_write} is the time taken to write a flag to the NIC, T_{PCI_write} is the time taken to write a word to the NIC, $T_{PCI\_read}(W)$ is the time taken to read W words from the NIC, T_s is the slot time, $T_{overhead}$ is the message length independent processing time, and W is the length of the message in words.

Eq. (4.1) breaks down the broadcast time into the summation of a number of smaller components. Each intermediate node in the tree must first receive a flag from its parent before it can set flags for its children. Since an intermediate node can set flags for its children only after its parent has set its own message flag, the time spent in reading the flag cannot be masked. The cost of reading one message flag is incurred at every level of the tree. The first component is the time spent by intermediate nodes in the tree reading message flags. The second and third components together give the cost of setting flags. The second component is the time spent at the lowest level of the tree setting message flags The third component is the time spent at intermediate nodes setting message flags, which cannot be masked by pipelining. The fourth component is the propagation delay for the message itself. The fifth and sixth components are PCI write and read latencies. When the message is being written, the propagation starts in parallel. However, the entire message must be received at the NIC before it can be read. So, the entire time spent in reading the message over the PCI bus cannot be masked. This is why only the time for one PCI write is counted whereas the time for reading the entire message over the PCI bus is counted. The seventh component is the fixed message-length independent software overhead time spent at the source for such tasks as memory allocation for the message buffer.

Eq. (4.2) gives the time taken to complete a barrier using the hierarchical barrier algorithm.

$$T_{barrier} = \lceil \log_r(N) \rceil * \begin{bmatrix} (r-1)*T_{flag\_read} + T_{PCI\_write} \\ +3*(N_{ring}-1)*T_s \end{bmatrix} \qquad (4.2)$$

where T_{flag_read} is the time taken to read a flag from the NIC, T_{PCI_write} is the time taken to write a word to the NIC, T_s is the slot time, and N_{ring} is the total number of nodes on the ring.

The time taken for a barrier is given by the product of time spent at each step and the number of steps. There are $log_r(N)$ steps. At each step, a node writes a flag, then reads $(r-1)$ flags. There is a propagation delay between the write and the reads. The three components in the parentheses correspond to flag read time, flag write time and propagation delay respectively.

Eq. (4.3) gives the time taken to complete an all-reduce using the simultaneous broadcast algorithm.

$$\begin{aligned} T_{all-reduce} = &\, T_{PCI\_write} \\ &+ (W-1)*N*T_s \\ &+ (N-1)*T_{PCI\_write} \\ &+ (N-1)*T_{PCI\_read}(W) \\ &+ T_{overhead} \end{aligned} \qquad (4.3)$$

where T_{flag_write} is the time taken to write a flag, T_{PCI_write} is the time taken to write a word to the NIC, $T_{PCI\_read}(W)$ is the time taken to read W words from the NIC, T_s is the slot time, and $T_{overhead}$ is the message length independent processing time.

Eq. (4.3) breaks down the time taken for an all-reduce into the summation of 5 components. In an all-reduce, all nodes simultaneously write their arrays to the shared memory, then set *N-1* flags, and then read *N-1* arrays. The first two components in eq. (4.3) are the time spent writing the message. The first component is the time spent writing the first word t over PCI which cannot be masked. The second component is the propagation delay. Note that the propagation delay in this case is greater than that in case of a single broadcast. The third component is the time spent in setting flags for all the broadcasts. Each node sets *N-1* flags. The fourth component is the time spent reading the arrays over the I/O bus. The fifth component is the message-length independent software processing overhead time.

5   Performance Evaluation

The three algorithms described in the preceding section have been implemented and incorporated into the BBP. Their performance was evaluated on a 4-node SCRAMNet Cluster of 300 MHz Pentium II workstations. These experimental results were used to validate the analytical model discussed above.

For comparison, we also measured the time taken for equivalent operations on MPIFM on Myrinet on the same cluster. Myrinet is a 1Gb/s point-to-point network which is a popular interconnect used for clustered systems. MPIFM is the most popular communications software that provides collective communication support on Myrinet. FM [4], the communication layer on top of which MPIFM is built, is at the same layer as BBP. FM does not provide any collective communication support. In addition, MPIFM adds only a little overhead to FM. Therefore we have chosen MPIFM for our comparison.

For each operation, the following results are presented. First, for a 4-node system, measured results are presented for SCRAMNet and MPIFM/Myrinet. These are labeled "SCRAMNet (Measured)" and "MPIFM (Measured)" respectively in the figures. Estimated times for SCRAMNet using the model and parameters for SCRAMNet are also presented. These are labeled "SCRAMNet (Modeled)". The purpose of presenting both numbers is to check for validity of the model. Simulated results for the RM model network are also presented. These were calculated using equations (4.1)-(4.3) and parameters for the RM model as described in section 4. These results are labeled "RM (Modeled)". Simulated results for each operation are also presented for bigger system sizes. MPIFM uses well-known algorithms for the three operations under study. These have been implemented on top of point-to-point messages. We measured times taken for point-to-point messages and used them to compute the time taken for collective operations for larger system sizes. These results are labeled "MPIFM (Modeled)" in the figures.

Figures 1, 2 and 3 show the performance of broadcast. Fig. 1 compares measured values of broadcast timings for MPIFM and SCRAMNet, and the RM model for a 4-node system with varying message length and *r=4*. It can be noted that the modeled values for SCRAMNet are very close to actual measured values. Since Myrinet has the highest bandwidth, it has the lowest slope, but it has higher latency. Hence, for short messages SCRAMNet and the RM model network do better. Figs. 2 and 3 show the performance of broadcast for zero byte and 64 bytes for increasing system size. It can be observed that the performance depends on the value of *r*. A value of *r=4* is the best for a 32 node system. However, this may not be the case for larger systems. Figs. 2 and 3 show that in general, as the system size increases so does the ideal value of *r*.

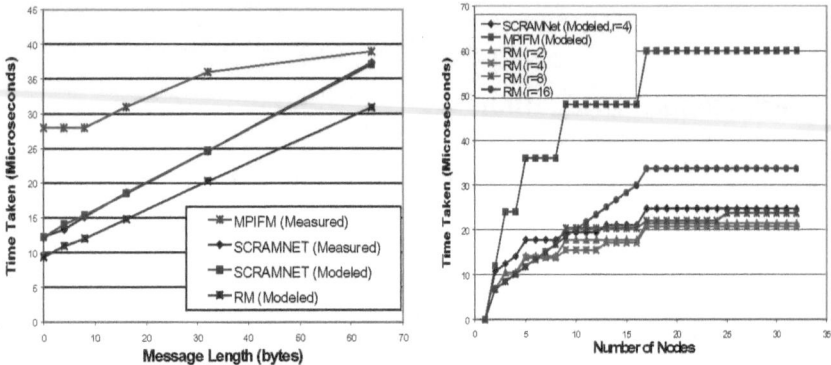

Fig. 1. Broadcast Performance on a 4 node system

Fig. 2. Broadcast Performance (0 byte)

Figures 4 and 5 show the performance of the Barrier algorithm. As can be seen in Fig. 4, the modeled performance closely tracks the actual measured performance on SCRAMNet. The curve marked MPIFM shows the measured performance of the MPIFM Barrier implementation on Myrinet. A 4-node barrier takes 32 microseconds on MPIFM and only 13.9 microseconds on BBP on SCRAMNet. The hierarchical barrier algorithm on the RM model network (for *r=4*) takes only 10.7 microseconds.

Fig. 5 shows the performance of the barrier algorithm for larger systems, up to 32 nodes and compares the performance of our algorithm on a reflective memory network with that of the *O(log(N))* scheme used in MPIFM. Note that the performance depends on the value of *r* used. For systems up to 32 nodes, the algorithm works best with *r=4*. A trend similar to broadcast is observed here. In general, as system size increases so does the ideal value of *r* to be used in this algorithm.

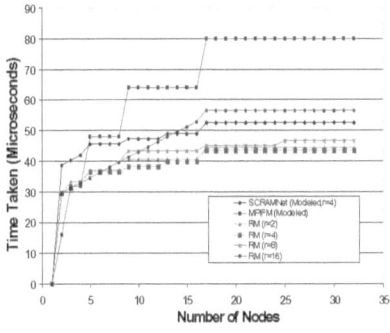

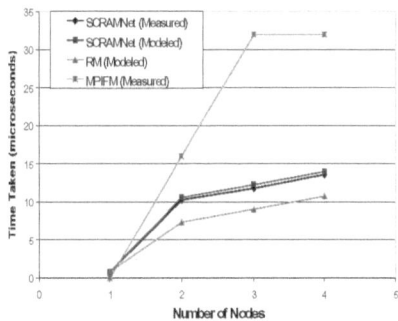

Fig. 3. Broadcast Performance (64 bytes)   **Fig. 4.** Barrier Performance on a 4-node system

Figures 6, 7 and 8 show the performance of the All-Reduce algorithm. Fig. 6 shows the performance on a 4-node system. It can be observed that for SCRAMNet, the modeled values closely follow actual measured times. For short message sizes, SCRAMNet and the RM model network do better than Myrinet, but Myrinet does better for longer messages. Figs. 7 and 8 show the performance of All-Reduce for 4 byte and 64 byte lengths for systems larger than 4 nodes. The same pattern is observed. For the shorter message size, SCRAMNet and the RM model network do better.

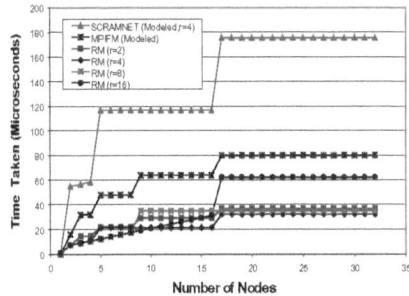

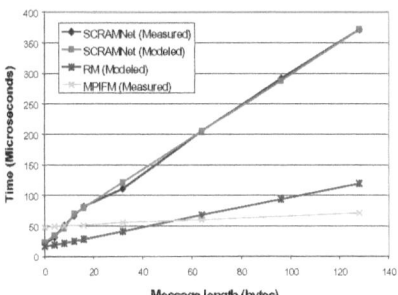

Fig. 5. Barrier Performance on up to 32 nodes   **Fig. 6.** All-Reduce Performance on a 4-node system

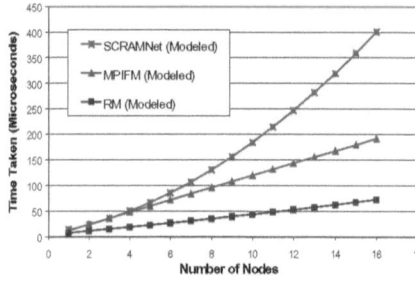
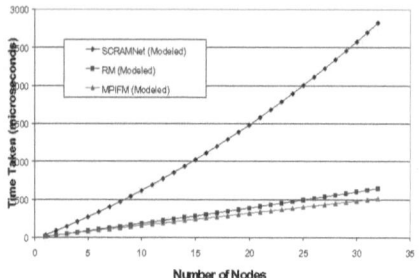

Fig. 7. All-Reduce Performance (4 bytes)   **Fig. 8.** All-Reduce Performance (64 bytes)

It can be observed that the RM model network does well for short message lengths, the best performance being for the broadcast algorithm. This shows that the performance is limited by the bandwidth of the network. Better performance can be expected of an RM network with higher bandwidth.

Another limitation of RM networks is that the amount of memory that is shared is limited. The broadcast and all-reduce algorithms require $O(N^2)$ space for control and $O(M)$ and $O(MN)$ space respectively for data, where M is the length of the message. The barrier algorithm also requires $O(N)$ space. The amount of shared memory eventually determines how much any algorithm for an RM network can scale. However, today RM NICs are available with up to 8 MB of shared memory [11]. Memory limitation, is therefore not a big problem for medium sized clusters. For instance, a 64-node system, the barrier operation needs only 8 bytes and broadcast and all-reduce need only 512 bytes for control. The size of shared memory does not limit the largest message length possible, as messages can be packetized.

6   Conclusions

In this paper, we have presented algorithms for Barrier Synchronization, Broadcast, and All-Reduce on reflective memory networks. These algorithms have been implemented and their performance compared with Myrinet, a high bandwidth network commonly used in cluster computing today. Current generation RM networks do not have bandwidths as high as point-to-point networks. Even with a bandwidth disadvantage, RM networks give good performance for short messages for the three collective communication operations studied. Furthermore, they offer a much simpler programming model and allow better overlap between computation and communication than many point-to-point networks. They also offer low latencies, which are useful for applications that exchange many short messages. The two limitations of RM networks are limited memory and limited bandwidth. RM networks have traditionally been used for specialized applications such as real time systems. With higher bandwidths, RM networks can give good performance for broadcast, barrier and all-reduce communication operations for a wider variety of cluster computing applications.

Additional papers related to this research can be obtained from the following Web pages: Network-Based Computing Laboratory (http://nowlab.cis.ohio-state.edu) and Parallel Architecture and Communication Group (http://www.cis.ohio-state.edu/~panda/pac.html).

References

1. T. Anderson, D. Culler, and D. Patterson.   A Case for Networks of Workstations (NOW). IEEE Micro, pages 54-64, Feb 1995.
2. D. J. Becker et al. Beowulf: A Parallel Workstation for Scientific Computation. In International Conference on Parallel Processing, 1995.
3. N. J. Boden, D. Cohen, et al. Myrinet: A Gigabit-per-Second Local Area Network. IEEE Micro, pages 29-35,Feb 1995.
4. S. Pakin, M. Lauria, and A. Chien.   High Performance Messaging on Workstations: Illinois Fast Messages (FM).   In Proceedings of Supercomputing'95.
5. T. Von Eicken, A. Basu, V. Buch, and W. Vogels. U-Net: A User-level Network Interface for Parallel and Distributed Computing.   In ACM Symposium on Operating Systems and Principles, 1995
6. M. G. Jacunski, V. Moorthy, P. P. Ware, M. T. Pillai, D. K. Panda, and P. Sadayappan. Low Latency Message-Passing for Reflective Memory Networks. In Workshop on Communication, Architecture and Applications for Network-Based Parallel Computing (CANPC), 1999, pages 211-224.
7. V. Moorthy, M.G Jacunski, M. T. Pillai, P. P. Ware, D. K. Panda, T. W. Page, Jr., P. Sadayappan, V. Nagarajan, J. Daniel. Low Latency Message-Passing on Workstation Clusters using SCRAMNet.   In Proceedings of International Parallel Processing Symposium (IPPS), 1999, pages 148-152.
8. M. Jovanovic, and Velijko Milutnovic. An Overview of Reflective Memory Systems. IEEE Concurrency, Vol 7:2,pages 56-64, 1999
9. M. T. Liu. Distributed Loop Computer Networks. In Advances in Computers, Academic Press, 1978
10. J. Misra. Phase Synchronization. Information Processing Letters 38, pages 101-105, 1991 .
11. T. Bohman. Shared Memory Computing Architectures for Real-Time Simulation – Simplicity and Elegance, Technical Report, Systran Corporation, 1994.
12. VMIC's Reflective Memory Network, VME Microsystems International Corp., 1995

13. R. Gillet. Memory Channel Network for PCI, IEEE Micro, Vol. 16, No.1, Feb 1996, pages 12-18.
14. M. A. Blumrich, C. Dubnicki, E. W. Felten, and K. Li. Protected User-level DMA for the SHRIMP interface. In Proceedings of the International Symposium on High Performance Computer Architecture (HPCA-2), 1996.
15. L. Wittie, G. Hermannsson, and A. Li. Eager Sharing for Efficient Massive Parallelism. In Proceedings of the International Conference on Parallel Processing (ICPP), 1992.
16. J. Duato , S. Yalamanchili and L. Ni. Interconnection Networks: An Engineering Approach. The IEEE Computer Society Press, 1997
17. C. B. Stunkel, R. Sivaram, and D. K. Panda Implementing Multidestination Worms in Switch-Based Parallel Systems: Architectural Alternatives and their Impact, International Symposium on Computer Architecture (ISCA'97), 1997
18. P. K. McKinley , H. Xu, A.-H. Esfahanian and L. M. Ni.. Unicast-Based Multicast Communication in   Wormhole-Routed Direct Networks,   IEEE Transactions on Parallel and Distributed Systems, vol. 5, no. 12, pp.   1254--1265, December 1994.
19. S. Ranka and S. Sahni, Hypercube Algorithms for Image Processing and Pattern Recognition, Springer-Verlag, 1990.

Broadcast/Multicast over Myrinet Using NIC-Assisted Multidestination Messages*

Darius Buntinas, Dhabaleswar K. Panda, Jose Duato, and P. Sadayappan

Network-Based Computing Laboratory
Dept. of Computer and Information Science
The Ohio State University, Columbus, OH 43210
{buntinas,panda,duato,saday}@cis.ohio-state.edu

Abstract. Broadcasting and multicasting are common operations in parallel and distributed programs. Some modern Network Interface Cards (NICs) have programmable processors which can be used to provide support for these operations. However these processors are 5-15 times slower than the host processor. In this paper we propose a design and an implementation of a multi-send primitive to support efficient broadcast/multicast that requires minimal assistance from the NIC. Our scheme is designed with the idea that as much processing as possible should be done by the host processor. This gives us more flexibility with, for example, creating multicast trees which would be optimal for a particular message size, or choosing a multicast tree dynamically based on requirements of bandwidth versus latency for a particular message. We have designed a multi-send primitive and implemented it as an addition to Fast-Messages (FM) 2.1 running over a Myrinet network. The proposed scheme does less processing at the NIC. The impact of adding such NIC-assisted multicast operation to a run-time system is also very small, less than 500ns for non-multi-send packets. To fully utilize the benefits of this primitive, we propose a method for constructing an optimal multicast tree using the new primitive. We have evaluated this scheme and obtained a speedup factor of up to 1.85 for multicasting 16K messages with 16 nodes.

1 Introduction

Broadcasting and multicasting are common operations in parallel and distributed programs. For example, MPI [8] has a broadcast operation defined as part of the standard. It would be beneficial to be able to reduce the latency of this operation as much as possible. Some modern network interface cards (NICs) have programmable processors which can be used to provide support for collective communications such as broadcast/multicast.

Using programmable network interface cards (NICs) to support broadcasting/multicasting in a cluster is not a new idea. Bhoedjang [3] and Verstoep [15]

---

* This research is supported in part by an NSF Career award MIP-9502294, NSF Grant CCR-9704512, and Ameritech Faculty Fellowship Award, and grants from the Ohio Board of Regents.

have implemented NIC-supported multicasting, and Kesavan [6] and Sivaram [12] have evaluated different aspects of NIC-supported multicasting. In each of these schemes, the NIC is responsible for all aspects of the operation, including creating the tree and handling flow control. However, the processors found on current generation NICs are usually much slower than the host processors, for example, the processors on current generation clusters are 300-500MHz while the processors on the Myrinet NICs are 33-66MHz, this is roughly 5-15 times slower. This limits the amount of work that can be done by the NIC without compromising performance.

This raises a challenge whether new communication mechanisms can be developed for clusters to support broadcast/multicast with minimal NIC assistance, while delivering good performance. In this paper we take on such a challenge. We introduce a multidestination message passing mechanism. Such a mechanism has been developed earlier for router-based parallel systems [11, 10, 13] to support efficient collective communication.

In this paper we design and implement a *multi-send* primitive to support efficient broadcast/multicast that requires minimal assistance from the NIC. Our scheme is designed with the idea that as much processing as possible should be done by the host processor. This gives us more flexibility with, for example, creating multicast trees which would be optimal for a particular message size, or choosing a multicast tree dynamically based on requirements of bandwidth versus latency for a particular message. Also, because the proposed scheme does less processing at the NIC, the impact of adding such NIC-assisted multicast operation to a run-time system is very small (less than 500ns for non-multi-send packets) when compared with others (a $5\mu s$ additional per-packet overhead in the NIC alone in [15]).

We have implemented the multi-send primitive as an addition to Illinois Fast-Messages (FM) 2.1 [9, 7] running over a Myrinet [5] network. To fully utilize the benefits of this primitive, we propose a method for constructing an optimal multicast tree using the new primitive. We have evaluated this scheme and obtained a factor of improvement of up to 1.85 for multicasting 16K messages with 16 nodes.

Section 2 describes the new multi-send primitive, followed by Section 3 which describes broadcasting and multicasting using the new primitive. Construction of the optimal multicast tree is described in Section 4. The implementation details are discussed in Section 5 followed by our experimental results in Section 6. Related work is discussed in Section 7. Finally we conclude and discuss future work in Section 8.

2   NIC-Assisted Multidestination Message Passing

The basic idea is to create a *multi-send* primitive in which the host writes the packet data to the NIC only once followed by a list of destinations. The NIC would then transmit copies of the packet to each of those destinations. Figure 1 shows two diagrams where host 0 is sending packets to hosts 1 through 3. The left diagram shows host 0 making three unicast (point-to-point) sends, each of which is forwarded by the NIC to its destination. The diagram on the right shows the host making a single multi-send operation to the NIC which then forwards a copy of the packet to each of the destinations.

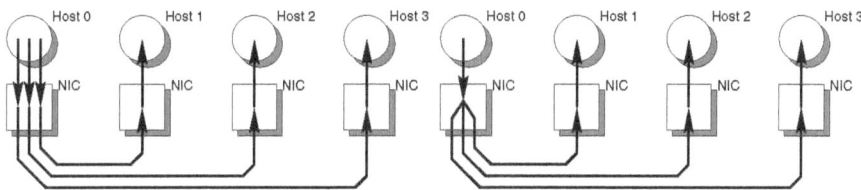

Fig. 1. Multiple host-based point-to-point operations (left) and a NIC-assisted multi-send operation (right) to four destinations.

Figure 2a shows the timing diagram for a multi-send operation sending a packet to four destinations, and the receive time for the last destination. Figure 2b shows the corresponding timing diagram for host-based point-to-point operations. In the figure the interval marked *Send* corresponds to the time it takes the host to assemble a packet and write it to the send queue on the NIC, and the interval marked *Xmit* corresponds to the time it takes the NIC to transmit the packet from the send queue to the network. The interval marked *Recv* corresponds to the combined time for the NIC to receive the packet, (including the network latency), for the NIC to forward the packet to the host, and for the host to process the packet. Notice that in both diagrams the receive time for a packet at the last receiver is overlapped with the transmission time at the sender for that same packet. In Figure 2b, for the first three packets, the network transmit time of one packet is overlapped with the host send time of the next and so it is not shown. As indicated below, timing parameters for FM over Myrinet are such that this will always be the case, regardless of the packet size. Though it is not shown in these figures, packet reception can also be pipelined between the NIC and the host.

Let us compare the latency of sending a packet to k destinations using a multi-send operation with the latency of sending a packet to k destinations using the usual host-based point-to-point operations. The time for the kth destination to receive the packet using a multi-send operation would be $(t_{Send}+(k-1) \times t_{Xmit} + t_{Recv})$, and $(k \times t_{Send} + t_{Recv})$ using host-based point-to-point operations. We have timed the host send, the NIC transmit and the receive operations in FM 2.1 on our cluster consisting of 300MHz Pentium II machines with 33MHz LANai 4.3 Myrinet cards. We estimate the send time to be $(2.7863\mu s+0.0301\mu s \times m)$[1], the NIC transmit time to be $(1.3958\mu s+0.0075\mu s \times m)$ and the receive time to be $(4.2820\mu s+0.0230\mu s \times m)$, where m is the packet size in bytes. Thus for sending a 1,536 byte packet to six destinations, t_{Send} would be $49.0199\mu s$, t_{Xmit}

---

[1] See the Appendix on how we arrived at these estimates.

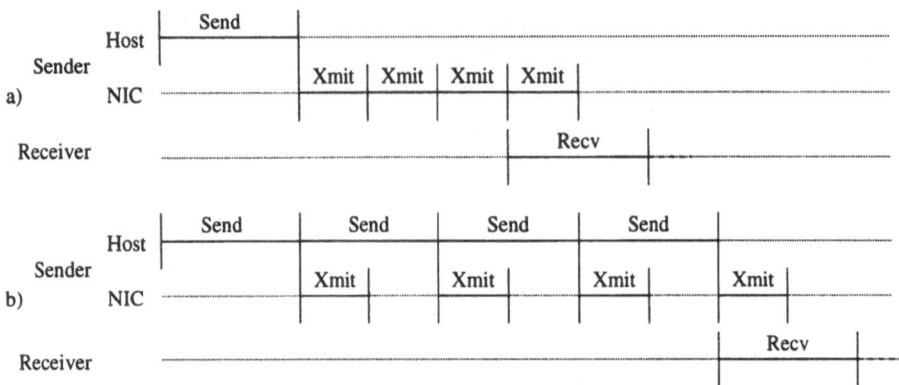

Fig. 2. Timing diagram comparing latencies for sending one packet to four destination using a) a multi-send operation and b) host-based point-to-point operations.

would be $12.9158\mu s$, and t_{Recv} would be $39.61\mu s$. The multi-send operation would take $153.2089\mu s$ and the usual host-based point-to-point method would take $333.7294\mu s$. This leads to a factor of improvement of 2.18. We can see that multi-send is a powerful primitive.

The estimates above were made without write-combining support[2]. Without write-combining, we achieve about 31.7 megabytes per second throughput when the host is writing a packet to the NIC. Assuming write-combining is enabled, we could get 90 megabytes per second throughput[1]. Then the send time would be $(2.7863\mu s+0.0106\mu s\times m)$ which would be $19.0679\mu s$ for a 1,536 byte message. The multi-send operation would then take $123.2569\mu s$ while the usual host-based point-to-point method would take $154.0174\mu s$. This would lead to a factor of improvement of 1.25. While the improvement is not as great as without write-combining, it is still significant.

3   Broadcast/Multicast with the Multi-send Primitive

While the multi-send primitive is powerful, for covering a large number of destinations we need to perform broadcasts and multicasts hierarchically in order to minimize the overall broadcast/multicast latency. This can be done by having the host at each intermediate node receive the message, then issue another multi-send operation to forward the message to its child nodes. This raises a challenge: how to create an optimal tree? It is also interesting to analyze how this scheme is different from the NIC-based multicast schemes described in [3, 15, 12, 6].

In the NIC-based scheme [3, 15, 12, 6], the incoming multicast packet is transmitted to the child nodes by the NIC after it has been forwarded to the host.

---

[2] In our configuration, the write-combining feature does not seem to be working in the Myrinet driver supplied with the FM distribution.

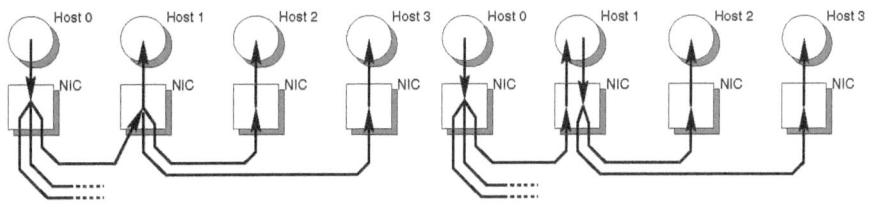

Fig. 3. NIC-based multicast (left) and a NIC-assisted multicast (right).

Figure 3 illustrates the difference in the two methods. This figure shows two diagrams where node 0 sends a message to multiple destinations, one of which is node 1. Node 1 then sends to nodes 2 and 3. The diagram on the left shows a completely NIC-based scheme where the packet coming into node 1 from node 0 is sent to nodes 2 and 3 by the NIC after being forwarded to the host. The diagram on the right shows node 1 forwarding the incoming packet to the host. The host then issues a multi-send operation to transmit the packet to nodes 2 and 3.

While it may seem that the completely NIC-based scheme would always be better than the method we are proposing, we believe that that is not the case. The completely NIC-based approach puts more responsibility on the NIC which, as previously mentioned, has a processor 5-15 times slower than the host. We believe that the additional processing power available at the host will allow greater flexibility in, for instance, tree construction. So that depending on the message size and quality of service requirements, a tree optimal in either bandwidth or latency, for that message size can be used for sending the message. This could be done on a per-message basis. This paper will examine how to construct a multicast tree that is optimal for latency, and study the performance of such a tree.

4   Constructing an Optimal Multicast Tree

In this section, we show how to construct an optimal multicast tree using the proposed new multi-send primitive. The basic idea is to construct a tree such that the maximum number of nodes will be sending at any time. Such a tree would be optimal in terms of latency.

Bar-Noy and Kipnis [2] have shown that in the postal model, a broadcast tree optimal in terms of latency is based on the following recurrence relation. In the postal model, a broadcast to $F_\lambda(t)$ nodes can be completed in t time.

$$F_\lambda(t) = \begin{cases} 1 & \text{if } 0 \leq t < \lambda, \\ F_\lambda(t-1) + F_\lambda(t-\lambda) & \text{if } t \geq \lambda. \end{cases}$$

In this recurrence relation, λ is defined as the ratio of (i) the total amount of time from when the sender of a packet starts sending it to when the receiver receives the complete packet and (ii) the amount of time that the sender spends sending the packet. One unit of time is defined as the time the sender spends sending a packet. It then takes λ time for a recipient to fully receive a packet after the sender starts sending it. It is assumed that as soon as a node receives a packet, it will start sending it to its children nodes.

Intuitively, one can think of $F_\lambda(t)$ as the number of nodes which have received the packet at time t. This is equal to the number of nodes which had already received the packet previously (i.e. $F_\lambda(t-1)$), plus the number of nodes which have just received the packet. The packets which were just fully received at time t must have been sent at λ time before then. Since, at that time there were $F_\lambda(t-\lambda)$ nodes which would have sent these packets, there would be that many new nodes receiving the packet at time t.

In our design, the NIC will be transmitting the packets to different nodes. So we need to apply the postal model from the point of view of the NIC. Specifically, when a packet is sent from a node, say, node 0, to another node, node 1, which will receive it and send it to a third node, node 2, then λ is defined as the ratio of i) the time from when the NIC at node 0 starts transmitting the packet to node 1 until the NIC at node 1 is ready to transmit the packet to node 2 and ii) the time it takes the NIC to finish transmitting the packet. Note that part i) of the ratio is simply the one way latency of a packet (i.e. the time it takes for the NIC to transmit the packet plus the time it takes for the host to receive it plus the time for the host to send the packet to the NIC).

To construct the tree, we used an algorithm similar to the "simple top-down greedy algorithm" in [4]. The tree is stored as a list of destination lists, one per host. The algorithm uses two queues called the *new* queue and the *old* queue. We start with the root node and enqueue it in the *new* queue with time 0. Then, for each node p in $(p_1, p_2, \ldots p_{n-1})$ we do the following:

- dequeue the node q that has the minimal time t of both of the queues.
- add p to the destination list of q
- enqueue p onto the *new* queue with time $t + \lambda$
- enqueue q onto the *old* queue with time $t + 1$

While there are algorithms which may construct the tree faster [4], this algorithm is simple and general. Because we were constructing the tree off-line in our test program, we were not concerned with the running time of this algorithm. This algorithm does, however, produce a tree that is optimal in the postal model for a given λ [4, 2].

So far we have focused on multicasting a single packet. For multi-packet messages, there are two ways for intermediate nodes to forward the message to it children. One way would be for the node to receive the whole message, then send the message to its children. The other method would be for the node pipeline the message in a packet-wise fashion. In other words, the node would receive the message one packet at a time, and forward the packets to its children as soon as they are received rather than waiting for the whole message to be received.

The decision on whether to pipeline the message or not will mostly depend on whether the run-time system supports it. FM, for instance, does not support message pipelining in general (though we were able to do this in a special case). In Section 6 we will show performance results with and without pipelining.

5   Our Implementation of the Multi-send Primitive

We used Illinois Fast Messages (FM) version 2.1 from the HPVM 1.0 distribution for the base of our experiments. This version was used because it is the latest version of FM available for Linux.

In FM 2.1, a message is associated with a stream. In order to send a message, a stream is created between the node and the destination with the FM API call **FM_begin_message()**. Data can then be sent on the stream using the **FM_send_piece()** API call. When enough data is sent to fill a packet, FM creates a packet and writes it to the NIC which in turn transmits it to the destination node. On the receiving side, FM calls a message handler to optionally re-assemble the message, packet by packet, into the user buffer. A stream is terminated using the **FM_end_message()** API call, at which time any remaining data is assembled into a packet and written to the NIC.

To avoid loosing packets due to buffer overflow at the receiver, FM uses a flow control scheme using credit management. One credit corresponds to one packet buffer at the receiver. On starting FM, each sender starts with a certain amount of credits for each receiver. Before any packet is sent FM checks if the sender has sufficient credits for the receiving node. If there are no available credits at the receiver, then the sender blocks until it receives more credits, otherwise, the sender decrements the number of credits it has for that receiver and sends the packet. Whenever a node receives a packet it increments a counter of the number of credits it needs to return to the sender. These credits are returned to the sender either by piggybacking the credits on a data packet sent to that node, or via an explicit credit packet.

We modified FM by adding a new API call, **FM_begin_message_multi()** which creates a stream between the sender and all destinations specified in the destination list given as an argument. As with a regular FM stream, data is sent using **FM_send_piece()** and the stream is terminated with **FM_end_message()**. The flow control mechanism was also modified. Before a packet is sent credits are checked for every one of the destinations. If there are not enough credits for any destination, the operation blocks until there are. Basically, rather than just verifying that we have credits for a single destination, we check that we have enough credits for each destination. For returning credits normal FM unicast packets have a field for piggybacking them. In our scheme we use piggyback credits for each destination as described below.

When a packet is ready to be sent, the packet is assembled for the first destination and written to the send frame on the NIC. Next a list of information on each additional destination is assembled and written to a new field which is added to the send frame. Each entry in the list holds the logical node number, the physical node number and the returned credits for that destination. These are be used to update the corresponding fields in the packet header so that the packet can be sent to each destination.

Since the host assembles the packet such that it is ready to be sent to the first destination, the NIC can transmit the packet without checking whether it is a multi-destination packet. Only after the NIC has initiated the transmit DMA and is waiting for it to complete, will it check for additional destinations. This way our modifications add no overhead at the NIC for sending standard FM messages. The NIC then updates the logical node number, credit and route fields of the packet for the next destination. This is done as soon as the transmit DMA pointer has passed those fields but without waiting for the entire DMA to finish. This allows the header field updates to be overlapped with the DMA for all but the smallest messages. After updating the fields, the NIC waits for the DMA to finish then the DMA is immediately initiated to transmit the packet to the next destination. This is repeated for each additional destination.

6   Experimental Results

The performance tests were run on a cluster of 16 300MHz Pentium II machines each with 128MB of RAM running RedHat 5.2 Linux with kernel version 2.0.36. The machines are connected by a Myrinet LAN network with LANai 4.3 cards via a 16 port switch.

We tested the performance of the multi-send primitive and compared it with multiple unicast sends. In every iteration of our test routine, the root would send messages to the destinations, and then the last destination would send a zero byte message back to the root after receiving a copy of the message. This was timed for 1,000 iterations, then the average was taken for the result. This was done varying the message size and number of destinations. Figures 4 and 5 show the results of this test. Notice that for messages less than 32 bytes, our scheme performs slightly worse than the host-based scheme. This is due to the fact that the NIC transmit time is not smaller than the host send time and due to the overhead of adding the multi-send primitive to FM. However, the NIC-assisted scheme performs clearly better than the host-based scheme for larger messages. It can be observed that the multi-send primitive achieves a factor of improvement of 3.51 for sending a 16K message to 15 destinations.

To test the performance of a multicast operation using the multi-send primitive, we ran a test similar to the one described above. One iteration of the test routine would send a message along a multicast tree, then one of the leaf nodes would send a zero byte message back to the root. This was timed for 1,000 iterations then the average was taken. Because we couldn't be sure which leaf node would receive the message last, we ran the loop several times, each time changing the leaf node which would return the message, then taking the maximum value. In order to cut down on the number of leaf nodes to test we only tested the leaf nodes which were the last children of their parents. This was then varied for message size and number of destinations. When we were using the optimal multicast tree in our tests, we needed to use a value for λ which would produce

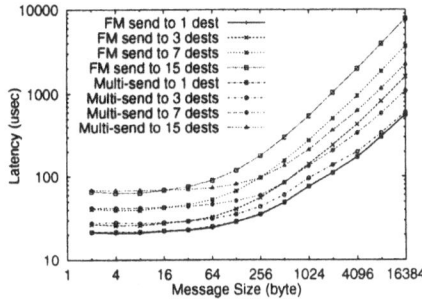 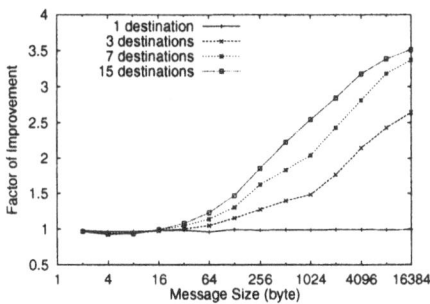

Fig. 4. Latency for NIC-assisted multi-send operation and multiple FM send operations.

Fig. 5. Speedup for NIC-assisted multi-send operation versus multiple FM send operations.

the best performance. Since the value of λ depends on the message size, in our test program, for each message size we constructed a new tree based on integer λ values from 1 to the number of nodes participating, and took the minimum. So each point in our multicast performance graphs is the minimum over each tree, of the maximum for each responding leaf node in that tree, of the average of 1,000 iterations.

Also, to study the performance impact of pipelining for multi-packet messages, we incorporated modifications to our test program as outlined in Section 4. As soon as a packet was received by the intermediate node, it would be sent out, rather than wait for the whole message to arrive. To pipeline a message, the application would have to open a stream to its destination(s), then receive the incoming message one packet at a time until it has received it completely, then close the stream.

This cannot normally be done in FM 2.1 because while a stream is open, FM does not allow the application to make a call to receive parts of a message. This is done to avoid certain deadlock conditions. When a stream is opened with `FM_begin_message()` or `FM_begin_message_multi()`, FM sets a lock so that any calls to receive a message return immediately without receiving. To get around this, we used a version of this call, `FM_unsafe_begin_message_multi()` which does not set a lock. This version is intended to be used only inside a message handler. We used it outside a message handler in our main routine. Since the lock is not set when we open the stream, we are then able to receive the packets of the incoming message and send them out. Though this approach may lead to deadlock in the general case, because our test programs ran one multicast at a time, there were no cyclical dependencies and no deadlock could occur. We used this method, not to show how to pipeline messages in FM, but rather to demonstrate the performance of our scheme when pipelining is possible.

We will next compare NIC-assisted multicasting to host-based multicasting. Because the binomial tree is most often used for host-based multicast operations,

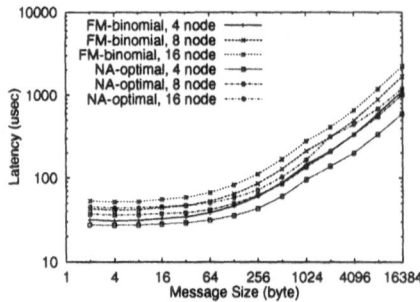
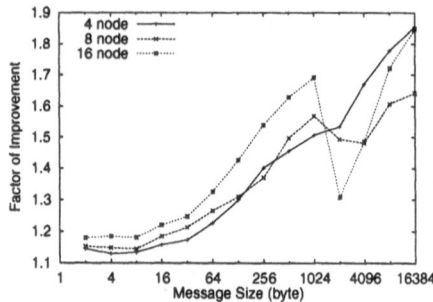

Fig. 6. Multicast latency for NIC-assisted multicast using an optimal tree *with packet-wise pipelining* (NA-optimal), and multicast using binomial tree with FM unicast send (FM-binomial).

Fig. 7. Multicast factor of improvement for NIC-assisted multicast using an optimal tree *with packet-wise pipelining*, compared to multicast using binomial tree with FM unicast send.

as used in MPI, we will use the binomial tree for the host-based multicast, and compare it to the NIC-assisted multicast using an optimal tree as discussed in Section 4. Then, because the binomial tree may not be the best tree for host-based multicast, we will use an optimal tree for the host-based multicast and compare that with the NIC-assisted multicast also using an optimal tree. In each case, we will show the impact of message pipelining.

Figures 6 and 7 compare NIC-assisted multicast using an optimal tree with pipelining against the host-based multicast using a binomial tree. Notice that the NIC-assisted scheme is better for every message size and every number of destinations. The dip in the factor of improvement for 2048 byte messages with 16 nodes is due to packetization effects. The graph also shows a factor of improvement of 1.86 for multicasting a 16K message to four nodes and a factor of improvement of 1.85 for multicasting a 16K message to 16 nodes.

Figures 8 and 9 show the same comparison as above but without message pipelining. We can see that the when compared to the pipelined case, performance does not change for one packet messages (FM packets are 1,536 byte) or for four nodes of any size. This is because pipelining does not occur for single packet messages, and for a four node broadcast the optimal tree is flat ($\lambda = 2$), i.e., the root sends the message directly to all the three destinations, so again no pipelining would occur. While the performance improvement is not as great for multi-packet messages with eight and 16 nodes, when compared to the case when messages are pipelined, there is still a 1.53 and 1.30 factor of improvement for 16K messages with eight and 16 nodes, respectively.

To see what impact the shape of the tree had on the performance we are seeing, the optimal tree algorithm was used with the host-based unicast primitive and compared with the same data for the multi-send primitive above. Figures 10, 11, 12 and 13 show the results of this comparison. In this test, our scheme

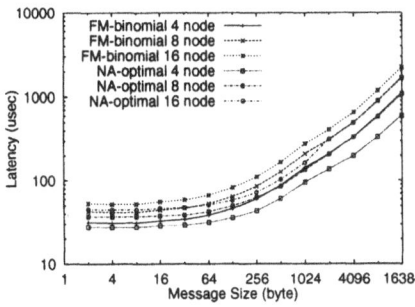
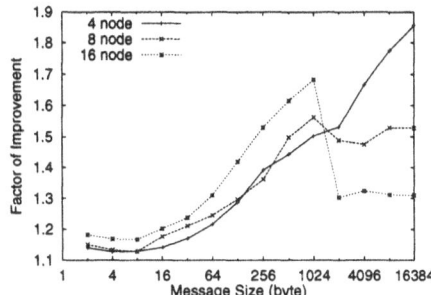

Fig. 8. Multicast latency for NIC-assisted multicast using an optimal tree *without packet-wise pipelining* (NA-optimal), and multicast using binomial tree with FM unicast send (FM-binomial).

Fig. 9. Multicast factor of improvement for NIC-assisted multicast using an optimal tree *without packet-wise pipelining*, compared to multicast using binomial tree with FM unicast send.

performs a little worse than the host-based method for messages less than 32 bytes. We believe that this is due to the overhead of the additions to FM similar to that observed for Figure 4. For multi-packet messages, the optimal tree for the host-based method turned out to be a binomial tree (i.e. $\lambda = 1$), so the performance improvement for those messages is the same as in the previous graphs.

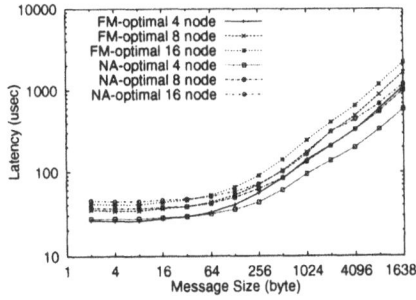
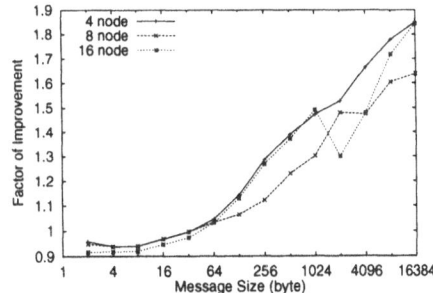

Fig. 10. Multicast latency for NIC-assisted multicast using an optimal tree *with packet-wise pipelining* (NA-optimal), and multicast using an optimal tree with FM unicast send (FM-optimal).

Fig. 11. Multicast factor of improvement for NIC-assisted multicast using an optimal tree *with packet-wise pipelining*, compared to multicast using an optimal tree with FM unicast send.

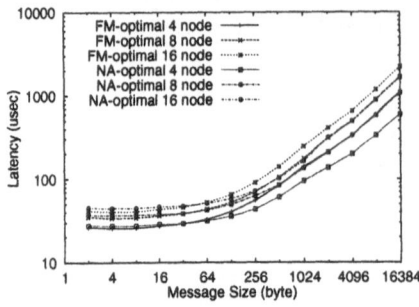 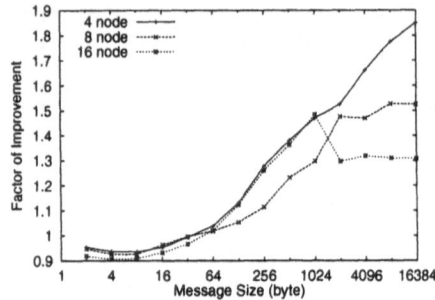

Fig. 12. Multicast latency for NIC-assisted multicast using an optimal tree *without packet-wise pipelining* (NA-optimal), and multicast using an optimal tree with FM unicast send (FM-optimal).

Fig. 13. Multicast factor of improvement for NIC-assisted multicast using an optimal tree *without packet-wise pipelining*, compared to multicast using an optimal tree with FM unicast send.

7   Related Work

NIC-based multicasting has been previously proposed by Verstoep et.al. [15] and Bhoedjang et.al. [3]. Their schemes perform the entire multicast operation at the NIC, as opposed to our scheme which uses a multi-send operation as a primitive for multicast.

Verstoep, et.al. extend FM 1.1 to include NIC-based multicasting. In their scheme (called FM/MC)[15], the multicast is performed completely at the NIC-level. At intermediate nodes, the packet is forwarded to the host, but then immediately transmitted to the child nodes without involving the host. The host receive queues are divided into multicast queues and unicast queues. In order to prevent buffer overflow, credits are managed separately for each. One multicast credit corresponds to one packet buffer in *each* host in the network, rather than just for one host, as with unicast credits. One NIC on the network is designated as a credit manager which distributes and collects the multicast credits. A NIC must request credits from the manager before multicasting a packet. However, once a multicast has been initiated, the intermediate nodes do not need to check for credits and can immediately forward the packet to their children when they receive it.

Bhoedjang et.al. propose a new message passing protocol called Link-level Flow Control (LFC)[3]. This system does all flow control at the NIC and also performs the multicast completely at the NIC. In this system data for a packet is copied to a buffer pool on the NIC by the host, then the host writes a descriptor to the send queue. The NIC polls the send queue and transmits the packets when there are sufficient credits. In order to send a multicast packet, the host simply has to add one descriptor for each destination but refer them to the same data. At an intermediate node, the NIC receives the packet then adds descriptors for its children to the send queue.

The main difference between our scheme and the schemes described above, is that a multicast operation in the schemes described above is done completely at the NIC. Also, our scheme keeps the receive queues and credit management unified for both unicast and multicast messages.

8   Conclusions and Future Work

We have introduced a new multi-send primitive, which uses the NIC to transmit multiple copies of a packet to different destinations. We then showed how this primitive can be used in a multicast tree to further improve performance for large numbers of destinations.

The multi-send primitive gave us a 3.51 factor of improvement over conventional host-level iterative sends for 16K messages. We also observed a 1.85 factor of improvement for 8K messages and 16 nodes when using the primitive in a multicast operation using an optimal tree versus using a binomial tree with the traditional host-level unicast sends.

The current evaluations are based on a 16-node cluster with a 16 port myrinet switch. Thus, there is no network contention during the multicast operation. For larger systems, network contention will play an important role. We plan to develop a method for constructing trees for multicast using multi-send primitives which would give minimal contention for arbitrary irregular networks. Also it would be interesting to study the effects of a workload on such an algorithm and the resulting performance on the multicast.

On a more general level we intend to investigate whether other collective communication operations, such as barriers, reductions, or personalized multicast could benefit from similar NIC-assisted primitives.

Additional Information: Additional papers related to this research can be obtained from the following Web pages: Network-Based Computing Laboratory (`http://nowlab.cis.ohio-state.edu`) and Parallel Architecture and Communication Group (`http://www.cis.ohio-state.edu/~panda/pac.html`).

Appendix

This appendix explains how we arrived at the estimates shown in Section 2. We used the RDTSC Pentium assembly instruction[14] which reads the Pentium's internal 64 bit cycle counter. If one knows the speed of the processor, one can use this counter for accurate timings.

To estimate t_{Send} we timed the send portion of a simple ping-pong program and averaged it over 10,000 iterations. We did this for various message sizes up to one packet size (1,536 bytes).

To estimate t_{Xmit} we used the RTC register on the NIC's LANai chip. This register is incremented at a regular interval. To time this interval we did the following. First, we read the NIC's RTC register from the host then immediately read the Pentium cycle counter. We then repeatedly slept for one second, read the RTC and Pentium cycle counter, and compared the values to the initial reading, then calculated the elapsed time. This was done until the resulting value converged. By looping until the value converged, we were able to eliminate, to an arbitrary degree of accuracy, the delay of reading the RTC register over the PCI bus.

Once we calibrated the RTC register period, we timed the NIC transmit time by subtracting the RTC time from the variable storing the total transmit time as soon as the NIC noticed that a packet was added to the send queue. Then as soon as the transmit DMA was completed, we added the value of the RTC register to this variable. This was done for sending 10,000 packets, then this value was read by the host and divided by 10,000. To make sure that no other packets were sent during this time, such as credit packets, the FM library code was modified to prevent such packets from being sent.

Note that $t_{Send} + t_{Xmit}$ does not include the time between when the host finishes copying the packet to the NIC and when the NIC notices that the packet is there. We expect this time to be small.

We timed the interval for the NIC to receive a message and DMA it to the host similarly to how we timed the t_{Xmit} value. We took the time from when the NIC started the DMA from the network to a receive buffer, until the packet had finished being DMAed to the host. We then timed the interval for the host to perform the copy of the packet from the DMA region where the NIC had placed it, to the application buffer. We took the sum of these two measurements for the value of t_{Recv}.

Note that this time does not include the network latency, which should be very small because we have only one switch, and the time from when the NIC finishes DMAing the packet until when the host notices that the packet is there. Again, we feel that this should be a small value.

References

1. S. Araki, A. Bilas, C. Dubnicki, J. Elder, K. Konishi and J. Philbin, "User-Space Communication: A Quantitative Study". *Proceedings of the 1998 SC'98 Conference.* November, 1998.
2. A. Bar-Noy and S. Kipnis, "Designing Broadcast Algorithms in the Postal Model for Message-Passing Systems". *Mathematical Systems Theory*, 27(5), pp. 431-452, September 1994.
3. R.A.F. Bhoedjang, T. Ruhl and H.E. Bal, "Efficient Multicast On Myrinet Using Link-Level Flow Control". *International Conference on Parallel Processing*, pp. 381-390, August 1998.
4. J. Bruck, L. De Coster, N. Dewulf, C. Ho and R. Lauwereins, "On the Design and Implementation of Broadcast and Global Combine Operations using the Postal Model". *IEEE Transactions on Parallel and Distributed Systems*, 7(3), pp. 256-265, March 1996.
5. N. Boden, D. Cohen, R. Felderman, A. Kulawik, C. Seitz, J. Seizovic, and W. Su, "Myrinet: A Gigabit-Per-Second Local Area Network". *IEEE Micro* 15(1), pp. 29-36, February 1995.

6. R. Kesavan and D.K. Panda, "Optimal Multicast with Packetization and Network Interface Support". *International Conference on Parallel Processing (ICPP 1997)*, pp. 370-377.

7. M. Lauria, S. Pakin and A. Chien, "Efficient Layering for High Speed Communication: Fast Messages 2.x". *Proceedings of the 7th High Performance Distributed Computing (HPDC7) Conference*, July 28-31, 1998.

8. Message Passing Interface Forum, *MPI-2: Extensions to the Message-Passing Interface*. July 1997.

9. S. Pakin, M. Lauria and A. Chien, "High Performance Messaging on Workstations: Illinois Fast Messages (FM) for Myrinet". *In Supercomputing '95*.

10. D.K. Panda, "Fast Barrier Synchronization in Wormhole k-ary n-cube Networks with Multidestination Worms". *International Symposium on High Performance Computer Architecture (HPCA '95)*, pp. 200-209, 1995.

11. D.K. Panda, S. Singal, and R. Kesavan, "Multidestination Message Passing in Wormhole k-ary n-cube Networks with Base Routing Conformed Paths". *IEEE Transactions on Parallel and Distributed Systems*, Vol. 10, No. 1, pp. 76-96, January 1999.

12. R. Sivaram, R. Kesavan, D.K. Panda, and C.B. Stunkel, "Where to Provide Support for Efficient Multicasting in Irregular Networks: Network Interface or Switch?" *International Conference on Parallel Processing (ICPP 1998)*, pp. 452-459.

13. C.B. Stunkel, R. Sivaram, and D.K. Panda "Implementing Multidestination Worms in Switch-Based Parallel Systems: Architectural Alternatives and their Impact". *International Symposium on Computer Architecture (ISCA '97)*, Vol. 25, No. 2, pp. 50-61, June 2-4 1997.

14. *Using the RDTSC Instruction for Performance Monitoring*. available from http://developer.intel.com/drg/pentiumII/appnotes/RDTSCPM1.HTM

15. K. Verstoep, K. Langendoen, and H.E. Bal, "Efficient Reliable Multicast on Myrinet". *1996 International Conference on Parallel Processing*, Vol. 3, pp. 156-165, August 1996.

Simulation Studies of Gigabit Ethernet Versus Myrinet Using Real Application Cores

Helen Chen and Pete Wyckoff

Sandia National Laboratories
MS 9011, P.O. Box 969, Livermore, CA 94551 USA
{hycsw,wyckoff}@ca.sandia.gov

Abstract. Parallel cluster computing projects use a large number of commodity PCs to provide cost-effective computational power to run parallel applications. Because properly load-balanced distributed parallel applications tend to send messages synchronously, minimizing blocking is as crucial a requirement for the network fabric as are those of high bandwidth and low latency. We consider the selection of an optimal, commodity-based, interconnect network technology and topology to provide high bandwidth, low latency, and reliable delivery. Since our network design goal is to facilitate the performance of real applications, we evaluated the performance of myrinet and gigabit ethernet technologies in the context of working algorithms using modeling and simulation tools developed for this work.

1 Introduction

A group of enthusiasts of commodity high-performance computing platforms has lived at the fringes of the computing community for many years now, and this bunch is seeing its numbers grow following the general demise of the massively parallel processor (MPP) manufacturers. Even the government research laboratories are joining the fray. Sandia National Laboratories is a United States Department of Energy research facility which can no longer satisfy its thirst for FLOPS by buying monolithic multi-million dollar machines, as there is not sufficient market demand to keep vendors in business.

The idea of cluster computing is to aggregate machine rooms full of relatively cheap hardware, connected with some sort of network, and apply the combined force of the individual machines on a single calculation. Problems arise, though, in attempting to operate this set of machines as a single unit. As it is not feasible to run a single instance of the operating system on the entire cluster, the alternate paradigm of message passing is used instead. Each processor (which could also be a small shared-memory multiprocessor) maintains a disjoint address space, and messages are passed between machines as driven by the requirements of each application.

The hardware employed in a cluster is generally the most readily available in the volume personal computing market, so as to leverage the cost advantages of buying commodity hardware. The down side to this is that some critical pieces

B. Falsafi and M. Lauria (Eds.): CANPC 2000, LNCS 1797, pp. 130–144, 2000.

of hardware for cluster computing are completely irrelevant for the mass market, namely the interconnect. The advent of shared 10 Mb/s ethernet [3] was a giant step, and remains the basis of the standard "fast" networking infrastructure, as it has been for the last 15 years. Within the last few years, though, the price of 100 Mb/s ethernet cards have approached the reach of most users, and commodity gigabit network components are on their way. High-end cluster users can afford both gigabit ethernet and myrinet [9] as the message passing infrastructure. More esoteric networking components, such as HiPPi [10] and Giganet [12] are available to those willing to incur the additional costs, and are becoming cheaper and faster with time.

The remainder of this paper discusses the technologies we simulated, and methods we used which involve a mix of "artificial" basic tests and simulations of core algorithms from real parallel applications. Our results tally the positive and negative aspects of each technology.

2   Interconnect Technologies

The following three subsections describe the network fabrics we considered in the simulations discussed in Section 3. In each section we calculate the current pricing for a prototypical 256 node cluster, a size which should be familiar to many cluster builders.

2.1   Myrinet

Myricom's myrinet is a cost-effective, high-performance communication and switching technology. It interconnects hosts and switches using 1.28 Gb/s full-duplex links. The myrinet PCI host adapter can be programmed to interact directly with the host processors for low-latency communications, and with the network to send, receive, and buffer packets.

Myricom supplies open source software that runs on common hosts and operating systems. This software maps the network periodically to find available paths between communicating hosts. All myrinet packets carry a source-based routing header to provide intermediate switches with forwarding directions. Therefore, myrinet switches do not need to run routing algorithms or maintain a routing table. Because myrinet does not impose a size limitation on its packets, it can easily encapsulate any protocol's packet format (e.g. TCP [8], IP, etc.), thereby providing interoperability. While the simplicity in the myrinet switch offers a low per-port cost, it lacks management capability to maintain robustness in large clusters.

The current myrinet switch is a 16-port crossbar, although there should soon be available a 64-port switch. These ports can be used to interconnect either switches or processors, thereby allowing arbitrary network topologies. Normally, more interswitch connections implies more diverse paths, which can reduce blocking within the switching fabric. However, there will then be fewer ports available to interconnect processing nodes.

The severe cable length restriction is the greatest impediment to creating complex topologies. Optical converters are available from Myricom, at a cost of $3600 per connection, which would more than double the per-host connection cost. On the small scale, one can easily build hypercubes and large-dimensional tori using 35 foot LAN cables. For our large scale simulations, we chose a two dimensional torus as the best tradeoff in terms of area and cost. It scales in two physical dimensions just as our hardware scales in two dimensions on the machine-room floor. Our plans for 10 000 compute nodes and our budget do not permit a hypercube topology on that scale.

Myrinet sells a network interface card for $1700, 16-port switches for $5000, and cables for $200. For the topology described above, the total cost for 256 nodes is $256 \times \$1700 + 32 \times \$5000 + 12 \times 32 \times \$200 = \$670k$.

2.2 Gigabit Ethernet

The most popular Local Area Network (LAN) technology is ethernet. Ethernet has evolved from the 3 Mb/s technology, invented by Bob Metcalfe in 1973, to the 10-, 100- (or fast), and 1000-Mb/s (or gigabit) ethernet standards of today [7], gigabit ethernet is fast becoming a commodity item and therefore, we believe it can be a cost-effective alternative to interconnect parallel computers. Moreover, there are already discussions of 10- and even 100-gigabit per second ethernet [4], which could provide the next generation parallel computers with a smooth upgrade path to their communication subsystem.

Conventional routers, however, are not scalable because they use designs based on a backplane bus or crossbar switch. The largest non-blocking switch available today supports only 64 nodes, and cascading is required to build a cluster beyond that size. These routers use the spanning tree algorithm to calculate a loop-free tree that has only a single path for each destination, using the redundant paths as hot stand-by links, precluding the use of, say, a mesh topology. Without diverse paths, cascaded switches will suffer performance bottlenecks due to output port contention.

Due to the lack of switch scalability and the necessity to remain backward compatible with slower ethernet implementations, we believe the applications of a conventional gigabit ethernet switch fabric are limited to small parallel systems. We decided to conduct a simulation study of a 256-node cluster, nevertheless, in order to evaluate the effects of ethernet's packet framing, inter-frame gap, maximum and minimum packet size, and store-and-forward switching mechanism on the performance of parallel applications.

Network cards for gigabit ethernet are around $700, and 64-port switches can be found for $30k. Including fiber and thinking forward to inter-switch trunking gives a total 256-node cost of $256 \times \$700 + 5 \times \$30\,000 + 280 \times \$75 = \$350k$.

2.3 Avici Terabit Switch Router

The Avici router uses two direct-connect networks [2] as its switching fabric to achieve high performance, economical scalability, and robustness. The dual fabric connects switching nodes (or line cards) using twelve 20-Gbps full duplex links to form two 3-D toroidal meshes [1]. Each set of five line cards is grouped into a quadrant which is connected via a backplane to form a loop in the z-dimension. The x and y dimensions are formed by connecting neighboring quadrants along the backplane in folded tori, which allows uniformly short wires to be used for all connections, thereby lowering wiring costs as well as latency variations. With this arrangement, an Avici router can be incrementally expanded to include up to $14 \times 16 \times 5 = 1120$ line cards. At 16 gigabit ethernet ports per line cards, this configuration can interconnect a parallel system of 17 920 compute processors.

Similar to myrinet, the Avici router uses wormhole routing inside the fabric to achieve low latency. Unlike myrinet, however, rather than buffering the entire message inside the network, the Avici router segments its messages into 72-byte scheduling units and exercises credit-based flow control to prevent flit loss. Together with its per-connection buffer management, and overprovisioned fabric links relative to the line card I/O demands, the Avici router implements an output-buffered virtual crossbar to eliminate the blocking problem in wormhole routing. Because of the huge speed mismatch between gigabit ethernet and the fabric link (1:20), the Avici router will store incoming gigabit ethernet packets before forwarding to prevent buffer underrun within the fabric. Unlike conventional switches, however, the number of store-and-forward operations in the Avici reaches an upper bound of two, once at the incoming and the other at the outgoing gigabit ethernet port. Moreover, because the Avici router is designed for telecommunications applications, it is extremely robust and has extensive SNMP-based management capabilities, a feature that is essential to building reliable large parallel systems.

Replacing the switches in the cost calculation for conventional gigabit ethernet, and dropping a few unneeded fibers gives a total $256 \times \$700 + \$250\,000 + 256 \times \$75 = \$450k$.

3   Simulation Methodologies

We adapt existing simulation packages to capture important characteristics of a technology, such as its link level protocol and switch architecture. Because these characteristics are unique to the technology it represents, we are not concerned with effects due to differences in implementation. Instead, we ensure the fidelity of our simulation results by extending these packages to use the same set of parallel algorithms to generate traffic. We also code an identical interface layer to handle details of packet transmission and reception. Since the goal of our study is to identify potential interconnect technologies, we do not consider end station overhead. We plan to address the performance issues involving the host adapter, device driver, and end-system protocol processing in a future study.

Because many users share the use of a parallel computer system, each will allocate a number of processors from the pooled resources to solving his or her problems. Therefore, we chose to conduct our simulation study using a 256-node network to represent a typical user's problem solving environment. The

following subsections discuss the intermediate interface layers and the details of
the low-level simulators.

3.1   Opnet

MIL3's Optimized Engineering Tools [11] is a comprehensive engineering system capable of simulating large communication networks with detailed protocol
modeling and performance analysis. Its features include graphical specification
of models, event-scheduled simulation kernel, and hierarchical object-based modeling. We selected Opnet to simulate the conventional gigabit ethernet switch
because Opnet has an existing model that simulates the gigabit ethernet protocol.

On the top level, we used Opnet's network editor to compose our network
using components such as switches, nodes, and links. The network consists of
five conventional gigabit ethernet switches, 256 compute nodes, and full-duplex
links to interconnect them. We populated four switches each with 64 end nodes,
which are in turn connected via a fifth switch. We chose a star topology because
it offers the lowest hop count between the most distant nodes in the network.

At the next lower level, we used Opnet's node editor to construct our compute and switch nodes. A compute node consists of a module to run the parallel
application models that we wrote, a gigabit ethernet protocol entity, a transmit-
ter, and a receiver. The process model contains a state transition diagram which
represents the parallel code. Each of the 256 nodes in the system runs the state
machine which transitions between sending, receiving, and computing states.

3.2   Avici Simulator

Allen King and coworkers at Avici wrote a simulator [5] to be used in planning
the switch hardware they built. We inserted hooks into the simulator by which
we could feed our own traffic patterns into the switch: **sendPacket()** inserts a
packet into the fabric, while **receivedPacket()** is called up from the fabric to
notify our modules of the receipt of a packet at a destination line card. The
function **nextFlitTime()** notifies our code that the simulator has advanced in
time, and we use that notification to fire any pending events. Various other calls
are used by the fabric and the application code modules to notify each other of
initialization, completion, and to acquire or change fabric parameters. We also
added the modeling of a line card which mates 16 gigabit ethernet ports into the
Avici backplane.

Our interface layer also handles the details of segmentation and reassembly
so that an application is insulated from the transport details. This layer ensures
that no packet is dropped by keeping lists of in-flight messages, which also aids
in the generation of statistics.

3.3   Myrinet Simulator

The myrinet simulator [6] was initially developed by Chen-Chi Kuo as a grad-
uate student in the Computer Science Department at the University of Utah

to be used in their full system simulator. We adapted just the myrinet part of the simulator, and added an event handling mechanism along with the packet tracking and upper layer frameworks written for the Avici simulator interface.

We generated hardware parameters from Myricom's documentation or by performing empirical tests on our cluster. Our connectivity topology is a two-dimensional (wrapped) torus of switches, with eight nodes to a switch, and was chosen for its scalability properties over more complex topologies. The links between switches consist of two parallel cables, giving a doubled hop-to-hop bandwidth of 2.56 Gb/s.

The same application codes designed for use with the Avici simulator couple directly to the interface we wrote to communicate with Utah's flit-level myrinet simulator, and similar parsing tools can be used to deduce statistics from the output of simulation runs.

4   Parallel Code Algorithms

Accurate characterization of network performance is a complex task. Simple numbers such as minimum latency or maximum bandwidth are not sufficient metrics to enable cross-technology comparisons. We augment these basic numbers with results from computational core algorithms from real parallel codes in use at Sandia. Results from the tests are deferred until the following section.

A code entitled `token_pass` is our simplest test. It arranges the participating processors in a virtual loop than iterates the passing of a "token" around the loop a certain number of times. Each processor awaits a message from its neighbor to the left, then delays a bit to simulate processing time, then sends a message to its neighbor on the right. By changing the size of the token to be large, we can perform accurate bandwidth measurements. By setting the payload to zero, we find the minimum message latency. Since only two processors at a time are ever involved in a communication, there are no contention effects to filter out from the results.

The codes `fan_in` and `fan_out` are generated from the same source file with different `#define` settings, as they perform quite similar functions. The former simulates a global reduction whereby each processor sends a message to the "host" processor. The sends are staggered slightly to avoid odd synchronization effects in the switches, and to simulate real life in which it is impossible to do clock-synchronized sends on a distributed machine. This test is good for measuring performance degradation due to internal fabric blocking. In the reverse mode, `fan_out` has the host processor sending staggered messages to all the other processors. This tests the blocking effects in the other direction. Performance numbers from `fan_in` and `fan_out` model the startup and shutdown events of parallel applications, which often include global broadcast and reduction phase.

The code `mesh` simulates a computational kernel from a two-dimensional finite element calculation. This class of structured grid codes is very common among the large scale calculations being performed today at the laboratories.

The processors are laid out in a virtual two-dimensional mesh, and each processor will communicate with its immediate neighbors in both the x and y directions. The code performs a number of iterations of computation and communication cycles, which represents the real code's explicit time stepping algorithm as it solves a generalized partial differential equation.

We have made some modifications to the `mesh` code to model a torus topology, which is necessary for a code simulating periodic boundary conditions and arises in calculations on a spherical domain or in free space, for instance. In the toroidal topology, each processor always has four neighbors, unlike in the mesh where edge and corner processors have fewer neighbors.

5   Results

Our results are presented in order of the algorithms we used to test the networks, followed by a summary of all the tests.

5.1   Technology Characterization

We ran the `token_pass` code with a one-byte payload to determine the minimum message latency between neighboring nodes in a 256-member virtual ring for all three technologies. As mentioned earlier, since only two processors at a time are involved in communication, there are no contention effects. We compiled our results and listed the minimum, maximum, average, and standard deviation values for each study in Table 1. As shown, the myrinet technology delivered very good latency and jitter (latency variation). Jitter in the absence of congestion is a function of network topology; it reflects the difference in distance between `token_pass` neighbors in the network. The raw fabric speed for the Avici switch is shown as the last line in Table 1.

Table 1. Minimum message latency results, in μs.

	Min	Avg	Max	σ^2
Myrinet	0.388	0.427	0.869	0.093
Avici GigE	1.380	1.386	1.530	0.024
Conventional GigE	1.564	1.595	3.532	0.244
Avici fabric	0.180	0.186	0.330	0.024

As a result of the Avici's higher fabric speed and path diversity in the 3D-torus topology, myrinet's performance is inferior to that of the Avici, as we configured a 2D torus for myrinet due to its physical constraints. As expected, since the Avici gigabit ethernet routes its packet through the Avici fabric, it had inherited the fabric's low jitter. The increases in its latency amounts to the sum of two transmission delays, when the packet arrives at the input and when it reaches the output of the Avici gigabit ethernet line cards. Store-and-forward switching is necessary here in order to prevent buffer underrun at the outgoing line card switch due to the large speed mismatch; a fabric link is 20 times that of the gigabit ethernet speed. Furthermore, because the ethernet standard imposes a minimum packet size of 64-byte, the original one-byte message was padded before transmission. Therefore, each of the transmission delays is actually $64 * 8/1000 = 0.512\ \mu s$. Two times this value is roughly the increase seen in comparing to the fabric's latency.

The existing Opnet switch model does not emulate processing delay; consequently, the latency values that we obtained through simulation (Table 1 row 3) are better than measured statistics. In our star topology, a packet will traverse either one or three hops depending on whether the immediate neighbor is on the same switch or not. Since switches today typically incur about 10 μs of processing delay, the values listed in Table 1 would have an additional latency of 10 μs at the lower bound, and 30 μs at the upper bound, making the performance of a conventional switch the least favorable of the three.

Using `token_pass` and a 15 MB message, we measured throughput for each technology to verify the correctness of our simulation code. We chose that message size because it is large enough to fill the end-to-end communication pipe, a criterion necessary for throughput measurements. The end-to-end communication pipe is the product of the theoretical bandwidth and the round-trip time. The simulation throughput values are different from the corresponding theoretical bandwidth by less than half a percent.

5.2   Fan-In and Fan-Out

Table 2 lists the maximum, minimum, average, and standard deviation latency results for a 2 kB message from our `fan_in` study. The results for smaller messages go linearly to zero, and are not shown. The simulations had 255 sources each sending one messages to a single destination, thereby causing contention at the destination host machine. Myrinet performance is roughly 20% better than both the conventional and the Avici gigabit ethernet, because it has an effective bandwidth of 1.28 Gb/s to the destination host as opposed to the 0.98 Gb/s of gigabit ethernet.

Table 2. Latency statistics for the `fan_in` code. Units are in μs.

	Min	Avg	Max	σ^2
Myrinet	13.19	1663.51	3313.83	956.55
Avici GigE	538.26	2941.32	4349.76	1055.05
Conventional GigE	24.83	2488.14	4345.48	1343.83
Avici fabric	4.68	129.72	233.49	66.55

Table 3 similarly shows the latency results for a 2 kB message in the `fan_out` studies. A message was broadcast from the source to all destinations. As shown in the table, the conventional gigabit ethernet switches offer the best end-to-end latency by far, because these switches implement multicast in hardware, where a multicast packet is referenced and sent simultaneously to all multicast members. On the other hand, wormhole routing emulates multicast in software; this mechanism requires a source host to send a multicast packet multiple times, one for each multicast destination. Therefore, myrinet exhibited the worst latency performance. The Avici fabric fared better because of its higher aggregate bandwidth and diverse paths.

Table 3. Latency statistics for the `fan_out` code. Units are in μs.

	Min	Avg	Max	σ^2
Myrinet	13.43	1666.60	3319.09	957.94
Avici GigE	63.24	159.54	258.60	45.13
Conventional GigE	24.83	46.17	54.76	11.13
Avici fabric	21.18	141.44	233.43	61.62

5.3 Mesh and Torus

The results for both the **mesh** and **torus** algorithms are included in this section as the codes are identical save for the extra edge connections in **torus**. Similar results will also be seen in both.

Message Latency. The first data we present is a message latency. All messages sent (and received) are recorded with timestamps across all the iterations of the algorithm. The data in Table 4 list the average time for a message to pass through the respective network, along with the standard deviation of the measurements and the maximum and minimum times. It is seen by comparing the average and maximum values for each technology that the maximum message transfer time can be up to an order of magnitude more than the average in the case of myrinet and conventional gigabit ethernet due to the presence of link contention. Only with the Avici switch are the numbers more comparable. These maximum numbers tend to pull up the averages.

The average transfer times for both the Avici and for myrinet are seen to be similar, while the conventional ethernet is larger due to the bottleneck at the second-stage switch in the center of the topology. It would be reasonable to use trunked links from the first-stage switches to the central switch to provide improved bandwidth and alleviate the bottleneck, but this type of scalability will not go too far as commodity switch vendors only provide small numbers of ports per switch. A fat tree using multiple switches is a possible solution, but expensive, and may also not reach high node counts as the switches directly connected to hosts will run out of ports in that case.

Up to a message size of 256 bytes, the myrinet network delivers average latencies about 1 μs lower than does the Avici ethernet. The y-axis intercept of the myrinet average line is about 1 μs while that for the Avici is 2 μs. This is due to the latency induced in the Avici switch core itself, which we measure to be the same amount. Myrinet switches add about 300 ns per hop, with an average of 3 hops per route in a 8×4 two-dimensional torus, to give the y-intercept seen there.

Table 4. Latency simulation results from **mesh** algorithm.

	Avici				Myrinet			
Size	Min	Avg	Max	σ^2	Min	Avg	Max	σ^2
32	1.38	2.57	5.28	0.87	0.58	1.57	5.74	0.90
64	1.65	3.27	7.11	1.10	0.78	2.23	9.85	1.44
128	2.76	5.34	9.72	1.75	1.18	3.74	17.58	2.54
256	4.86	9.18	17.37	3.02	1.98	7.85	55.75	7.07
512	9.09	16.97	30.93	5.44	3.58	16.73	226.71	18.83
1024	17.49	32.56	55.95	10.25	6.78	36.54	441.90	43.75
2048	22.20	59.20	112.59	20.21	13.18	75.89	906.86	93.33

	Ethernet			
Size	Min	Avg	Max	σ^2
32	1.56	49.55	174.77	19.82
64	1.85	49.35	175.06	19.90
128	2.88	49.30	190.47	20.65
256	4.92	48.18	214.20	26.61
512	9.02	48.32	333.28	52.31
1024	17.21	84.04	586.44	98.29
2048	29.52	151.36	1088.28	188.40

In the large message extreme, a 2 kB packet takes on average 59 μs to transfer through the Avici ethernet network, or 76 μs to transfer through the myrinet network; however, the worse case transfer time is a factor of eight greater for the myrinet, almost as bad as in the conventional gigabit ethernet network. Note that these are not raw transfer times, but the result of the interactions with transfers between other pairs of nodes on the network. This leads us to conclude that the effect is from the blocking induced by obstructing messages in the network traffic. The Avici switch is configured to be non-blocking by its extreme path redundancy and the fact that we do not overload the ports on each line card, so any difference between the maximum message transfer time and the average is due to output port contention, *i.e.*, when multiple messages are waiting to enter a single destination host. In the case of the conventional gigabit ethernet, messages may be blocked at the output ports of each of the up to three switches in the path from the source to the destination. The case for Myrinet involves up to six switches, but the bottleneck is not as great as in ethernet due to the multiple routes of the switches.

The message latency values for the related algorithm, torus, are well inside of one standard deviation away from those presented for mesh, and offer no solid conclusions. The algorithmic difference is that slightly more communication is occurring, and it is becoming more regular in that each processor talks to exactly four neighbors in torus. The underlying network is identical in both algorithms. This regularity seemed to help myrinet to provide fairer bandwidth sharing during contention, where results show a decrease in average and maximum latencies and standard deviations for all message sizes. This phenomenon is absent in the Avici case because of its much higher internal fabric speed. Conventional gigabit ethernet switches lack path diversity, and thus the increased offered load presented by the torus algorithm increased the queue depths at the output ports of the switches.

Completion Times. The second data analysis we perform takes into account more of the details of the algorithm. Figure 1 shows plots of the results at a 256 byte message size, for each of the three technologies, and for both of the algorithms.

Each plot shows, for each iteration, and for each processor, the time when that processor completed that iteration. The unlabeled vertical axis is the iteration number of the algorithm, from 1 to 10. The horizontal axis is the global time, in microseconds, and varies from plot to plot as the completion times are quite different with respect to both message size and to network technology.

Each integral band of y-axis is broken up into 256 points, one for each processor, and a dot is placed in a processor's strip in a given iteration number at the time that processor has sent and received all messages necessary to proceed with the calculation of that timestep, or equivalently, when the processor has received the results of the previous iteration from all its neighbors.

One thing to notice in the plots is that some processors always complete much earlier than the others. For the mesh case, these are usually the ones on the corner which have fewer messages to exchange with their neighbors, as there are fewer neighbors. In the torus case, this is not true, and the individual bunches of dots tend to be more even, as the corner and edge processors can not advance too far ahead of the rest of the fray in the middle.

At the relatively small 256 byte message size shown in the figure, the iteration bunches are well separated from each other as most of the time to completion of each iteration is taken up by computation time, represented in our simulation by a sleep of 10 μs. An ideal network which used no time to transfer messages would show perfectly vertical lines at each iteration, with the last line (between 9 and 10) at 90 μs. Anything more than this is the effect of waiting for communications.

Unshown are the plots for the rest of the studied range of message sizes, where looking at just the Avici results, we observe that the total time to completion is gradually increasing, from 140 μs for 32 byte messages, to 900 μs at 2 kilobyte messages, and that each iteration bunch is becoming separated into individual

Fig. 1. Completion times, 256 byte messages, for the three technologies and the two algorithms.

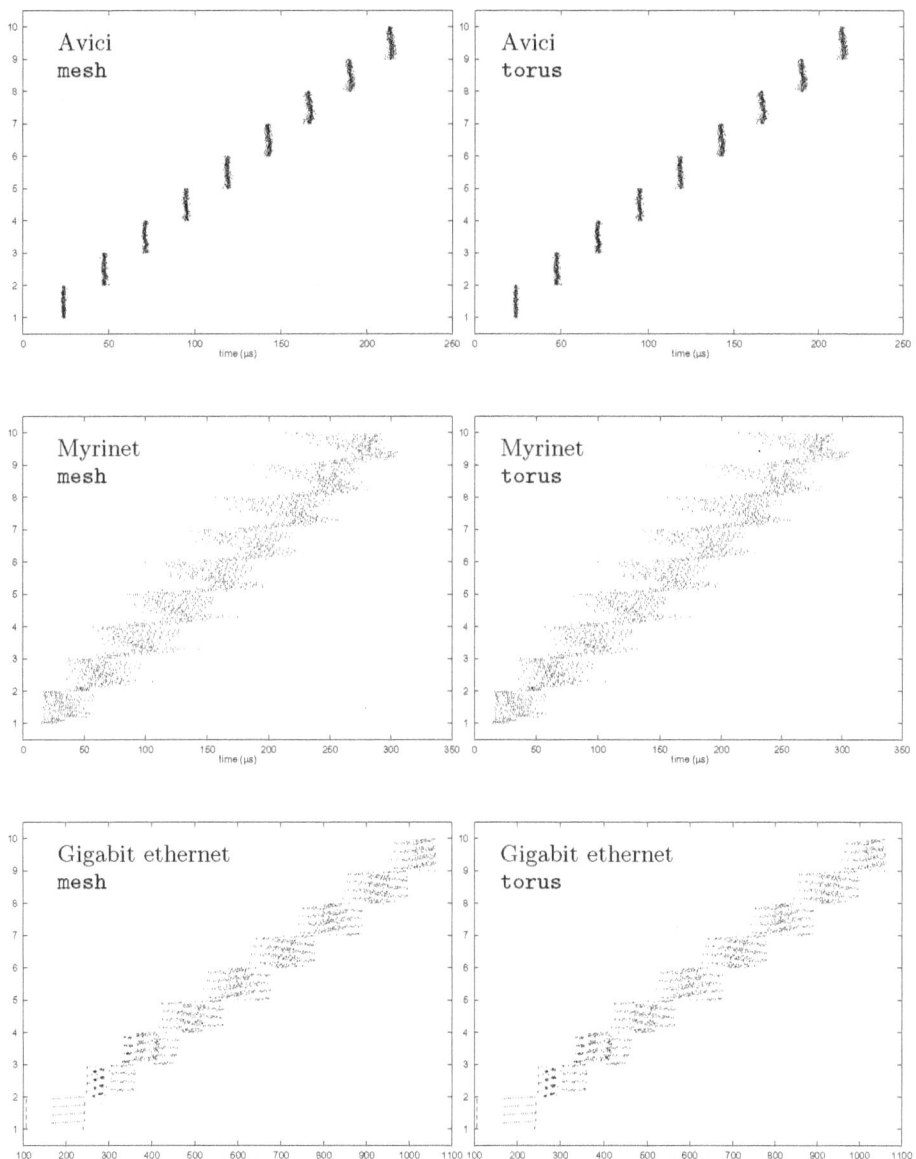

stripes, with the edge processors finishing earlier than the bulk in the center. For the **torus** case there is no obvious striping.

In the myrinet network case, where the groups are fuzzier as the effect of the larger maximum communication times listed in Table 4. The apparent patterns in the large message size plots show the discrepancy in transfer time between nearby nodes and distant nodes in the mesh (or torus) as messages sent farther through the network are subject to more potential points of blocking. Total time to completion for these simulations are the same as for Avici at small message sizes, to about three times longer in the large message case.

The results for the conventional gigabit ethernet cascade of switches feature x-axis ranges consistently three to six times larger than those for the Avici plots. Great multi-millisecond stripes can be seen in the large message size plots for the ethernet where whole regions of the two dimensional mesh proceed into later iterations while other regions are still working on the communications associated with earlier iterations. In the **torus** case this horizontal striping is more pronounced but the iterations are forced to be more temporally bunched as the added toroidal communication patterns introduce more dependencies between processors.

This spread in iteration number is able to occur since there is no global synchronization step between iterations – each processor is permitted to proceed to the next iteration as long as it has received results from the previous iteration from all its neighbors. Following this thought, it can be seen that a certain processor can get up to two iterations in time away from those processors which are neighbors of its immediate neighbors. This continues up to the boundaries of the mesh, which for our 16×16 case means that the spread can proceed up to eight iterations apart.

Fig. 2. Total time for completion, **mesh** and **torus** topologies, with slope of linear fit.

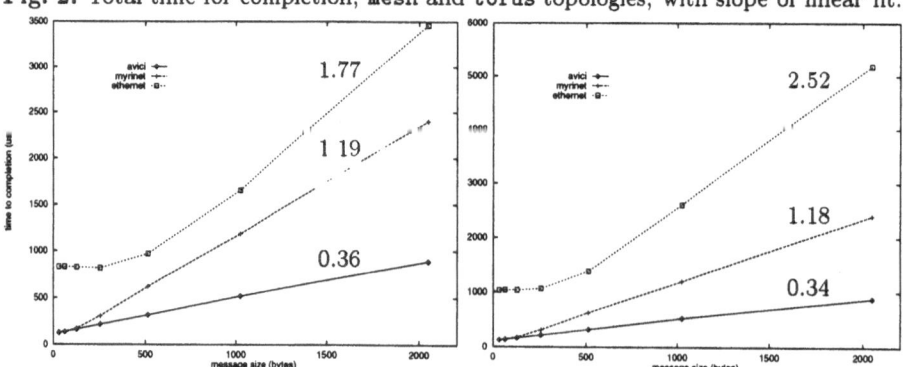

It is interesting to notice the rate of degradation of network performance with increasing message size. This is shown in Figure 2 for the two algorithms. A linear fit of the largest two points for each technology and each algorithm is overlaid on the plot near the corresponding curve. This slope represents the scalability of the given network technology to the two algorithms under increasing message size. Both codes give the same scalability performance on the first two networks, but for conventional gigabit ethernet, the increased offered load seen in the **torus** algorithm renders the network less scalable as message sizes grow.

Summary. The average message latency delivered by the three network technologies is affected both by available bandwidth and the presence of bottlenecks. The conventional cascaded gigabit ethernet without trunking is hampered severely by both these factors. Fabric blocking is seen to be bad for parallel algorithms in that it increases the maximum latency seen by any particular message, and since all messages must eventually reach their destination before the code can complete, that maximum latency value is crucial to the wall-clock performance of a code. The Avici switch is seen to have the smallest amount of fabric blocking, while the myrinet fabric offers potential blocking points at every switch along the path of a message.

The algorithm we tested was chosen due to its ubiquity in parallel scientific computing. It emphasizes the nature of locality in many algorithms in production use today, but points out in the results above that not all communications will physically be local even though in the virtual topology they may appear to be nearest neighbor. This mapping of algorithmic topology to physical topology is crucial for application performance. We did not model an algorithm which involved a global synchronization, which are also common especially for those that do disk input and output. The effects of this communication pattern can be discerned by looking at the **fan_in** and **fan_out** results of Section 5.2.

6 Conclusions

We have presented the results of analysis of three different major network architectures for parallel commodity computing. It is important to choose the network correctly as it can have a large impact on all but the most embarrassingly parallel applications, and may be the source of up to half of the cost of the entire machine. Important factors to consider are raw performance figures such as bandwidth and latency, as well as more complex parameters such as jitter, routing, multicast support, and distribution of blocking in the fabric.

Since our network design goal is to facilitate the performance of real applications, we evaluated the performance of the three network technologies when applied to specific application cores important to our users. In this context we analyzed timing results gathered from the networks and drew conclusions from our knowledge of the network about its effect on performance of the application.

Our simulation results show that myrinet behaves well in the absence of congestion. Under heavy load, its latency suffers due to blocking in wormhole routing. Also myrinet is limited from scaling too far due to the short cable length problem. Future development by Myricom may alleviate that constraint, although the cost to latency or budgets is unknown. The simplicity in the myrinet switch results in low per-connection cost; however, the non-commodity nature of the host network interface cards keep that side of the connection expensive.

Conventional gigabit ethernet switches can not scale to support more than 64 gigabit ethernet ports, which lead to the introduction of a topology which involves cascading multiple stages of small switches. The presence of multiple hops in a path between hosts, and the store-and-forward nature of legacy ethernet leads to unacceptable message delays. Bandwidth bottlenecks at the topmost switch in the cascade are also a problem.

The Avici terabit switch router has an internal fabric which is quite similar to myrinet, in that it is a very high-bandwidth three-dimensional torus using source routing and simple non-buffering switches. The line cards present standard gigabit ethernet connections to hosts, though, in keeping with the current commodity favorite. Our simulations show that the Avici switch outperformed myrinet on large messages (above 512 bytes), and was comparable in the small-message regime. From a cost standpoint, Avici is only slightly cheaper than myrinet for a comparable topology, and is expected to reduce in cost with further penetration of gigabit ethernet into the market.

References

1. Dally, W. "Scalable Switching Fabrics for Internet Routers." Computer Systems Laboratory, Stanford University and Avici Systems. July 1999.
2. Duato, J., Yalmanchili, S., and Ni, L. "Interconnection Networks: an Engineering Approach." *IEEE Computer Society Press.* 1997. pp. 11–16.
3. Held, G. *Ethernet networks: design, implementation, operation, management.* John Wiley & Sons, Inc. 1998, pp. 78–95.
4. Jacobsen, O. J., ed. "From the editor." *The Internet Protocol Journal.* **2**, n. 3, pp. 1ff, 1999.
5. King, A. "Terasim: the Simulator for Avici TSR." Avici Systems, Inc., 1997.
6. Kuo, C. C. "The Avalanche Myrinet Simulation Package." Department of Computer Science. University of Utah. 1997.
7. Seifert, R. *Gigabit Ethernet: technology and applications for high speed LANs,* Addison-Wesley, 1998, pp. 141 280.
8. Stevens, W. *TCP/IP Illustrated.* Addison-Wesley, 1994–1996.
9. Myricom. http://www.myri.com/myrinet/overview/index.html. 1999.
10. High performance networking forum. http://www.hnf.org. 1998.
11. MIL3. http://www.mil3.com/products/modeler/home.html. 1999.
12. Giganet. http://www.giganet.com. 1999.

Comparison and Evaluation of Design Choices for Implementing the Virtual Interface Architecture (VIA)*

Mohammad Banikazemi[1], Bulent Abali[2], and Dhabaleswar K. Panda[1]

[1] Network-Based Computing Laboratory
Dept. of Computer and Info. Science, Columbus, OH 43210
{banikaze,panda}@cis.ohio-state.edu
[2] System Design & Performance, IBM T.J. Watson Research Center
Yorktown Heights, NY 10598
abali@watson.ibm.com

Abstract. The Virtual Interface Architecture (VIA) specification has been developed to standardize user-level network interfaces that provide low latency, high bandwidth communications. Few hardware and software implementations of VIA exist. Since the VIA specification is flexible, different choices exist for implementing various components of VIA such as doorbells, address translation methods, and completion queues. Although previous studies have evaluated the overall performance of different VIA implementations, there has not been a comparative study on the performance of VIA components. In this paper, we evaluate and compare the performance of different implementations of essential VIA components. We discuss the pros and cons of each design approach and describe the required support for implementing each of them. As a user application, we use the NAS Parallel Benchmarks to study the effect of caching the address translation tables on the NIC and to study design issues involved in implementing completion queues. As a hardware platform we use the IBM Netfinity SP cluster running the NT 4.0 operating system and a Myrinet connected cluster of PCs running the Linux operating system.

1 Introduction

Distributed and high performance applications require a low latency, high bandwidth communication facility for exchanging data and synchronization operations. Raw bandwidth of networks have increased significantly in the past few years and networking hardware supporting bandwidths in the order of gigabits per second have become widely available. However, the traditional networking architectures and protocols do not reach the performance of the hardware at the application level. The layered nature of the legacy networking softwares and

---

* This research is supported in part by an IBM Cooperative Fellowship award, an NSF Career Award MIP-9502294, NSF Grant CCR-9704512, an Ameritech Faculty Fellowship award, and grants from the Ohio Board of Regents.

B. Falsafi and M. Lauria (Eds.): CANPC 2000, LNCS 1797, pp. 145–161, 2000.
© Springer-Verlag Berlin Heidelberg 2000

the usage of expensive system calls and extra memory–to–memory copies required in these systems are some of the factors responsible for degradation of the communication subsystem performance as seen by the applications.

In recent years, communication systems [12] such as AM [21], VMMC [8], FM [14], U-Net [20, 22], LAPI [17], and BIP [15] have been proposed by the research community and industry to address these issues. All of these communication systems use much simpler communication protocols in comparison with legacy protocols such as the TCP/IP. The role of the operating system has been much reduced in these systems and in most cases user applications are given direct access to the network interface. The Virtual Interface Architecture (VIA) specification has been developed to standardize these user-level network interfaces and to make their ideas available in commercial systems [4]. The VIA specification has been influenced mostly by the U-Net and VMMC. Since the introduction of VIA, few software and hardware implementations of VIA have become available. The Berkeley VIA [11, 10], Giganet VIA [18], Servernet VIA [18], MVIA [2], and FirmVIA [7] are among these implementations. Different components of VIA have been implemented in different ways in these implementations. Although, the performance of these implementations have been evaluated, there has not been a detailed study of the design choices for implementing different components of VIA.

In this paper, we discuss the essential components of VIA and present different approaches for implementing these components. We discuss the pros and cons of each approach and present the required support for their implementations. In particular, we discuss different possible approaches for implementing components such as software doorbells, virtual-to-physical address translation, and completion queues. We use the NAS Parallel Benchmarks to study the effect of caching the address translation tables on the NIC and to study different completion queue implementations. We use a subset of VIA implemented on an IBM SP-connected Netfinity cluster [7] running the MS Windows NT operating system and a Myrinet-connected cluster of PCs running the Linux operating system to evaluate different components of VIA.

The rest of this paper is organized as follows: In Section 2, we briefly overview the Virtual Interface Architecture, discuss the VIA send and receive operations in detail, and identify different important components involved in these operations. Different design alternatives for implementing different components of VIA are discussed in Section 3. The performance evaluation results are presented in Section 4. Related work is discussed in Section 5. In Section 6, we present our conclusions.

2   Virtual Interface Architecture (VIA)

In this section we first present an overview of VIA. Then, we discuss different events that occur during the send and receive operations and present the basic components involved in performing these operations. We focus on systems with programmable NICs.

2.1   Overview

The Virtual Interface Architecture (VIA) is designed to provide high bandwidth, low latency communication support over a System Area Network (SAN). A SAN interconnects the nodes of a distributed computer system[4]. The VIA specification is designed to eliminate the system processing overhead associated with the legacy network protocols by providing user applications a protected and directly accessible network interface called the Virtual Interface (VI).

Each VI is a communication endpoint. Two VI endpoints on different nodes can be logically connected to form a bidirectional point-to-point communication channel. A process can have multiple VIs. A send queue and a receive queue (also called as work queues) are associated with each VI. Applications post send and receive requests to these queues in the form of VIA descriptors. Each descriptor contains one Control Segment (CS) and zero or more Data Segments (DS) and possibly an Address Segment (AS). Each DS contains a user buffer virtual address. The AS contains a user buffer virtual address at the destination node. Immediate Data mode also exists where the immediate data is contained in the CS. Applications may check the completion status of their VIA descriptors via the *Status* field in CS. A doorbell is associated with each work queue. Whenever an application posts a descriptor, it notifies the VIA provider by ringing the doorbell. Each VI work queue can be associated with a Completion Queue (CQ) too. A CQ merges the completion status of multiple work queues. Therefore, an application need not poll multiple work queues to determine if a request has been completed.

The VIA specification requires that the applications *register* the virtual memory regions which are going to be used by VIA descriptors and user communication buffers. The intent of the memory registration is to give an opportunity to the VIA provider to pin (lock) down user virtual memory in physical memory so that the network interface can directly access user buffers. This eliminates the need for copying data between user buffers and intermediate kernel buffers typically used in traditional network transports.

The VIA specifies two types of data transfer facilities: the traditional send-receive messaging model and the Remote Direct Memory Access (RDMA) model. In the send/receive model, there is a one to one correspondence between send descriptors on the sending side and receive descriptors on the receiving side. In the RDMA model, the initiator of the data transfer specifies the source and destination virtual addresses on the local and remote nodes, respectively. The RDMA write operation is a required feature of the VIA specification while the RDMA read operation is optional. In this paper, we focus on the send/receive messaging facilities of VIA.

2.2   Message Passing in VIA

For sending and receiving messages, the following major steps are taken:
Constructing the Descriptor: The application creates a descriptor in a registered memory region. This descriptor includes the virtual address of the send or receive buffer and its length. The message buffer is allocated from a registered memory region. The descriptor also contains a status field which the VIA provider updates upon completion of the operation. **Posting the Descriptor:** The application posts the descriptor using the `VipPostSend` or `VipPostRecv` function call. Through the doorbell mechanism, the NIC is informed about the existence of the posted descriptor. **Obtaining the Descriptor by the NIC:** The NIC retrieves from the descriptor the information required for sending or receiving a message. The information includes the address and the length of the user buffer and the address of the status field of the descriptor. **Performing the Operation:** The NIC performs the send operation by injecting the data into the network after it is transferred from the user buffer to the NIC. For the receive operation, the message is received from the network into the NIC memory and then into the user buffer. **Marking the Descriptor as Complete:** After performing the send or receive operation, the NIC marks the status field of the VIA descriptor as complete. If a CQ is associated with the VI, the NIC also makes an entry in the CQ so that the application can detect the completion through CQ as well. **Application Detecting the Completion of the Operation:** The application can check the status of the operation using `VipSendDone` and `VipRecvDone` in a non-blocking fashion, `VipSendWait` and `VipRecvWait` in a blocking fashion, and `VipCQDone` and `VipCQWait` if a CQ is associated with the corresponding work queue.

2.3   Basic Components of VIA

Considering different operations involved in sending and receiving messages, three major components can be identified as the basic components of the message passing operations. These components are: 1) informing the NIC of an outstanding send or receive request, 2) the NIC obtaining information about the outstanding operation and corresponding user data buffers and performing the operation, and 3) the NIC informing the user program of the completion of send and receive operations. In order to implement the send and receive operations efficiently, it is crucial to implement these components as efficiently as possible. In the next section, we present different design alternatives for implementing these components and present the pros and cons of each of them. It should be noted that we only consider the methods which do not require any unnecessary data copies.

3   Design Alternatives

In this section, we discuss the implementation of doorbells which are related to the first component of message passing operations and are used for informing the NIC of the existence of outstanding send or receive descriptors. We also study different implementations of virtual-to-physical address translation and the possibility of caching descriptors. These two issues relate to the second basic component or the mechanism through which the NIC obtains information about the outstanding operations and corresponding user data buffers. The third component, the mechanism through which the user program is informed of the completion of send and receive operations, is also discussed with respect to the implementation of completion queues.

3.1 Doorbells

VIA specifies that each VI be associated with a pair of doorbells. The purpose of a doorbell is to notify the NIC of the existence of newly posted descriptors. Doorbells can be implemented in hardware or software. However, most of the current generation NICs do not provide any hardware support for doorbells, they need to be implemented in software. Therefore, in this paper, we focus on the design choices for implementing doorbells in software.

Approach 1 (D1): One approach for implementing doorbells in software is allocating space for each doorbell in the NIC memory and mapping it to the address space of the process. The user application rings the doorbell by simply setting the corresponding bit in the NIC memory or by writing the address of the descriptor (or the descriptor itself) in the NIC memory. To protect a doorbell from being tampered by other processes, doorbells of different processes need to be on separate memory pages in the NIC since protection granularity of a kernel is one page (e.g. 4KB). The advantage of using this mechanism is that there is no need to go through the kernel for ringing the doorbells and this operation can be implemented in user space. The disadvantage of this approach is the cost of polling the VIs for send descriptors. As the number of active VIs increases, the NIC spends more time polling the send doorbells to check if there is any send descriptor to be processed. This limits the scalability of the communication subsystem. The other shortcoming of this approach when a single word or bit is used for each VI is that when a descriptor is posted, the subsequent post cannot proceed until the NIC becomes aware of the first posted descriptor. To overcome this shortcoming, a circular buffer can be used as a queue for each VI such that multiple descriptors can be posted by the user application even when the NIC firmware is busy performing other operations (such as sending and receiving messages) and hasn't become aware of some of the posted descriptors yet.

Approach 2 (D2): In order to avoid the cost of polling of VIs for send descriptors, a second approach in which the kernel intervention is required can be used. In this approach, a centralized queue of send descriptors (or handles to descriptors) are maintained by the NIC. Since all VIs share the same centralized queue, a mechanism is required to guarantee that this queue is accessed in an operating system safe fashion. Thus kernel intervention is required. In this approach, the need for polling all the active VIs is eliminated and the NIC needs to only look at the centralized queue for send descriptors. The disadvantage of this approach is the added delay of going through the kernel. The advantage of this approach is the elimination of the NIC polling active send requests.

The problem of polling send descriptors does not occur for receive descriptors. When a message is received at the NIC, the VI id of the received message is used to obtain the receive descriptor posted for that particular VI. If for some reasons the posted receive descriptors need to be preprocessed before the messages arrive (for example to perform the virtual-to-physical address translation which will be discussed later) then finding receive descriptors requires polling the active VIs and causes a similar problem.

3.2 Caching Descriptors

As discussed in Section 2.2, when the NIC recognizes that a descriptor is posted, it needs to obtain the information about the message (such as the user buffer address and the size of the message) from the descriptor. The descriptors are constructed by the VIA applications and therefore are stored in the host memory. The question is whether the host initiates the transfer of the descriptor or the NIC. Since DMA is the only way by which most NICs can access the host memory but the host can use PIO for transferring data to the NIC, there is a tradeoff between these two approaches with respect to the size of the descriptor being transferred from the host memory to the NIC memory. For the receive descriptors, the advantage of moving the descriptors to the NIC memory when the descriptors get posted is that the time for this transfer is not part of the the message latency. It should be noted that the host processor is required to be involved in PIO operations while the DMA operations are performed without the involvement of the host processor. We'll have a performance evaluation of these methods in Section 4.2.

3.3 Address Translation

Most NICs (including the widely used PCI based NICs) use physical addresses for performing DMA operations, whereas VIA descriptor elements, e.g. user buffer addresses, are virtual addresses. Therefore virtual-to-physical address translation is required. This address translation is required not only for transferring data, but also for accessing descriptors (if they are not cached in the NIC memory) and updating the status of operations by NIC. VIA specifies a memory registration mechanism to ensure that the page frames which are accessed by the NIC are present in the physical memory. Registered virtual memory pages are pinned down in physical memory. Before data is transferred to or from these memory regions, the virtual addresses should be translated to physical addresses. It should be noted that using approaches such as using a preallocated pinned contiguous buffer (at the boot time) from which user buffers are allocated or using DMA regions through which data transfers to and from NIC are performed is not reasonable. Allocating user buffers from a preallocated buffer requires modifications to the applications to use a custom routine for user buffer allocations. Using DMA regions for data transfers is not a viable choice because of the required extra data copies to and from these regions at the sending and receiving nodes.

Two critical issues in implementing the address translation for VIA are the location of address translation tables (commonly known as Translation Lookaside Buffers or TLBs) and the method of accessing them (i.e. whether the host or the NIC performs the translation). The VIA TLBs can be located in the host or NIC memory and can be accessed by the host or the NIC. Therefore, there are four possible approaches for performing the address translation: 1) the TLB is in the host memory and host performs the address translation, 2) the TLB is stored in the NIC memory and the NIC does the address translation, 3) the TLB is located in the host memory and the NIC performs the translation, and 4) the TLB is in the NIC memory and the host performs the address translation. Among these approaches, the fourth approach does not provide any advantage over the other approaches and has no practical use. In the rest of this section, we discuss the other three approaches in more detail.

Approach 1 (AT1): In this approach, the TLB is located in the host memory and the address translation is performed by the host. Since the user processes can not be trusted to provide the physical addresses, the translation (the TLB lookup) is performed in kernel space. The disadvantage of this approach is the need for user to kernel context switching. Since the VIA requires all data buffers to be in registered memory regions, the TLB lookup cost can be minimized by the creation of an address translation table for each registered memory region. This table should include the addresses of all the physical page frames which correspond to the memory region. By creating such a table at the memory registration time, the address translation can be efficiently done by indexing this table. The advantage of this approach is that the NIC memory requirement is small since the TLB is located in the host memory.

Approach 2 (AT2): In this approach, the TLB is located in the NIC memory and the NIC is responsible for performing the virtual-to-physical address translation. The limitation of this approach is the size of memory required for the TLB. For example, in order to support 256 MB of registered memory, a TLB of 256 KB is required. The available memory of the NIC is usually much smaller than that of the host, and the memory required for storing the TLB puts a heavy burden on the NIC resources and makes the implementation not scalable.

Approach 3 (AT3): In this approach, the TLB is located in the host memory but the translation is done by the NIC. The advantage of using this approach is that there is no need for using a big portion of the NIC memory for storing the TLB. The disadvantage of this approach is that the NIC requires to access the host memory for obtaining the translation. This access is usually done by a DMA operation and may have a high DMA startup delay. In order to minimize this problem, a portion of the NIC memory can be used to cache the translations such that future references to a particular page frame can be resolved without accessing the host memory. The size and characteristics of this cache along with the behavior of the application programs affect the overall performance of the address translation operation, if this approach is used.

We discuss the cost of implementing these approaches for the virtual-to-physical address translation in Section 4.3.

3.4   Completion Queues

As mentioned in Section 2.1, each work queue can be associated with a Completion Queue (CQ). In these cases, the notification of completed requests should be directed to a CQ on a per-VI work queue basis. The description of the `VipCQDone` states that it is possible to have multiple threads of a process wait on a CQ and its associated work queues [4]. Therefore, the VIA provider updates both the work queue and its associated CQ upon the completion of a request. Marking a descriptor as complete (in the work queue) is done by DMAing the status field of the descriptor (with the bit corresponding to the completion of the operation set) from the NIC to the host. For supporting the CQs, there are two possible approaches.

Approach 1 (CQ1): In this approach, the NIC in addition to updating the status field of the descriptor, inserts the descriptor handle into the associated CQ. The disadvantage of this approach is that an extra DMA operation is required for the insertion of the descriptor handle to the CQ. The advantage of this approach is that the application spends constant time checking for a completed operation regardless of the number of work queues associated with a CQ.

Approach 2 (CQ2): In this approach, no entries are added into the CQ. In fact there is no CQ in the host memory. The completed operations are simply found by polling the work queues associated with the CQ. That is, the `VipCQDone` function is implemented such that either `VipSendDone` or `VipRecvDone` is called for each work queue associated with the CQ. The advantage of this approach is that NIC need not perform a DMA operation for inserting the handle of the completed descriptor into the CQ. The disadvantage of using polling in this manner is that the method does not scale well with the increase in the number of work queues associated with a CQ. However, since in many applications each node communicates only with a small set of other processes, and therefore a limited number of work queues are associated with each CQ, this approach may be viable for implementing CQs.

We compare the cost of the implementation of these two approaches in Section 4.4. We also investigate how the scalability issue of the second approach can be dealt with.

4   Performance Evaluation

In order to evaluate different design alternatives discussed in Section 3 of this paper, we implemented a subset of VIA on two different systems. The first system consisted of 300 MHz Pentium II PCs with 128 MB of SDRAM and a 33 MHz/32-bit PCI bus and ran the Linux 2.0 operating system. The Myrinet switches and 33 MHz LANAI 4.3 NICs were used as the interconnect [9]. The second system was an IBM Netfinity SP switch-connected Cluster [7]. This cluster consisted of 450 MHz Pentium III PCs. Each node had 128 MB of SDRAM and a 33 MHz/32-bit PCI bus and ran the NT 4.0 operating system. These PCs were interconnected by an IBM SP switch and 100 MHz TB3PCI NICs [7]. These two testbeds represent a wide range of available network-based computing platforms.

In the rest of this section, we first present the cost of the basic operations in these two systems. Then, we evaluate and compare different alternatives for implementing different components of VIA.

4.1 Basic Operations

Since Programmed I/O (PIO) and DMA are the major methods for transferring data between the host and the NIC, we measured the cost of these operations. We also measured the cost of user to kernel space switch for both systems. For our NT testbed we used the Fast IO Dispatch method [19] and for our Linux testbed, we used a fast trap. These measurements are presented in Table 1.

Table 1. Cost of basic operations in the Myrinet-Linux and SP-NT testbeds.

Operation	Myrinet–Linux	SP-NT
Host PIO Write	0.16 μs/word	0.33 μs/word
Host PIO Read	0.49 μs/word	0.87 μs/word
User-space to Kernel-space	1.06 μs (Fast Trap)	2.27 μs (Fast IO Dispatch)
DMA Startup (host to NIC)	1.72 μs	1.78 μs
DMA Startup (NIC to host)	1.47 μs	1.61 μs

4.2 Caching Descriptors

As discussed in Section 3.2, the choice of caching the send descriptors when they are posted depends on the cost PIO and DMA operations. From the cost of these operations in our testbeds (Table 1), it can be seen that transferring up to five words through PIO is less time consuming than using the DMA in the Netfinity SP system. In the Myrinet-Linux testbed, transferring up to ten words can be done in a faster manner by using PIO. It should be noted that in neither of our testbeds, PCI write combining was used. If a system supports PCI write combining, a larger number of words can be transferred by PIO before the point where using DMA becomes more efficient. Another factor which affects the decision about caching send descriptors is the CPU utilization. While the host processor is not involved if DMA is used, using PIO requires the host to perform the transfer and increases the host CPU cycles used for send operations.

The situation is slightly different for receive descriptors. If the receive descriptors are to be accessed by DMA operations, a simple implementation performs the DMA when the corresponding message is received at the NIC of the receiving node. This will result in an increase in the latency by the cost of transferring the descriptor to the NIC. However, if the descriptor is cached at the time it gets posted, in most cases the cost of this transfer is not part of the send and transmission times of the message. Even if the NIC is responsible for the transfer, it is possible to mask the transfer time for receive descriptors by transferring the descriptors before the corresponding messages arrive at the NIC. However, implementing this feature requires an increase in the complexity of the NIC firmware. Furthermore, the NIC may need to poll all the receive queues of active VIs to see if there is any posted receive descriptor to be processed. Since the NIC processors are usually much slower than the host processors (4.5 times in our Netfinity cluster and 10 times in our Myrinet network), the increase in the complexity of firmware and the need for polling can degrade the performance of the firmware and increase the latency of messages. Furthermore, if the rate of incoming messages is high and/or the rate of messages being sent out from a particular node is high, the NIC may not get a chance to get the receive descriptor before the message arrives. In these situations, before NICs can retrieve the information about the descriptor, it has to store the message in a temporary location. If the message is kept in the NIC memory, messages might be dropped or the reception of messages might need to be stalled because of the usually small amount of available NIC memory. If the temporary storage is in the host memory (with an address known to the NIC), there will be an unnecessary data copy. Either way, the performance of the communication subsystem will degrade.

It is to be noted that the whole descriptor need not to be cached. Only those portions of the descriptor which are required by the NIC should be cached. In particular, the address and size of the data buffer, the control field of the descriptor (which includes the information such as the type of the operation) and the address of the status field of the descriptor should be cached on the NIC.

4.3   Address Translation

Three approaches for performing the address translation were discussed in Section 3.3. In the first approach (AT1), where the TLB is in the host memory and the host performs the translation, the cost of the address translation is essentially the one time user space to kernel space switch for each send or receive operation and the cost of the table lookup for each page frame of the send or receive buffer. In order to reduce the TLB lookup cost, one table for each registered memory can be created upon the registration of the memory region. This table includes the physical addresses of (the beginning of) all the page frames that the memory region spans over. By creating such a table, the virtual-to-physical address translation can be done by indexing the address translation table without any need for searching the table or multiple indirections. The Average cost of the address translation when the AT1 approach is used, is shown in the first row of Table 2. The overall cost of the translation is this additional cost plus the time required for accessing the TLB for each page frame of the send or receive buffer.

In the second approach (AT2), where the TLB is located in the NIC memory, a similar mechanism can be used. In this method, there is no need to go through the kernel for the address translation. The second line in Table 2 shows the additional cost for performing the translation by using this approach. It can be seen that this additional cost is zero. The overall cost of the translation for each send or receive operation is equal to the number of page frames of the send or receive buffers times the time required to access an element of the TLB. The cost of registering memory regions is increased in this method because the

Table 2. Cost of different methods of implementing the virtual-to-physical address translation. (See Figures 1 through 4 for the value of Miss Rate for different benchmarks.)

AT Method	Location/ Translator	NIC Memory Requirement	Myrinet-Linux Avg. Additional Cost	SP-NT Avg. Additional Cost
AT1	host/host	None	1.06	2.27
AT2	NIC/NIC	Proportional	0	0
AT3	host/NIC	Constant	$1.72 \times Miss\ Rate$	$1.78 \times Miss\ Rate$

TLB should be created and transferred to the NIC. Creating the TLB on the NIC requires multiple PIO write operations (based on the size of the registered memory). However, since the memory registration happens infrequently, this increase in the cost of memory registration can be tolerated. The more limiting factor for implementing this approach is the large memory space required for keeping the TLBs on the NIC. While there are NICs with large amount of memory, most NICs provide a limited amount of memory. On the other hand, with the increase in the size of available host physical memory and registered memory regions, the required memory on the NIC increases. These requirements make the third approach a more realistic and scalable approach for implementing the address translation.

In the third approach (AT3), the NIC perform the translation while the TLB is stored in the host memory. Since the TLB is stored in the host memory, the memory requirement on the NIC is minimal. However, if for every address translation the NIC is required to access the host memory (through DMA) this approach performs much worse than the second approach. In order to reduce the cost of the address translation while the size of required NIC memory is kept low, caching the address translations is used. If the translation of a particular physical address is found in a software cache (kept in the NIC memory), the translation can be performed quickly by accessing the corresponding cache entry. If the translation is not found in the cache, an access to the TLB in host memory (through DMA) is required (Table 2).

In order to evaluate the effectiveness of caching and estimating the required cache size, and in the absence of the existence a wide variety of applications and benchmarks for VIA, we used the NAS Parallel Benchmarks (NPB) [3,5] version 2.3 to gather the list of addresses being referred in these benchmarks. We profiled the NAS benchmarks to record the addresses of the send and receive buffers being used in these benchmarks. We ran the benchmark with 4, 16, and 64 processes and used two different problem sizes: class A and class B. We used different TLB cache sizes and degrees of associativity. It should be noted that the TLB cache is implemented in software and is stored in the NIC memory. (We haven't presented the data for the Embarrassingly Parallel (EP) and Fast Fourier Transform (FT) benchmarks because the communication operations used in these benchmarks are such that the performance of the address translation does not affect the execution time of the program significantly.)

Figure 1 shows the cache miss rates for the class A NAS benchmarks on a system with 128-entry direct-mapped caches. The results for running these pro-

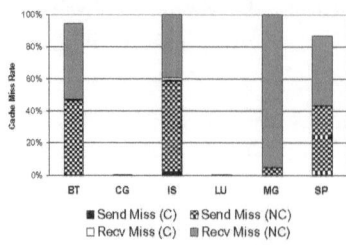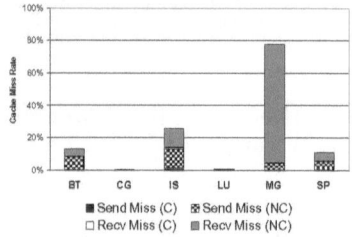

Fig. 1. The cache miss rate for the NAS benchmarks (class A) using four processes (left) and 16 processes (right) with 128-entry direct-mapped caches. C and NC denote compulsory and non-compulsory misses, respectively.

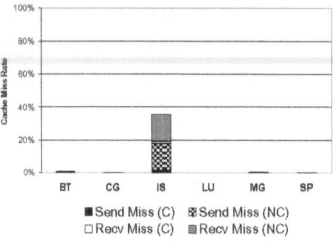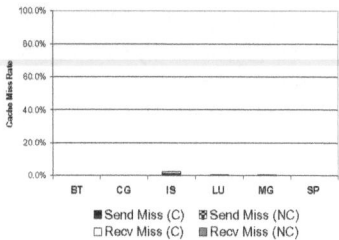

Fig. 2. The cache miss rate for the NAS benchmarks (class A) using four processes (left) and 16 processes (right) with 1024-entry direct-mapped caches and 128-entry 8-way associative caches. (The miss rates are identical for both of these cache types.) C and NC denote compulsory and non-compulsory misses, respectively.

grams on four and 16 processes are shown and cache misses are broken down into send and receive misses (compulsory and non-compulsory). It can be seen that with such a small cache and when four processes are used, in four of the benchmarks more than 80% of memory accesses result in a cache miss. When the programs are run on 16 processes the number of cache misses reduces significantly. If the cache size is increased to 1024 (Fig. 2), the cache miss rates for all benchmarks other than IS become negligible. Increase in the number of processes result in an decrease in message sizes and this compensate the effect of the increase in the number of messages being transmitted. It is interesting to see that miss rates are identical for a 1024-entry direct mapped cache or a 1024-entry cache with the degree of associativity of eight. The access time of a software direct-mapped cache is less than that for a software associative cache. Therefore, given the same performance, using a direct-mapped cache is preferred over an associative cache when implemented in software.

Figure 3 shows the cache miss rates for the class B NAS benchmarks on a system with 128-entry direct-mapped caches. Note that the results shown in this figure have been obtained from running these programs using 16 and 64 processes. The cache miss rates for systems with 1024-entry caches are shown in Figure 4. A similar pattern to those for class A benchmarks (smaller problem

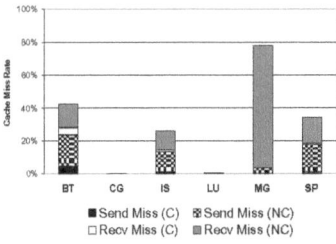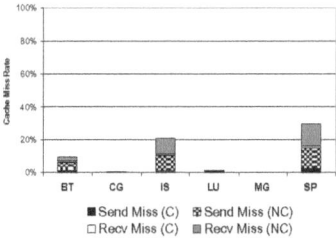

Fig. 3. The cache miss rate for the NAS benchmarks (class B) using 16 processes (left) and 64 processes (right) with 128-entry direct-mapped caches. C and NC denote compulsory and non-compulsory misses, respectively.

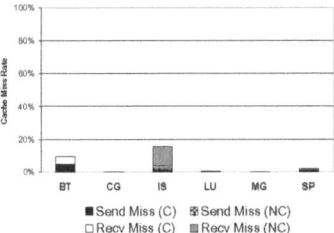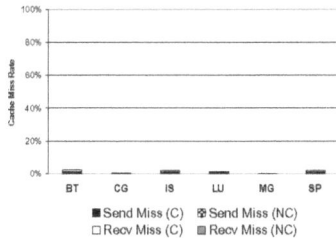

Fig. 4. The cache miss rate for the NAS benchmarks (class B) using 16 processes (left) and 64 processes (right) with 1024-entry direct-mapped caches and 128-entry 8-way associative caches. (The miss rates are identical for both of these cache types.) C and NC denote compulsory and non-compulsory misses, respectively.

size) can be seen. It is interesting to compare the cache miss rates for these benchmarks with different problem sizes. When the benchmarks use 16 processes, increasing the problem size (from class A to class B) result in an increase in the cache miss rates. Using caches with 1024 entries are shown to be enough to make the cache miss rates for all class A benchmarks negligible. However, when the problem size is increased, the BT and IS benchmarks produce a significant number of misses.

It can be seen that providing a larger cache size reduces the number of misses significantly. The required cache size for making cache misses negligible is shown to be very small. We have also studied the effect of using victim caches. The results show that the gain obtained from using victim caches is minimal. (We do not present the results for victim caches here because of the space limitation.) It should be noted that the NAS benchmarks are only representative of scientific applications and other applications and benchmarks need to be used to evaluate the caching for VIA too.

It should be noted that for receive operations, the cost of address translation might be hidden if the translation is done before the message arrives. The AT1 method can be easily used to take advantage of this characteristic. But the AT2 and AT3 methods can be implemented more easily if the translation is done when the message arrives. When the AT2 and AT3 methods are used, performing the translation before the message arrives increases the complexity of the firmware and can decrease the overall performance of the communication subsystem. Another issue which should be considered is that while for performing the address translation by using the AT3 approach the host processor is not involved, the AT1 approach requires the host to perform the translation.

Another important issue worth mentioning is the translation of the address of the status field of descriptors. Since after the completion of an operation, the status field of the corresponding descriptor should be updated, the NIC needs to know the physical address of the status field. (Obviously, this update could be done by issuing an interrupt to the host, but this approach will be too costly to be used in situations where the application is polling for the completion of an operation.) If the address translation is to be done by the NIC, there will be a need to access the TLB one more time to perform the translation of the status field address for each operation.

4.4   Completion Queues

We presented two approaches for implementing the completion queues in Section 3.4. The cost for the first approach (CQ1) is practically the cost of NIC performing a DMA operation to add an entry to the CQ. In the second approach (CQ2) the work queues associated with a CQ are polled. CQ2 approach won't be scalable if the number of work queues associated with a CQ is large. On the other hand in many real-life applications each process usually communicates only with a small set of processes. In order to evaluate the performance of CQ2, we used the NAS benchmarks. Among the NAS benchmarks, the LU and MG benchmarks use the MPI_Waitany function to receive any message from a collection of processes. Usage of this primitive is similar to waiting to receive a message by examining the completion queue associated with a set of VI receive queues. In order to find out the number of work queues associated with a CQ, we recorded the number of processes with which a process communicates and waits for the completion of the transfers by using the MPI_Waitany function. Table 3 shows the average number of processes a process communicates with using MPI_Waitany function in a 64-process system running the LU and MG benchmarks. The data shows that processes communicate with only a small set of processes. For example, in MG benchmark running on 64 nodes, each process communicates to 6.5 other processes on the average. Polling the VI work queues of these 6.5 processes is less time consuming (0.52 microseconds) than the NIC adding a completion entry to CQ (1.61 microseconds). It can be seen that the cost of the CQ2 approach is less than that of the CQ1 approach for these applications. It should be noted that the host CPU utilization is higher for the CQ2 approach.

Table 3. Comparison between different approaches for implementing CQs.

Bench-mark	Number of Processes	Avg. # of Recv Queues / CQ	Average CQ2 Cost	Myrinet-Linux CQ1 Cost	SP-NT CQ1 Cost
LU	4	2	0.16	1.47	1.61
LU	16	3	0.24	1.47	1.61
LU	64	3.5	0.28	1.47	1.61
MG	4	3	0.24	1.47	1.61
MG	16	4.6	0.37	1.47	1.61
MG	64	6.5	0.52	1.47	1.61

5   Related Work

There have been several implementations of VIA. The Berkeley VIA (Version
1) [11] is one of the first software implementations of the VIA. (This implementation is a partial implementation of VIA mainly done to obtain a better insight
on different aspects of the implementation of the VIA.) In this implementation,
a memory page on the NIC memory has been used for the implementation of
a pair of doorbells. The doorbells for send queues are polled for finding outstanding send descriptors. This polling is expensive and increases linearly with
the number of active VIs. The Berkeley VIA does not perform any caching of
descriptors. In other words, for sending messages NIC has to access the host
memory twice: once for obtaining the descriptor and once for obtaining the data
itself. In this implementation, only a subset of descriptors are moved between
the host and the NIC to reduce the high cost of transferring the descriptors.
The Berkeley VIA (Version 2) [10] is based on the the Berkeley VIA (Version 1)
implementation and adds memory registration and increased VI/user support.
In this implementation each memory page on the NIC can support up to 256
pairs of doorbells that belong to a single process. For the address translation a
buffer with limited size on the NIC is used for the TLB. If the size of registered
memory is bigger than what can be supported with this table, the translation
of some portions of the registered memory won't be present in the NIC TLB. In
these cases the host memory is accessed to obtain the translation. The location of
the host buffers holding the complete translations for registered memory regions
are known to the NIC. The FirmVIA [7] is an experimental implementation of
the Virtual Interface Architecture for the IBM SP Switch-Connected NT cluster
which is one the newest clustering platforms available. In this implementation,
the address translation is performed by the host. Descriptors are also cached
for improving the performance. The performance of GigaNet cLAN [1] and the
Tandem ServerNet VIA implementations are studied in [18].

The effect of using caching for address translation for user-level network interfaces (and in particular U-Net) has been presented in [22]. The address translation issues have also been studied in [16] and the address translation methods
are classified according to where lookup and the miss handling are performed.
The major difference between the address translation in systems discussed in
these papers and that in systems supporting VIA is the memory registration

mechanism required by VIA. In VIA, all the memory locations used as send and receive buffers are in registered memory regions and VIA implementations are not concerned with the possibility of accessing a location which belongs to swapped page frames.

The Virtual Interface Benchmark (VIBe) [13] has been recently developed for evaluating the performance of VIA implementations under different communication scenarios and with respect to the implementation of different components of VIA.

6 Conclusions

In this paper, we studied different components of VIA for sending and receiving messages. We presented various approaches for implementing different components of VIA and evaluated these approaches on two different platforms. We showed that caching the descriptors in the NIC memory can improve the performance of the communication subsystem by overlapping some portions of the receive overhead with those of send and transmission overhead. Using the NAS benchmarks, we showed that a small caching area for the address translation entries eliminates the need for accessing TLBs stored in the host memory for most of the send and receive operations. We also discussed the issues related to the implementation of completion queues. We showed that a software implementation (polling) performs well for the NAS benchmarks because of the limited number of processes with which a given process communicate. We also presented a few approaches for implementing VIA doorbells in software. We are currently engaged in the design and implementation of doorbells in hardware. We plan to study and evaluate design choices for implementing RDMA operations and different levels of reliability provided by VIA. We also plan to study the effect of different design choices on the overall performance of the communication subsystem under a wide variety of workloads.

Acknowledgements: We would like to thank Darius Buntinas, Sencer Kutlug, and the anonymous reviewers for their invaluable suggestions and helpful comments.

Additional Information: A number of papers related to this research can be obtained from the following Web pages: Network-Based Computing Laboratory (http://nowlab.cis.ohio-state.edu) and Parallel Architecture and Communication Group (http://www.cis.ohio-state.edu/~panda/pac.html).

References

1. GigaNet Corporations. http://www.giganet.com/.
2. M-VIA: A High Performance Modular VIA for Linux.
   http://www.nersc.gov/research/FTG/via/.

3. NAS Parallel Benchmarks. http://www.nas.nasa.gov/Software/NPB/.
4. Virtual Interface Architecture Specification. http://www.viarch.org/.
5. D. H. Bailey, E. Barszcz, L. Dagum, and H.D. Simon. NAS Parallel Benchmark Results. Technical Report 94-006, RNR, 1994.
6. M. Banikazemi, R. K. Govindaraju, R. Blackmore, and D. K. Panda. Implementing Efficient MPI on LAPI for IBM RS/6000 SP Systems: Experiences and Performance Evaluation. In *Proceedings of the 13th International Parallel Processing Symposium*, pages 183–190, April 1999.
7. M. Banikazemi, V. Moorthy, L. Hereger, D. K. panda, and B. Abali. Efficient Virtual Interface Architecture Support for IBM SP Switch-Connected NT Clusters. Accepted for presentation at International Parallel and Distributed Processing Symposium, May 2000.
8. M. Blumrich, C. Dubnicki, E. W. Felten, K. Li, and M. R. Mesarina. Virtual-Memory-Mapped Network Interfaces. In *IEEE Micro*, pages 21–28, February 1995.
9. N. J. Boden, D. Cohen, et al. Myrinet: A Gigabit-per-Second Local Area Network. *IEEE Micro*, pages 29–35, Feb 1995.
10. P. Buonadonna, J. Coates, S. Low, and D.E. Culler. Millennium Sort: A Cluster-Based Application for Windows NT using DCOM, River Primitives and the Virtual Interface Architecture. In *Proceedings of the 3rd USENIX Windows NT Symposium*, July 1999.
11. P. Buonadonnaa, A. Geweke, and D.E. Culler. An Implementation and Analysis of the Virtual Interface Architecture. In *Proceedings of the Supercomputing (SC)*, pages 7–13, Nov. 1998.
12. D. E. Culler and J. P. Singh. *Parallel Computer Architecture: A Hardware-Software Approach*. Morgan Kaufmann, March 1998.
13. S. N. Kutlug, M. Banikazemi, D. K. panda, and P. Sadayappan. VIBe: A Microbenchmark Suite for Evaluating Virtual Interface Architecture (VIA) Implementations. Technical Report OSU-CISRC-01/00-TR02, The Ohio State University, January 2000.
14. S. Pakin, M. Lauria, and A. Chien. High Performance Messaging on Workstations: Illinois Fast Messages (FM). In *Proceedings of the Supercomputing*, 1995.
15. Loc Prylli and Bernard Tourancheau. BIP: A New Protocol Designed for High Performance Networking on Myrinet. *In Proceedings of the International Parallel Processing Symposium Workshop on Personal Computer Based Networks of Workstations*, 1998. http://lhpca.univ-lyon1.fr/.
16. Ioannis Schoinas and Mark D. Hill. Address Trnslation Mechanisms in Network Interfaces. In *Proceedings of the 4th International Symposium on High Performance Computer Architecture*, February 1998.
17. G. Shah, J. Nieplocha, J. Mirza, C. Kim, R. Harrison, R. K. Govindaraju, K. Gildea, P. DiNicola, and C. Bender. Performance and Experience with LAPI - a New High-Performance Communication Library for the IBM RS/6000 SP. In *Proceedings of the International Parallel Processing Symposium*, March 1998.
18. E. Speight, H. Abdel-Shafi, and J. K. Bennett. Realizing the Performance Potential of the Virtual Interface Architecture. In *Proceedings of the International Conference on Supercomputing*, June 1999.
19. P. G. Viscarola and W. A. Mason. *Windows NT Device Driver Development*. Macmillan Technical Publishing, 1999.
20. T. von Eicken, A. Basu, V. Buch, and W. Vogels. U-Net: A User-level Network Interface for Parallel and Distributed Computing. In *ACM Symposium on Operating Systems Principles*, 1995.
21. T. von Eicken, D. E. Culler, S. C. Goldstein, and K. E. Schauser. Active Messages: A Mechanism for Integrated Communication and Computation. In *International Symposium on Computer Architecture*, pages 256–266, 1992.
22. M. Welsh, A. Basu, and T. von Eicken. Incorporating Memory Management into User-Level Network Interfaces. In *Proceedings of Hot Interconnects V*, Aug. 1997.

Efficient Communication Using Message Prediction for Cluster of Multiprocessors

Ahmad Afsahi and Nikitas J. Dimopoulos

Department of Electrical and Computer Engineering, University of Victoria
P.O. Box 3055, Victoria, B.C., Canada, V8W 3P6
{aafsahi,nikitas}@ece.uvic.ca

Abstract. With the increasing uniprocessor and SMP computation power available, interprocessor communication has become an important factor that limits the performance of clusters of workstations. Many factors including communication hardware overhead, communication software overhead, and the user environment overhead (multithreading, multiuser) affect the performance of the communication subsystems. A significant portion of the software communication overhead is attributed to message copying. Ideally, it is desirable to have a true zero-copy protocol where the message is moved directly from the send buffer in its user space to the receive buffer in the destination. However, because the send side does not know the final receive buffer address, early arriving messages have to be buffered at a temporary area. In this work, we show that there is a message reception communication locality in message-passing applications. We have utilized this communication locality and devised different message predictors at the receiver sides of communications. In essence, these message predictors can be used to drain the network and cache the incoming messages even if the corresponding receive calls have not been posted yet. The performance of these predictors, in terms of hit ratio, on some parallel applications is quite promising and suggest that prediction has the potential to eliminate most of the remaining message copies.

1 Introduction

With the increasing uniprocessor and SMP computation power available today, interprocessor communication has become an important factor that limits the performance of workstations clusters. Communication overhead is one of the most important factors affecting the performance of parallel computers. Many factors affect the performance of communication subsystems. Specifically, communication hardware and its services, communication software, and the user environment (multi-programming, multiuser) are the major sources of the communication overhead.

Communication software overhead currently dominates communication time in cluster of workstations. In the current generation of parallel computer systems, the software overhead is in the tens of microseconds [15]. This is worse in cluster of workstations. Even with high performance networks [9, 21] available today, there is still a gap between what the network can offer and what the user application can see. The communication software overhead cost comes mainly from three different

B. Falsafi and M. Lauria (Eds.): CANPC 2000, LNCS1797, pp. 162-178, 2000.

sources; crossing protection boundaries between the user space and the kernel space, passing several protocol layers, and involving a number of memory copying.

Several researchers are working to minimize the cost of crossing protection boundaries, and using simpler protocol layers by utilizing *user-level messaging* techniques such as active messages (AM) [40], fast messages (FM) [32], VMMC-2 [17], U-Net [41], LAPI [36], BIP [33], VIA [18], and PM [39].

A significant portion of the software communication overhead is attributed to message copying. Ideally, message protocols should transfer messages in a single copy (this is called a true zero-copy). That is, the protocol should copy the message directly from the send buffer in its user space to the receive buffer in the destination. However the send side does not know the receive buffer address and, hence, the communication subsystem at the receiving end copies messages from the network interface to a system buffer, and then from the system buffer to the receive buffer when the receiving application posts the receive call. Some researchers have tried to avoid memory copying [17, 27, 34, 6, 38, 37]. While they have been able to remove the memory copying between the application buffer space and the network interface at the sender side by using user-level messaging techniques, they haven't been able to remove the memory copying at the receiver sides completely. Zero-copy messaging at the receiver side is achieved only if the receive call is already posted, a rendez-vous type communication is used for large messages, or the destination buffer address is already known by a pre-communication. Although MPI-2 [30] supports remote memory access, this is mostly suitable for receiver-initiated communications arising from the shared-memory paradigm.

We are interested in bypassing the memory copying at the destination in the general case, synchronous or asynchronous, eager or rendez-vous and for sender-initiated communications as in MPI [29, 30]. In this work, we argue that it is possible to address the message copying problem at the receiving side by speculation. We support our claim by showing that messages display a form of locality at the receiving ends of communications.

This work, for the first time, introduces the notion of message prediction at the receiving side of message-passing systems. Predicting the next receive communication call, and hence the next destination buffer address, before the receive call is posted will enable us to transfer the message directly to the CPU cache speculatively before it is needed so that an effect of a zero-copy can be achieved.

The first contribution of this work is that we show evidence that there exists message communication locality at the receiver sides of message-passing parallel applications. The second contribution is the introduction and evaluation of different message predicting techniques for the receiving side of message-passing systems. Our tools are not ready for measuring the effectiveness of our predictors on the application run-time yet. Our preliminary evaluation measures the accuracy of the predictors in terms of hit ratio. The results are quite promising and suggest that prediction has the potential to eliminate most of the remaining message copies.

In Section 2.0 of this paper, we explain the motivation behind this work and discuss related work. We elaborate on how prediction would help eliminate the message copies at the receiving side of communications, in Section 3.0. Our experimental methodology used to gather communication traces from a number of parallel benchmarks is explained in Section 4.0. In Section 5.0, we show communication frequency and unique message identifier distributions in the benchmarks studied, and present evidence of message locality at the receiver sides. In Section 6.0, we propose our message predictors and present their performance on the applications. Finally, we conclude our paper in Section 7.0.

2   Motivation and Related Work

High performance computing is increasingly concerned with efficient communication across the interconnect due to the availability of high-speed highly-advanced processors. Modern switched networks, called *System Area Networks* (SAN), such as Myrinet [9] and ServerNet [21], provide high communication bandwidth and low communication latency. However, because of high processing overhead due to communication software including network interface control, flow control, buffer management, memory copying, polling and interrupt handling, users cannot see much difference compared to traditional local area networks.

Fortunately, several user-level messaging techniques have been developed to remove the operating system kernel and protocol stack from the critical path of communications [40, 32, 17, 41, 18, 33, 36, 39]. This way, applications can send and receive messages without operating system intervention which often greatly reduces the communication latency.

A significant portion of the software communication overhead is due to the number of message copying. With the traditional software messaging layers, there are usually four message copying operations from the send buffer to the receive buffer, as shown in Figure 1. These copies are namely from the send buffer to the system buffer (1), from the system buffer to the *network interface* (NI) (2), and at the other end of communication from the network interface to the system buffer (3), and from the system buffer to the receive buffer (4) when the receive call is posted. Note that, we haven't considered data transfer from the network interface (NI) at the sending process to the network interface at the receiving process as a separate copy.

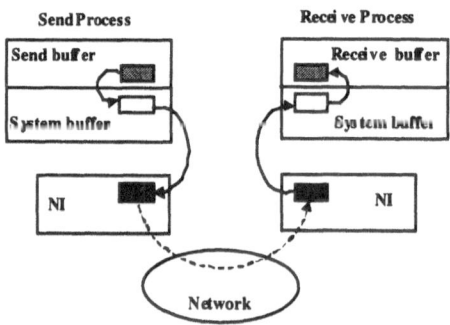

Fig. 1. Data transfers in a traditional messaging layer

At the send side, some user-level messaging layers use programmed I/O to avoid system buffer copying. FM uses programmed I/O while AM-II and BIP do so only for small messages. Some other user-messaging layers use DMA. VMMC-2, U-Net, and PM use DMA to bypass the system buffer copy while AM-II and BIP do so only for large messages. In systems that use DMA, applications or a library dynamically pins and unpins pages in the user space that contain the send and the receive buffers. Address translation can be done using a kernel module as in BIP, or by caching a limited number of address translations for the pinned pages as in VMMC-2, U-Net/MM [7], and PM. Some network interfaces also permit bypassing message copying at the network interface by directly writing into the network.

Contrary to the send side, bypassing the system buffer copying at the receiving side may or may not be achievable. Processes at the sending sides do not know the destination buffer addresses. Therefore, when a message arrives at the receiving side it has to be buffered if the receive call has not been posted yet. VMMC [8] for the SHRIMP multicomputer is a communication model that provides direct data transfer between the sender's and receiver's virtual address space. This is achieved by the receiver exporting its buffer address by sending a message to the sender before the actual transmission can take place.

VMMC-2 [17], uses a *transfer redirection* mechanism instead. It uses a default, redirectable receive buffer for a sender who does not know the address of the receive buffer. When a message arrives at the receiving network interface, the redirection mechanism checks to see if the receiver has already posted its buffer address. If the receive buffer has been posted earlier than the message arrival, the message will be directly transferred to the user buffer achieveing a zero-copy transfer. If the buffer address is not posted, the message is buffered in the default buffer. It will be transferred when the receive buffer is posted achieving a one-copy transfer.

Fast sockets [34] has been built using active messages. It uses a mechanism at the receiver side called *receive posting* to avoid the message copy in the fast socket buffer. If the message handler knows that the data's final memory destination is already known upon message arrival the message is directly moved to the application user space. Otherwise, it has to be copied into the fast socket buffer.

FM 2.x [27] uses a similar approach as fast sockets, namely *layer interleaving*. FM collaborates with the handler to direct the incoming messages into the destination buffer if the receive call has already been posted.

MPI-LAPI [6] is an implementation of MPI on top of LAPI [36] for the IBM SP machines. In the implementation of the eager protocol, the header handler of the LAPI returns a buffer pointer to LAPI which tells LAPI where the packets of the message must be reassembled. If a receive call has been posted, the address of the user buffer is returned to LAPI. If the header handler doesn't find a matching receive, it will return the address of an *early arrival buffer* and hence a one-copy transfer is accomplished. Messages with sizes larger than those of eager transfer are transferred using a 2-phase rendez-vous protocol.

Some research projects have proposed solutions to multi-protocol message-passing interfaces on *cluster of multiprocessors* (Clumps) using both shared-memory for intra-node communications and message-passing for inter-node communications [37, 19, 28].

MPICH-PM/CLUMP [37] is an MPI library implemented on a cluster of SMPs. It uses a message-passing only model where each process runs on a processor of an SMP node. For inter-node communications, it uses *eager* and *rendez-vous* protocols internally. For short messages, it achieves one-copy using eager protocol as the message is copied into a temporary buffer if the MPI receive primitive has not been issued. For large message, it uses rendez-vous protocol to achieve zero-copy by using a remote write operation but it needs an extra communication. For intra-node communications, it achieves a one-copy using a kernel primitive that allows to copy messages from the sender to the receiver without involving the communication buffer.

BIP-SMP [19], uses shared memory for small messages (a two-copy transaction), and direct copy for large messages with a kernel overhead. For inter-node communications, it works like MPI-BIP which is a port of MPICH [20].

TOMPI [13] is a threaded implementation of MPI on a single SMP node. It copies a message only once by utilizing multiple threads on an SMP node. Unfortunately, it is not scalable to cluster of SMP machines.

Another technique to bypass extra copying is the *re-mapping* technique. A zero-copy TCP stack is implemented in Solaris by using copy-on-write pages and re-mapping to improve communication performance [11]. It achieves a relatively high throughput for large messages. However, it does not have a good performance for small messages.

fbufs [16] is also using the re-mapping technique to avoid the penalty of copying large messages across different layers of protocol stack. However, fbufs allows re-mapping only for a limited range of user virtual memory.

It is quite clear that the user-level messaging techniques may not achieve a zero-copy communication all the time at the receiver side of communications, while all page re-mapping techniques perform poorly for short messages which are extremely important in parallel computing.

Prediction techniques have been proposed in the past to predict the future accesses of sharing patterns and coherence activities in distributed shared memory (DSM) by looking at their observed behavior [31, 26, 23, 43, 12, 35]. These techniques assume that memory accesses and coherence activities in the near future will follow past patterns. Sakr and his colleagues have used time series and neural networks for the prediction of the next memory sharing requests [35]. Dahlgren and his colleagues devised hardware regular stride techniques to prefetch several blocks ahead of the current data block [12]. More elaborate hardware-based irregular stride prefetching approaches have been proposed by Zhang and Torrellas [43]. Kaxiras and Goodman have recently proposed an instruction-based approach which maintains the history of load and store instructions in relation to cache misses and predicting their future behavior [23]. Mukherjee and Hill proposed a general pattern-based predictor to learn and predict the coherence activity for a memory block in a DSM [31]. In a recent paper, Lai and Falsafi proposed a new class of pattern-based predictors, *memory sharing predictors*, to eliminate the coherence overhead on a remote access latency by just predicting the memory request messages [26].

As stated above, many prediction techniques have been proposed to reduce or hide the latency of a remote memory access in shared memory systems. Recently, Afsahi and Dimopoulos proposed some heuristics to predict the destination target of subsequent communication requests at the send side of communications in message-passing systems [1, 2]. To the best of our knowledge, no prediction technique has been proposed for the receive side of communications in message-passing systems to reduce the latency of a message transfer.

This paper, reports on an innovative approach for removing message copying at the receiving ends of communications for message-passing systems. We argue that it is possible to address the message copying problem at the receiving sides by speculation. We introduce message prediction techniques such that messages can be directly transferred to the cache even if the receive calls have not been posted yet.

3   Using Message Predictions

In this section, we analyze the problem with the early arrival of messages at the destinations in message-passing systems. In such systems, a number of messages arrive in arbitrary order at the destinations. The consuming process or thread will consume one message at a time. If we know which message is going to be consumed next, we can move the message upon its arrival to near the place that it is to be consumed (e.g. a staging cache).

For this, we have to consider three different issues. First, deciding which message is going to be consumed next. This can be done by devising receive call predictors, history-based predictors that predict subsequent receive calls by a given node in a message-passing program, Second, deciding where and how this message is to be moved in the cache. Third, efficient cache re-mapping and late binding mechanisms need to be devised for when the receive call is posted.

In this work, we are addressing the first problem. That is, devising message predictors and evaluating their performance. We are working on several methods to address the remaining issues. We shall report on these issues in the future.

4   Experimental Methodology

In exploring the effect that different heuristics have in predicting the next receive call, we utilized a number of parallel benchmarks, and extracted their communication traces on which we applied our predictors.

We have used some well-known parallel benchmarks form the *NAS parallel benchmarks* (NPB) suite [5], and the *Parallel Spectral Transform Shallow Water Model* (PSTSWM) application [42]. We used the MPI [29] implementation of the NPB suite (version 2.3), and version 6.2 of the PSTSWM application.

We are only interested in the patterns of the point-to-point communications between pair-wise nodes in our applications. For this, we executed these applications on an IBM SP2 machine. We wrote our own profiling code using the wrapper facility of the MPI to gather the communication traces. We did this by inserting monitor operations in the profiling MPI library for the communication related activities.

We considered different system sizes and problem sizes for our applications to evaluate the performance of our prediction heuristics. Specifically, we experimented with the workstation class "W", and the large class "A" of the NPB suite, and the default problem size for the PSTSWM application. The NPB results are almost the same for "W" and "A" classes. Hence, we report only for the "A" class here. Note that we also removed the initialization part from the communication traces of the PSTSWM application. Although the derived results are for the above mentioned parallel applications, we believe that these applications are representative of the existing scientific and engineering parallel applications.

5   Receiver-Side Locality Estimation

Our applications use synchronous and asynchronous MPI receive primitives, namely *MPI_Recv* and *MPI_Irecv* [29]. *MPI_Recv (buf, count, datatype, source, tag, comm, status)* is a standard blocking receive call. When it returns, data is available at the destination buffer. The PSTSWM application uses this type of receive call. *MPI_Irecv (buf, count, datatype, source, tag, comm, request)* is a standard nonblocking receive call. It immediately posts the call and returns. Hence, data is not available at the time of return. It needs another call to complete the call. All applications in our study use this type of receive call.

One of the communication characteristics of any parallel application is the frequency of communications. Figure 2, illustrates the minimum, average, and maximum number of receive communication calls in the applications under different system sizes. We ran our applications once for each different system size and counted the number of receive calls at each node. The average, minimum, and maximum number of receive calls is computed over all nodes of each application. It is clear that all nodes in the BT, SP, and CG applications have the same number of receive communication calls. While nodes in the PSTSWM application have different number of receive communication calls.

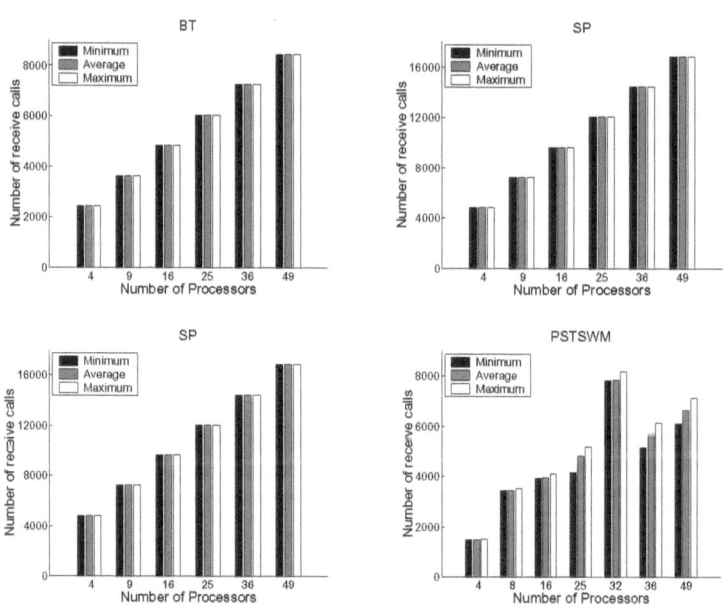

Fig. 2. Number of receive calls in the applications under different system sizes

Each of the MPI_Recv and MPI_Irecv calls is distinguished by a 7-tuple of parameters, namely: *source, tag, count, datatype, buf, comm,* and *status* or *request*. In order to choose precisely one of the received messages at the network interface and transfer it to the cache, our predictors need to consider all the details of a message envelop. That is, *source, tag, count, datatype, buf,* and *comm* (we don't consider *status* and *request* as they are just a handle when the calls return). We assign a different identifier for each unique 6-tuple found in the communication traces of the applications. Figure 3, shows the number of *unique message identifiers* in our applications under different system sizes. By average, minimum, and maximum, we mean the average, minimum, and maximum number of unique identifiers taken over all nodes of each application. It is evident that all nodes in the BT, and CG applications have the same number of unique message identifiers while nodes in the SP, and PSTSWM applications have different number of unique message identifiers (except when the number of processors is four for the SP benchmark).

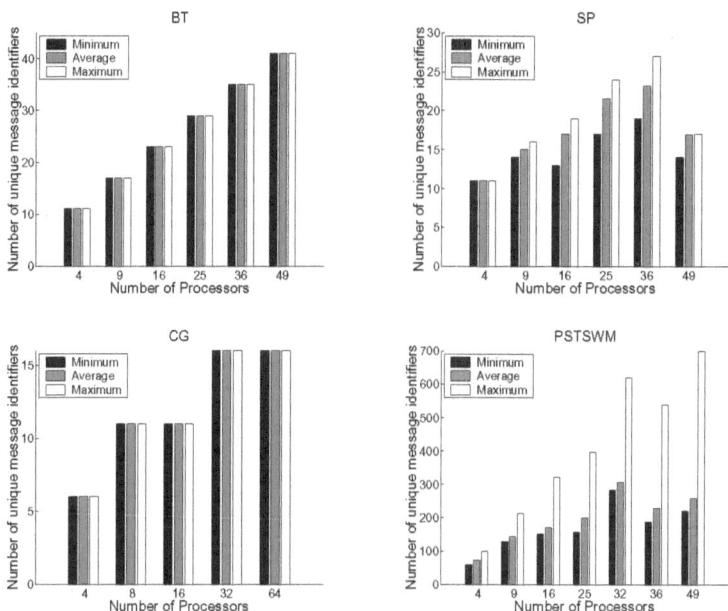

Fig. 3. Number of unique message identifiers in the applications under different system sizes

5.1   Communication Locality

In the context of message passing programming, many parallel algorithms are built from loops consisting of computation and communication phases. Therefore, communication patterns may be repetitive. This has motivated researchers to find or use the *communications locality* properties of parallel applications [1, 2, 24, 22, 25, 14, 10]. Kim and Lilja [24] have shown that there is a locality in message destination, message sizes, and consecutive runs of send/ receive primitives in parallel algorithms. They have proposed and expanded the concept of memory access locality based on the *Least Recently Used*, LRU, stack model to determine these localities. In [1, 2], Afsahi and Dimopoulos have shown the communication locality of message-passing application in terms of message destination locality. Karlsson and Brorsson [22] have compared the communication properties of parallel applications in message-passing systems using MPI, and shared memory systems using TreadMarks [4].

In conjunction with this work, *message reception locality* is understood to mean that if a certain message reception call has been used it will be re-used with high probability by a portion of code that is "near" the place that was used earlier, and that it will be re-used in the near future.

In the following subsection, we present the performance of the classical LRU, LFU, and FIFO heuristics on the applications to see the existence of locality or repetitive receive calls. We use the *hit ratio* to establish and compare the performance of these heuristics. As a hit ratio, we define the percentage of times that the predicted receive call was correct out of all receive communication requests.

5.2   The LRU, FIFO, and LFU Heuristics

The *Least Recently Used* (LRU), *First-In-First-Out* (FIFO), and *Least Frequently Used* (LFU) heuristics, maintain a set of k (k is the window size) unique message identifiers. If the next message identifier is already in the set, then a hit is recorded. Otherwise, a miss is recorded and the new message identifier replaces one of the identifiers in the set according to which of the LRU, FIFO or LFU heuristics is used.

Figure 4, shows the results of the LRU, FIFO, and LFU heuristics on the application benchmarks when the number of processors is 64 for CG and 49 for all other applications. Similar results have been produced for different system sizes [3]. It is clear that the hit-ratios in all benchmarks approach 1 as the window size increases. The performance of the FIFO algorithm is the same as the LRU for BT, and PSTSWM benchmarks, and almost the same for the SP and CG benchmarks. The LFU algorithm consistently has a better performance than the LRU and FIFO heuristics on the BT, CG, and PSTSWM applications. It also has a better performance than the LRU and FIFO heuristics on the SP benchmark for window sizes of greater than five.

The LRU, FIFO and LFU heuristics do not predict exactly the next receive call but shows the probability that the next receive call might be in the set. For instance, the SP benchmark shows nearly 60% hit ratio for a window size of five under the LRU heuristic. This means that 60% of the time one of the five most recently issued call will be issued next. These heuristics perform better when the window size k is sufficiently large. However, this large window adds to the hardware/software implementation complexity as one would need for example, to move all messages in the set to the cache in the likelihood that one of them is going to be used next. This is prohibitive for large window sizes.

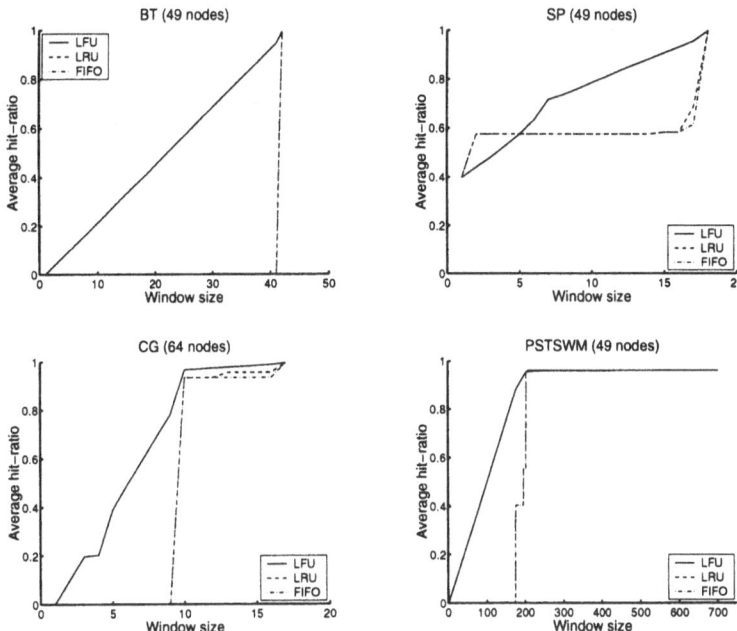

Fig. 4. Effects of the LR, FIFO, and LFU heuristics on the applications

We are interested to devise predictors that can predict the next receive call with a high probability. In Section , we introduce our novel message predictors employing different heuristics and evaluate their performance.

6   Message Predictors

The set of predictors introduced in this section predict the subsequent receive calls based on the past history of communication patterns on a per node basis. These heuristics were originally proposed in [1, 2] to predict the destination target of subsequent communication requests at the sender sides of communications. These predictors can be used dynamically at the communication assist with or without the help of a programmer or a compiler. In the following figures, by average, minimum, and maximum, we mean the average, minimum, and maximum hit ratio taken over all nodes of each application.

6.1   The Tag Predictor

The Tag predictor assumes a static communication environment in the sense that a particular communication receive call in a section of code, will be the same one with high probability. We attach a different *tag* (this is different than the tag in an MPI communication call; It may be a unique identifier or the program counter at the address of the communication call) to each of the receive calls found in the applications. This can be implemented with the help of the compiler or by the programmer through a *pre-receive (tag)* operation which will be passed to the communication subsystem to predict the next receive call before the actual receive call is issued.

To this tag and at the communication assist, we assign this receive call. A hit is recorded if in subsequent encounters of the tag, the requested communication is the same as the receive call already associated with the tag. Otherwise, a miss is recorded and the tag is assigned the newly requested receive call. The performance of the Tag predictor is shown in Figure 5. It is evident that this predictor doesn't have a good performance on the applications. It cannot predict the communication patterns of PSTSWM at all, and has a degrading performance for all other applications when the number of processors increases.

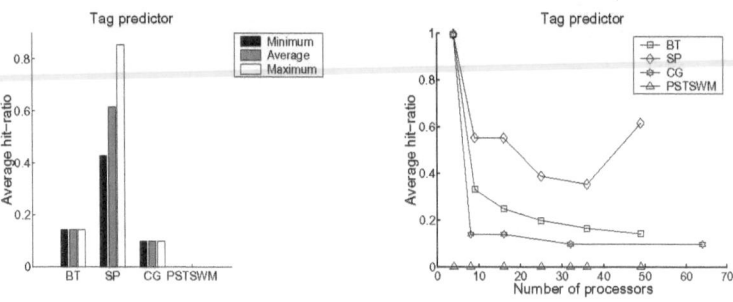

Fig. 5. Effects of the Tag predictor on the applications

6.2   The Single-Cycle Predictor

The *Single-cycle* predictor is based on the fact that if a group of receive calls are issued repeatedly in a cyclical fashion, then we can predict the next request one step ahead. The following example illustrates the single-cycle predictor. The top trace represents the sequence of requested receive calls, while the bottom trace represents the predicted sequence. The arrows with the cross represent misses, while the ones with the circle represent hits. The "dash" in place of a predicted request indicates that a cycle is being formed, and therefore no prediction is offered (note that this is also added to the misses).

Request sequence 1 3 5 6 1 3 5 6 7 7 1 3 5 6

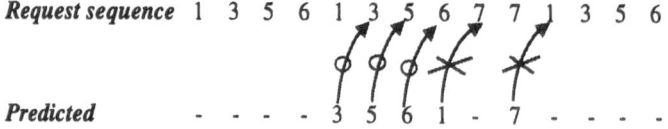

Predicted   - - - - 3 5 6 1 - 7 - - - -

This predictor implements a simple cycle discovery algorithm. Starting with a *cycle-head* receive call (this is the first receive call that is requested at start-up, or the receive call that causes a miss), we log the sequence of requests until the cycle-head receive call is requested again. This stored sequence constitutes a cycle, and can be used to predict the subsequent requests. If the predicted receive call coincides with the subsequent requested one, then we record a hit. If the requested receive call does not coincide with the predicted one, then we record a miss and the cycle formation stage commences with the cycle-head being the receive call that caused the miss. The performance of the Single-cycle predictor is shown in Figure 6. It is evident that its performance is consistently very high (hit ratios of more than 0.9).

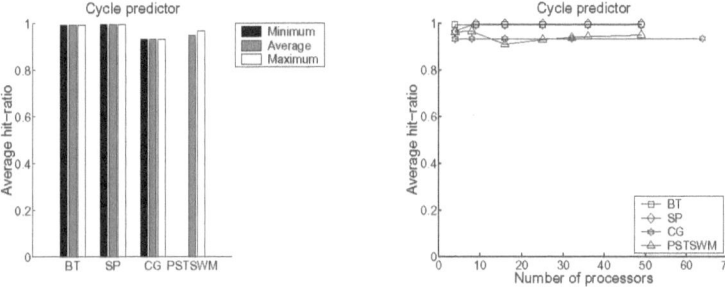

Fig. 6. Effects of the Single-cycle predictor on the applications

6.3   The Tag-Cycle Predictor

The Tag predictor didn't have a good performance on the applications while the Single-cycle predictor had a very good performance. We would like to see the impact of the cycle algorithm on the Tag predictor. Therefore, we combine the Tag algorithm with the Single-cycle algorithm and call it the *Tag-cycle* predictor.

In the Tag-cycle predictor, we attach a different tag to each of the communication requests found in the benchmarks and do a Single-cycle discovery algorithm on each tag. To this tag and at the communication assist, we assign the requested receive call, to be called *tagcycle-head* node (this is the first receive call that is requested at this tag, or the node that causes a miss). We log the sequence of the requests at this tag until the tagcycle-head node is requested again. This stored sequence constitutes a cycle at each tag, and can be used to predict the subsequent requests. The performance of the Tag-cycle predictor is shown in Figure 7. The Tag-cycle predictor performs well on all benchmarks. Its performance is the same as the Single-cycle predictor on BT and PSTSWM. However, it has a better performance on CG and a lower performance on SP.

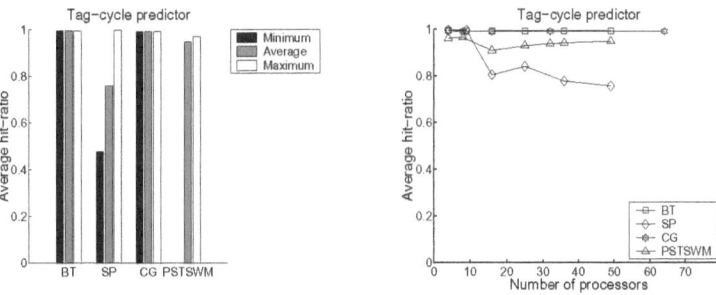

Fig. 7. Effects of the Tag-cycle predictor on the applications

6.4   The Tag-Bettercycle Predictor

In the Single-cycle and Tag-cycle predictors, as soon as a receive call breaks a cycle we remove the cycle and form a new cycle. In the *Tag-bettercycle* predictor, we keep the last cycle associated with each tagcycle-head encountered in the communication patterns of each node. This means that when a cycle breaks we maintain this cycle in memory for later references. If we haven't already seen the new tagcycle-head then we form a new cycle for it, otherwise we predict the next communication call based on the member of the cycle associated with this new tagcycle-head that we have from the past in memory. The performance of the Tag-bettercycle predictor is shown in Figure 8.

The Tag-bettercycle predictor performs well on all benchmarks. Its performance is the same as the Single-cycle and Tag-cycle predictors on BT and PSTSWM. However, it has a better performance on CG and a lower performance on SP relative to the Single-cycle predictor. The Tag-bettercycle predictor has a better performance on SP compared to the Tag-cycle predictor.

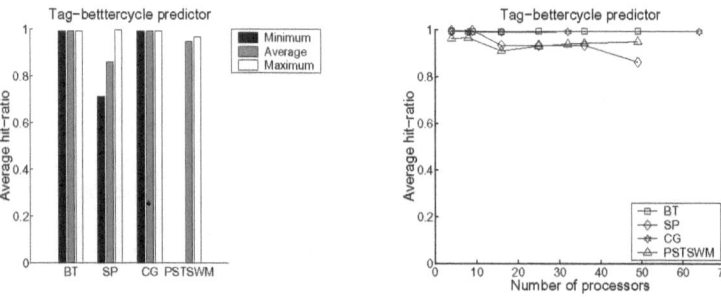

Fig. 8. Effects of the Tag-bettercycle predictor on the applications

6.5   Message Predictors' Comparison

Figure 9, presents a comparison of the performance of the predictors presented in this paper when the number of processors is 64 for CG and 49 for the other benchmarks. As we have seen so far, Single-cycle, Tag-cycle and Tag-bettercycle all perform well on the benchmarks. However, the performance of the Single-cycle is better on the SP benchmark while Tag-cycle and Tag-bettercycle have better performance for the CG benchmark. Similar results for other systems sizes can be found in [3].

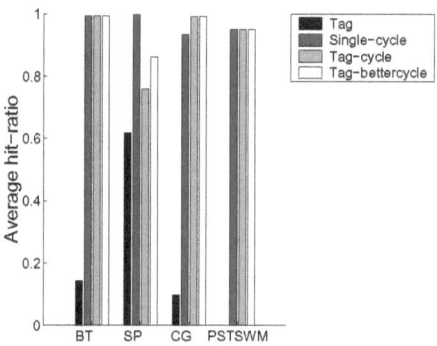

Fig. 9. Comparison of the performance of the predictors on the applications

7   Conclusion

Communication latency adversely affects the performance of networks of workstations. A significant portion of the software communication overhead belongs to a number of message copying operations. Ideally, it is very desirable to have a true zero-copy protocol where the message is moved directly from the send buffer in its user space to the receive buffer in the destination without any intermediate buffering. However, this is not always possible as a message may arrive at the destination where the corresponding receive call has not been issued yet. Hence, the message has to be buffered in a temporary buffer.

In this paper, we have shown that there is a message reception communication locality in message-passing applications. We have utilized this communication locality and devised different message predictors for the receiver sides of communications. By predicting receive calls early, a node can perform the necessary data placement upon message reception and move the message directly into the cache. We presented the performance of these predictors on some parallel applications. The performance results are quite promising and justify more work in this area.

We envision these predictors to be used to drain the network and place the incoming messages in the cache in such a way so as to increase the probability that the messages will still be in cache when the consuming thread needs to access them.

Further issues we are presently investigating include mechanisms for in-the-cache late binding and thread scheduling to guarantee that the consuming thread finds the message in the cache of the processor it executes on. We shall report on these issues in the future.

Acknowledgement

This work was supported by grants from NSERC and the University of Victoria. We would like to thank Dr. Murray Campbell at the IBM T J Watson Research Center for his kind help in accessing the IBM Deep Blue machine. We also would like to thank the anonymous referees for their valuable comments and suggestions.

References

1. A. Afsahi and N. J. Dimopoulos, "Hiding Communication Latency in Reconfigurable Message-Passing Environments", Proceedings of the of IPPS/SPDP 1999, 13th International Parallel Processing Symposium and 10th Symposium on Parallel and Distributed Processing, April 1999, pp. 55-60.
2. A. Afsahi and N. J. Dimopoulos, "Communication Latency Hiding in Reconfigurable Message-Passing Environments: Quantitative Studies", *13th Annual International Symposium on High Performance Computing Systems and Applications, HPCS'99*, June, 1999, pp. 111-126.
3. A. Afsahi and N. J. Dimopoulos, "Efficient Communication Using Message Prediction for Clusters of Multiprocessor", Technical Report ECE-99-5, Department of Electrical and Computer Engineering, University of Victoria, December, 1999.
4. C. Amza, A. L. Cox, S. Dwarkadas, P. Keleher, H. Lu, R. Rajamony, W. Yu and W. Zwaenepoel, "TreadMarks: Shared Memory Computing on Networks of Workstation", IEEE Computer, Volume 29, no. 2, February 1996, pp. 18-28.
5. D. H. Bailey, T. Harsis, W. Saphir, R. V. der Wijngaart, A. Woo and M. Yarrow, "The NAS Parallel Benchmarks 2.0: Report NAS-95-020", Nasa Ames Research Center, December 1995.
6. M. Banikazemi, R. K. Govindaraju, R. Blackmore and D. K. Panda, "Implementing Efficient MPI on LAPI for IBM RS/ 6000 SP Systems: Experiences and Performance Evaluation, *"Proceedings of the of IPPS/SPDP 1999, 13th International Parallel Processing Symposium and 10th Symposium on Parallel and Distributed Processing*, April 1999, pp. 183-190.
7. A. Basu, M. Welsh, T. V. Eicken, "Incorporating Memory Management into User-Level Network Interfaces", Hot Interconnects V, August 1997
8. M. Blumrich, K. Li, R. Alpert, C. Dubnicki, E. Felten, and J. Sandberg, "A Virtual Memory Mapped Network Interface for the SHRIMP Multicomputer", *Proceedings of the 21st Annual International Symposium on Computer Architecture*, 1994, pp. 142-153.
9. N. J. Boden, D. Cohen, R. E. Felderman, A. E. Kulawik, C. L. Seitz, J. N. Seizovic and W-K. Su, "Myrinet: A Gigabit-per-Second Local Area Network", *IEEE Micro*, February 1995.
10. S. Chodnekar, V. Srinivasan, A. Vaidya, A. Sivasubramaniam and C. Das, "Towards a Communication Characterization Methodology for Parallel Applications", Proceedings of the Third International Symposium on High Performance Computer Architecture, 1997.
11. H. Chu, "Zero-copy TCP in Solaris, *"Proceedings of the USENIX Annual Technical Conference*, 1996, pp. 253-263.
12. F. Dahlgren, M. Dubois and P. Stenström, "Sequential Hardware Prefetching in Shared-Memory Multiprocessors", *IEEE Transactions on Parallel and Distributed Systems*, 6(7), 1995.
13. E. D. Demaine, "A Threads-Only MPI Implementation for the Development of Parallel Programs", *Proceedings of the 11th International Symposium on High Performance Computing Systems, HPCS'97*, 1997, pp. 153-163.
14. B. V. Dao, Sudhakar Yalamanchili, and Jose Duato, "Architectural Support for Reducing Communication Overhead in Multiprocessor Interconnection Networks", *Proceedings of the*

Third International Symposium on High Performance Computer Architecture, 1997, pp. 343-352.

15. J. J. Dongarra and T. Dunigan, "Message-Passing Performance of Various Computers", *Concurrency: Practice and Experience*, Volume 9, Issue 10, 1997, pp. 915-926.

16. P. Druschel and L. L. Peterson, "Fbufs: A High-bandwidth Cross-domain Transfer Facility", *Proceedings of the Fourteenth ACM Symposium on Operating Systems Principles*, 1993, pp. 189-202.

17. C. Dubnicki, A. Bilas, Y. Chen, S. Damianakis and K. Li, "VMMC-2: Efficient Support for Reliable, Connection-Oriented Communication", *Proceedings of the Hot Interconnect'97*, 1997.

18. D. Dunning, G. Regnier, G. McAlpine, D. Cameron, B. Shubert, F. Berry, A. M. Merritt, E. Gronke and C. Dodd, "The Virtual Interface Architecture", *IEEE Micro*, March-April, 1998, pp. 66-76.

19. P. Geoffray, L. Prylli, and B. Tourancheau, "BIP-SMP: High Performance Message Passing Over a Cluster of Commodity SMPs", *SC99: High Performance Networking and Computing Conference*, November, 1999.

20. W. Gropp and E. Lusk, "User's Guide for MPICH, a Portable Implementation of MPI", *Argonne National Laboratory, Mathematics and Computer Science Division*, June, 1999.

21. R. W. Horst and D. Garcia, "ServerNet SAN I/O Architecture", *Proceedings of the Hot Interconnects V*, 1997.

22. S. Karlson and M. Brorsson, "A Comparative Characterization of Communication Patterns in Applications Using MPI and Shared Memory on an IBM SP2", *Proceedings of the Workshop on Communication, Architecture, and Applications for Network-based Parallel Computing, International Symposium on High Performance Computer Architecture*, February 1998.

23. S. Kaxiras and J. R. Goodman, "Improving CC-NUMA Performance Using Instruction-Based Prediction", *International Symposium on High Performance Computer Architecture*, 1999.

24. J. Kim and D. J. Lilja, "Characterization of Communication Patterns in Message-Passing Parallel Scientific Application Programs", *Proceedings of the Workshop on Communication, Architecture, and Applications for Network-based Parallel Computing, International Symposium on High Performance Computer Architecture*, February 1998, pp. 202-216.

25. D. G. de Lahaut and C. Germain, "Static Communications in Parallel Scientific Programs", *Proceedings of PARLE'94, Parallel Architecture and Languages*, July 1994.

26. A.-C. Lai and B. Falsafi, "Memory Sharing Predictor: The Key to a Speculative Coherent DSM", *Proceedings of the 26th Annual International Symposium on Computer Architectures*, 1999, pp. 172-183.

27. M. Lauria, S. Pakin and A. A. Chien, "Efficient Layering for High Speed Communication: Fast Messages 2.x", *Proceedings of the 7th High Performance Distributed Computing, HPDC7, Conference*, 1998.

28. S. S. Lumetta, A. M. Mainwaring, and D. E. Culler, "Multi-Protocol Active Messages on a Cluster of SMPs", *SC97: High Performance Networking and Computing Conference*, November, 1997.

29. *Message Passing Interface Forum: MPI: A Message-Passing Interface Standard.* Version 1.1 (June 1995).

30. *Message Passing Interface Forum: MPI-2: Extensions to the Message-Passing Interface*, (July 1997).

31. S. S. Mukherjee and M. D. Hill, "Using Prediction to Accelerate Coherence Protocols", *Proceedings of the 25th Annual International Symposium on Computer Architecture*, 1998.

32. S. Pakin, M. Lauria, and A. Chien, "High Performance Messaging on Workstation: Illinois Fast Messages (FM) for Myrinet," *Proceedings of the Supercomputing'95*, Nov., 1995.

33. L. Prylli and B. Tourancheau, "BIP: A New Protocol Designed for High Performance Networking on Myrinet", *Proceedings of the PC-NOW98: International Workshop on*

Personal Computer based Networks Of Workstations, in conjunction with IPPS/SPDP'98, 1998.

34. S. H. Rodrigues, T. E. Anderson and D. E. Culler, "High-Performance Local Area Communication with Fast Sockets", *USENIX 1997 Annual Technical Conference*, January 1997.

35. M. F. Sakr, S. P. Levitan, D. M. Chiarulli, B. G. Horne, and C. L. Giles, "Predicting Multiprocessor Memory Access Patterns with Learning Models", *Proceedings of the Fourteenth International Conference on Machine Learning*," 1997, pp. 305-312.

36. G. Shah, J. Nieplocha, J. Mirza and C. Kim, R. Harrison, R. K. Govindaraju, K. Gildea, P. DiNicola, and C. Bender, "Performance and Experience with LAPI -- a New High-Performance Communication Library for the IBM RS/6000 SP", *First Merged Symposium IPPS/SPDP 1998 12th International Parallel Processing symposium & 9th Symposium on Parallel and Distributed Processing,* 1998.

37. T. Takahashi, F. O'Carrol, H. Tezuka, A. Hori, S. Sumimoto, H. Harada, Y. Ishikawa, P.H. Beckman, "Implementation and Evaluation of MPI on an SMP Cluster", *Proceedings of the PC-NOW99: International Workshop on Personal Computer based Networks Of Workstations, in conjunction with PPS/SPDP'99,* 1999.

38. Y. Tanaka, M. Matsuda, M. Ando, K. Kubota and M. Sato, "COMPaS: A Pentium Pro PC-based SMP Cluster and its Experience", *Proceedings of the PC-NOW98: International Workshop on Personal Computer based Networks Of Workstations, in conjunction with IPPS/SPDP'98,* 1998.

39. H. Tezuka, F. O'Carroll, A. Hori, and Y. Ishikawa, "Pin-down Cache: A Virtual Memory Management Technique for Zero-copy Communication", *First Merged Symposium IPPS/SPDP 1998 12th International Parallel Processing symposium & 9th Symposium on Parallel and Distributed Processing,* 1998.

40. T. V. Eicken, D. E. Culler, S. C. Goldstein, and K. E. Schauser, "Active Messages: A Mechanism for Integrated Communication and Computation", *Proceedings of the 19th Annual International Symposium on Computer Architecture*, May 1992, pp. 256-265.

41. T. V. Eicken, A. Basu, V. Buch and W. Vogels, "U-Net: A User-Level Network Interface for Parallel and Distributed Computing", Proceedings of the 15th ACM Symposium on Operating Systems Principles, December, 1995.

42. P. H. Worley and I. T. Foster, "Parallel Spectral Transform Shallow Water Model: A Runtime-tunable parallel benchmark code", *Proceedings of the Scalable High Performance Computing Conference*, 1994, pp. 207-214.

43. Z. Zhang and J. Torrellas, "Speeding Up Irregular Applications in Shared-Memory Multiprocessors: Memory Binding and Group Prefetching", *Proceedings of the 22nd Annual International Symposium on Computer Architectures*, 1995, pp. 188-199.

Author Index

Lecture Notes in Computer Science

For information about Vols. 1–1785
please contact your bookseller or Springer-Verlag

Vol. 1829: C. Fonlupt, J.-K. Hao, E. Lutton, E. Ronald, M. Schoenauer (Eds.), Artificial Evolution. Proceedings, 1999. X, 293 pages. 2000.

Vol. 1830: P. Kropf, G. Babin, J. Plaice, H. Unger (Eds.), Distributed Communities on the Web. Proceedings, 2000. X, 203 pages. 2000.

Vol. 1831: D. McAllester (Ed.), Automated Deduction – CADE-17. Proceedings, 2000. XIII, 519 pages. 2000. (Subseries LNAI).

Vol. 1832: B. Lings, K. Jeffery (Eds.), Advances in Databases. Proceedings, 2000. X, 227 pages. 2000.

Vol. 1833: L. Bachmair (Ed.), Rewriting Techniques and Applications. Proceedings, 2000. X, 275 pages. 2000.

Vol. 1834: J.-C. Heudin (Ed.), Virtual Worlds. Proceedings, 2000. XI, 314 pages. 2000. (Subseries LNAI).

Vol. 1835: D. N. Christodoulakis (Ed.), Natural Language Processing – NLP 2000. Proceedings, 2000. XII, 438 pages. 2000. (Subseries LNAI).

Vol. 1836: B. Masand, M. Spiliopoulou (Eds.), Web Usage Analysis and User Profiling. Proceedings, 2000, V, 183 pages. 2000. (Subseries LNAI).

Vol. 1837: R. Backhouse, J. Nuno Oliveira (Eds.), Mathematics of Program Construction. Proceedings, 2000. IX, 257 pages. 2000.

Vol. 1838: W. Bosma (Ed.), Algorithmic Number Theory. Proceedings, 2000. IX, 615 pages. 2000.

Vol. 1839: G. Gauthier, C. Frasson, K. VanLehn (Eds.), Intelligent Tutoring Systems. Proceedings, 2000. XIX, 675 pages. 2000.

Vol. 1840: F. Bomarius, M. Oivo (Eds.), Product Focused Software Process Improvement. Proceedings, 2000. XI, 426 pages. 2000.

Vol. 1841: E. Dawson, A. Clark, C. Boyd (Eds.), Information Security and Privacy. Proceedings, 2000. XII, 488 pages. 2000.

Vol. 1842: D. Vernon (Ed.), Computer Vision – ECCV 2000. Part I. Proceedings, 2000. XVIII, 953 pages. 2000.

Vol. 1843: D. Vernon (Ed.), Computer Vision – ECCV 2000. Part II. Proceedings, 2000. XVIII, 881 pages. 2000.

Vol. 1844: W.B. Frakes (Ed.), Software Reuse: Advances in Software Reusability. Proceedings, 2000. XI, 450 pages. 2000.

Vol. 1845: H.B. Keller, E. Plöderer (Eds.), Reliable Software Technologies Ada-Europe 2000. Proceedings, 2000. XIII, 304 pages. 2000.

Vol. 1846: H. Lu, A. Zhou (Eds.), Web-Age Information Management. Proceedings, 2000. XIII, 462 pages. 2000.

Vol. 1847: R. Dyckhoff (Ed.), Automated Reasoning with Analytic Tableaux and Related Methods. Proceedings, 2000. X, 441 pages. 2000. (Subseries LNAI).

Vol. 1848: R. Giancarlo, D. Sankoff (Eds.), Combinatorial Pattern Matching. Proceedings, 2000. XI, 423 pages. 2000.

Vol. 1849: C. Freksa, W. Brauer, C. Habel, K.F. Wender (Eds.), Spatial Cognition II. XI, 420 pages. 2000. (Subseries LNAI).

Vol. 1850: E. Bertino (Ed.), ECOOP 2000 – Object-Oriented Programming. Proceedings, 2000. XIII, 493 pages. 2000.

Vol. 1851: M.M. Halldórsson (Ed.), Algorithm Theory – SWAT 2000. Proceedings, 2000. XI, 564 pages. 2000.

Vol. 1853: U. Montanari, J.D.P. Rolim, E. Welzl (Eds.), Automata, Languages and Programming. Proceedings, 2000. XVI, 941 pages. 2000.

Vol. 1854: G. Lacoste, B. Pfitzmann, M. Steiner, M. Waidner (Eds.), SEMPER — Secure Electronic Marketplace for Europe. XVIII, 350 pages. 2000.

Vol. 1855: E.A. Emerson, A.P. Sistla (Eds.), Computer Aided Verification. Proceedings, 2000. X, 582 pages. 2000.

Vol. 1857: J. Kittler, F. Roli (Eds.), Multiple Classifier Systems. Proceedings, 2000. XII, 404 pages. 2000.

Vol. 1858: D.-Z. Du, P. Eades, V. Estivill-Castro, X. Lin, A. Sharma (Eds.), Computing and Combinatorics. Proceedings, 2000. XII, 478 pages. 2000.

Vol. 1860: M. Klusch, L. Kerschberg (Eds.), Cooperative Information Agents IV. Proceedings, 2000. XI, 285 pages. 2000. (Subseries LNAI).

Vol. 1861: J. Lloyd, V. Dahl, U. Furbach, M. Kerber, K.-K. Lau, C. Palamidessi, L. Moniz Pereira, Y. Sagiv, P.J. Stuckey (Eds.), Computational Logic – CL 2000. Proceedings, 2000. XIX, 1379 pages. (Subseries LNAI).

Vol. 1862: P.G. Clote, H. Schwichtenberg (Eds.), Computer Science Logic. Proceedings, 2000. XIII, 543 pages. 2000.

Vol. 1863: L. Carter, J. Ferrante (Eds.), Languages and Compilers for Parallel Computing. Proceedings, 1999. XII, 500 pages. 2000.

Vol. 1864: B. Y. Choueiry, T. Walsh (Eds.), Abstraction, Reformulation, and Approximation. Proceedings, 2000. XI, 333 pages. 2000. (Subseries LNAI).

Vol. 1865: K.R. Apt, A.C. Kakas, E. Monfroy, F. Rossi (Eds.), New Trends Constraints. Proceedings, 1999. X, 339 pages. 2000. (Subseries LNAI).

Vol. 1866: J. Cussens, A. Frisch (Eds.), Inductive Logic Programming. Proceedings, 2000. X, 265 pages. 2000. (Subseries LNAI).

Vol. 1867: B. Ganter, G.W. Mineau (Eds.), Conceptual Structures: Logical, Linguistic, and Computational Issues. Proceedings, 2000. XI, 569 pages. 2000. (Subseries LNAI).

Vol. 1868: P. Koopman, C. Clack (Eds.), Implementation of Functional Languages. Proceedings, 1999. IX, 199 pages. 2000.

Vol. 1869: M. Aagaard, J. Harrison (Eds.), Theorem Proving in Higher Order Logics. Proceedings, 2000. IX, 535 pages. 2000.

Vol. 1872: J. van Leeuwen, O. Watanabe, M. Hagiya, P.D. Mosses, T. Ito (Eds.), Theoretical Computer Science. Proceedings, 2000. XV, 630 pages. 2000.

Vol. 1877: C. Palamidessi (Ed.), CONCUR 2000 – Concurrent Theory. Proceedings, 2000. XI, 612 pages. 2000.

Vol. 1880: M. Bellare (Ed.), Advances in Cryptology – CRYPTO 2000. Proceedings, 2000. XI, 545 pages. 2000.

Vol. 1881: C. Zhang, V.-W. Soo (Eds.), Design and Applications of Intelligent Agents. Proceedings, 2000. X, 183 pages. 2000. (Subseries LNAI).

Vol. 1893: M. Nielsen, B. Rovan (Eds.), Mathematical Foundations of Computer Science 2000. Proceedings, 2000. XIII, 710 pages. 2000.